DAC Guidelines and Reference Series

Managing Aid: Practices of DAC Member Countries

ORGANISATION FOR ECONOMIC CO-OPERATION AND DEVELOPMENT

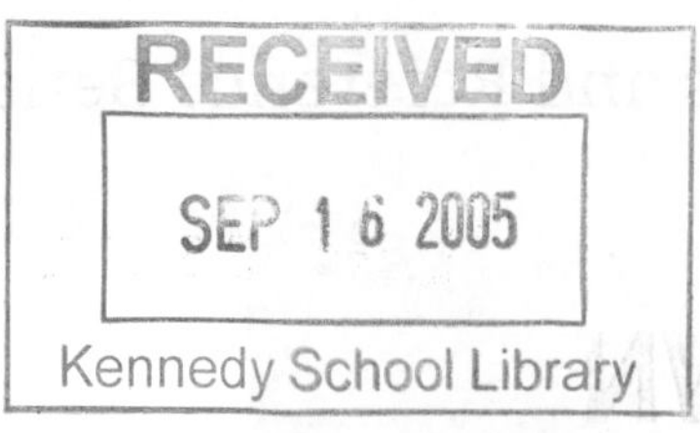

ORGANISATION FOR ECONOMIC CO-OPERATION AND DEVELOPMENT

The OECD is a unique forum where the governments of 30 democracies work together to address the economic, social and environmental challenges of globalisation. The OECD is also at the forefront of efforts to understand and to help governments respond to new developments and concerns, such as corporate governance, the information economy and the challenges of an ageing population. The Organisation provides a setting where governments can compare policy experiences, seek answers to common problems, identify good practice and work to co-ordinate domestic and international policies.

The OECD member countries are: Australia, Austria, Belgium, Canada, the Czech Republic, Denmark, Finland, France, Germany, Greece, Hungary, Iceland, Ireland, Italy, Japan, Korea, Luxembourg, Mexico, the Netherlands, New Zealand, Norway, Poland, Portugal, the Slovak Republic, Spain, Sweden, Switzerland, Turkey, the United Kingdom and the United States. The Commission of the European Communities takes part in the work of the OECD.

OECD Publishing disseminates widely the results of the Organisation's statistics gathering and research on economic, social and environmental issues, as well as the conventions, guidelines and standards agreed by its members.

This work is published on the responsibility of the Secretary-General of the OECD. The opinions expressed and arguments employed herein do not necessarily reflect the official views of the Organisation or of the governments of its member countries.

Also available in French under the title:
La gestion de l'aide : pratiques des pays membres du CAD

Foreword

The 23 members of OECD's Development Assistance Committee (DAC) disbursed in 2003 nearly USD 70 billion of public money, provided by taxpayers for the purposes of development. How do they plan, manage and assess the impact of these funds?

This study, based on a survey of DAC member countries' structures, systems and practices, is intended to help answer this question. I believe that it is an important and timely publication, and it offers a wealth of observations and analysis built up over years of research.

Since the DAC was established in 1960 it has served as a forum for the exchange of ideas and identification of best practices for managing development co-operation. All the DAC member countries are committed to maximising the effectiveness of their development co-operation, but different government systems and legislative and accountability frameworks are reflected in varying approaches to implementing aid programmes. This study sets out to provide aid managers, analysts, students and all other interested parties with perspectives on the diversity of solutions developed with the objective of enhancing the aggregate flows, timeliness and effectiveness of development co-operation efforts of the major donor countries.

Richard Manning
DAC Chairman

Acknowledgements. *This reference document stemmed from requests by DAC member countries and other participants and observers of the global development assistance system and follows from the 1999 study "A Comparison of Management Systems for Development Cooperation in OECD/DAC members". The publication was researched and written by Michael Laird supported by Jean Lennock and Julia Schweizer, with the assistance of Michelle Weston and Carola Miras. Numerous people in the OECD's Development Co-operation Directorate provided inputs and comments as the publication was being prepared. The work benefited from grants made by Austria, Canada, Germany, Ireland and Japan.*

In order to achieve its aims the OECD has set up a number of specialised committees. One of these is the ***Development Assistance Committee****, whose members have agreed to secure an expansion of aggregate volume of resources made available to developing countries and to improve their effectiveness. To this end, members periodically review together both the amount and the nature of their contributions to aid programmes, bilateral and multilateral, and consult each other on all other relevant aspects of their development assistance policies.*

The members of the Development Assistance Committee are Australia, Austria, Belgium, Canada, Denmark, Finland, France, Germany, Greece, Ireland, Italy, Japan, Luxembourg, the Netherlands, New Zealand, Norway, Portugal, Spain, Sweden, Switzerland, the United Kingdom, the United States and the Commission of the European Communities.

 MANAGING AID: PRACTICES OF DAC MEMBER COUNTRIES – ISBN 92-64-00761-X – © OECD 2005

Table of Contents

MANAGING AID: PRACTICES OF DAC MEMBER COUNTRIES – ISBN 92-64-00761-X – © OECD 2005

List of Boxes

List of Tables

List of Figures

Acronyms

ACIAR	Australian Centre for International Agricultural Research
ACP	Africa, Caribbean and Pacific
ADA	Austrian Development Agency
AECI*	Spanish Agency for International Co-operation
AfDB	African Development Bank
AFD*	French Development Agency
APAD	Portuguese Development Support Agency
APEC	Asia Pacific Economic Co-operation
AsDB	Asian Development Bank
AusAID	Australian Agency for International Development
BMZ*	Ministry of Economic Co-operation and Development (Germany)
BTC	Belgian Technical Co-operation
CAP	Consolidated Appeals Process
CG	(World Bank) Consultative Group
CHAP	Common Humanitarian Action Plan
CICID*	Inter Ministerial Committee for International Co-operation and Development (France)
CIDA	Canadian International Development Agency
CRS	Creditor Reporting System
DAC	Development Assistance Committee
DCD	Development Co-operation Directorate (Ireland)
DED*	German Development Service
DEG*	German Investment and Development Corporation
DFID	Department for International Development (United Kingdom)
DGCID*	Directorate General for International Co-operation and Development (France)
DGCS*	Directorate General for Development Co-operation (Italy)
DGDC*	Directorate General for Development Co-operation (Belgium)
DGIS*	Directorate General for International Co-operation (the Netherlands)
EBRD	European Bank for Reconstruction and Development
ECHO	European Commission Humanitarian Office
ECOSOC	(United Nations) Economic and Social Council
EDF	European Development Fund
EIA	Environmental Impact Assessment
GAVI	Global Alliance for Vaccines and Immunisation
GDP	Gross domestic product
GEF	Global Environment Facility
GFATM	Global Fund for AIDS, TB and Malaria
GNI	Gross national income
GNP	Gross national product
GTZ*	(German) Agency for Technical Co-operation
HIPC	Heavily Indebted Poor Country
ICP*	Portuguese Co-operation Institute

ICRC	International Committee of the Red Cross
IDA	International Development Association
IDB	Inter-American Development Bank
IDRC	International Development Research Centre (Canada)
IFAD	International Fund for Agricultural Development
IMF	International Monetary Fund
IPAD*	The Institute for Portuguese Development Support
JBIC	Japan Bank for International Co-operation
JICA	Japan International Co-operation Agency
KfW*	(German) Bank for Development
MDGs	Millennium Development Goals
MOPAN	Multi-Organisational Partnerships, Alliances and Networks
MTEF	Medium-Term Expenditure Framework
NEPAD	New Partnership for Africa's Development
NGO	Non-governmental organisation
NORAD	Norwegian Agency for Development Co-operation
NZAID	New Zealand Agency for International Development
OAG	Office of the Auditor General (Canada)
ODA	Official development assistance
OECD	Organisation for Economic Co-operation and Development
PCM	Project Cycle Management
PRGF	Poverty Reduction Growth Facility
PRSP	Poverty Reduction Strategy Paper
PRS	Poverty Reduction Strategy
PSA	Public Service Agreement (United Kingdom)
SAARC	South Asia Association for Regional Co-operation
SADC	Southern Africa Development Community
SDA	Service Delivery Agreement (United Kingdom)
SDC	Swiss Agency for Development and Co-operation
SDR	Special Drawing Right
SECIPI*	State Secretariat for International Co-operation and Latin America (Spain)
SECO*	State Secretariat for Economic Affairs (Switzerland)
Sida	Swedish International Development Co-operation Agency
SPA	Strategic Partnership with Africa
SWAp	Sector Wide Approach
UNAIDS	Joint United Nations Programme on HIV/AIDS
UNDP	United Nations Development Programme
UNECE	United Nations Economic Commissioner for Europe
UNEP	United Nations Environment Programme
UNFPA	United Nations Population Fund
UNHCR	United Nations High Commissioner for Refugees
UNICEF	United Nations Children's Fund
UNIFEM	United Nations Development Fund for Women
USAID	United States Agency for International Development
USD	United States dollar
WFP	World Food Programme
WHO	World Health Organisation
WTO	World Trade Organisation
ZSP*	Priority Zone for Partnerships (France)

* Denotes acronym in original language.

Introduction

This report aims to expand knowledge on the various practices and sometimes complex structures adopted by the 22 member countries of the OECD's Development Assistance Committee (DAC)[1] for managing their foreign assistance to developing and transition countries. It highlights relevant work within the DAC as well as good practices or noteworthy features of particular DAC member countries' programmes. The annexes provide information on DAC member country programmes, DAC statistics, the mainstreaming of cross-cutting issues and the management of development projects and programmes. This report builds on a similar study published by the OECD in 1999.[2]

The size and effectiveness of development programmes has been a central preoccupation of the DAC since its inception 40 years ago. The DAC's Peer Reviews make an important contribution to assessing the performance of each individual DAC member. This is a critical aspect of broader concerns to improve aid effectiveness which include evaluating the overall impact of aid programmes on partner countries or on certain sectors such as health or education.

Demonstrating and improving performance presents a significant challenge for DAC members. That at least nine DAC member countries underwent major reorganisation of some form in the last ten years highlights members' efforts to address some of these challenges through organisational reforms. Among the main aid management challenges that DAC member countries face and which are discussed in this report are:

- Establishing an appropriate legal and policy framework for the development programme.
- Improving public awareness and understanding of development issues.
- Maintaining and increasing levels of funding, and increasing the predictability of aid levels.
- Allocating development funds appropriately including between multilateral and bilateral channels.
- Improving co-ordination with other stakeholders.
- Promoting policy coherence.
- Managing human resources for development.
- Developing an effective organisational structure.
- Monitoring, evaluation and independent review of the programme.
- Promoting partnership and decentralisation.

An important input for this study has been the information and insights gained as part of the on-going peer reviews of DAC members' development co-operation policies and programmes. In addition, in order to collect information on aid management issues from a field perspective, a mission was organised to Mozambique, one of the least-developed countries in the world and a country where 19 DAC member countries are actively engaged and represented at field level. A mission to the Czech Republic was also conducted which provided an opportunity to gain an understanding of the issues faced by a non-DAC donor.

Notes

1. The DAC currently has 22 member countries: Australia, Austria, Belgium, Canada, Denmark, Finland, France, Germany, Greece, Ireland, Italy, Japan, Luxembourg, the Netherlands, New Zealand, Norway, Portugal, Spain, Sweden, Switzerland, the United Kingdom and the United States. The Commission of the European Communities is also a member of the DAC.
2. OECD (Organisation for Economic Cooperation and Development) (1999), *A comparison of management systems for development co-operation in OECD/DAC members*, OECD, Paris. Available at: *www.oecd.org/dataoecd/40/28/2094873.pdf.*

ISBN 92-64-00761-X
Managing Aid: Practices of DAC Member Countries

Chapter 1

Managing Development Co-operation in the New Millennium: The Context, Challenges and Way Forward

There is evidence that countries can lift themselves out of poverty and improve the quality of life of their people. At the same time, promoting development and reducing poverty remain major tasks. The efforts of developing countries themselves can be enhanced with foreign aid. The adoption in 2000 of the Millennium Declaration set out a partnership to support development, building on the DAC's own 1996 strategy, Shaping the 21st Century: The Contribution of Development Cooperation. *Key principles now receiving priority attention relate to partner country ownership, donor harmonisation and alignment with local strategies. Policy coherence for development, between donors' policies for development co-operation, trade, investment, migration and environment, to name but a few issues, is receiving increasing scrutiny given recognition of the impact these policies can have in a highly integrated world. The DAC has been at the forefront of the discussions of all these issues as member countries continue to work to improve the volume, targeting, effectiveness and efficiency of their aid programmes.*

The need to respond decisively to today's development challenges

Decades of experience have demonstrated that countries can lift themselves out of poverty and help people improve their quality of life. Across many countries, life expectancy and primary school enrolment rates have been increasing and infant mortality rates have been falling. Institutions that support democratic societies and market-based economies have been established or re-inforced. Scientific innovations have helped to raise agricultural production. Senegal, Thailand and Uganda have been notably successful in addressing their HIV/AIDS epidemics. Korea, Singapore and Chinese Taipei, amongst others, have graduated from needing foreign assistance altogether and today implement their own development co-operation programmes.

At the same time, the stark contrasts that characterise the world mean that promoting development and reducing poverty still remains a major and urgent task. Of the six billion people on our planet, the one billion living in developed countries earn four-fifths of all income while life is a struggle to survive on less than USD 1 a day for an estimated one billion people in developing or transition countries. Life expectancy at birth is 80 years or more in Japan, Sweden and Switzerland but less than 40 years in some countries ravaged by conflict or the spread of HIV/AIDS such as Botswana, Malawi, Sierra Leone, Zambia and Zimbabwe. The average maternal mortality ratio is 21 deaths per 100 000 live births in developed countries but rises to over 1 500 deaths in Burundi, Chad, Ethiopia, Rwanda, Sierra Leone and Sudan. Primary school enrolment rates are less than 40% in Angola, Burkina Faso, the Democratic Republic of Congo and Niger. In some countries – including Afghanistan, Cambodia, Chad and Ethiopia – fewer than 1 in 3 people have access to safe water.[1]

A recent survey commissioned by the World Bank found that overwhelming majorities of opinion leaders in both developed and developing countries believed that global peace and stability will not be achieved unless a major effort is made to reduce poverty around the world.[2] Furthermore, demographic projections suggest that the world in 2050 may not be stable and develop sustainably unless decisive action is taken to incorporate developing countries more into an increasingly integrated world economy. According to current projections, the population in developed countries will still be around one billion people in 2050 but there will be a substantial contraction in the number of working-age people. Meanwhile, the population in developing countries will rise from five billion to nearly 7.7 billion, with a massive expansion in the number of people of working age.[3] If unchecked, the disparities between conditions in developed and developing countries could increase pressures further on international migration.

While developing and transition countries[4] have primary responsibility for their social and economic development as well as to ensure good governance, their efforts can be significantly enhanced with foreign assistance.[5] A robust conclusion of recent research is that aid is indeed effective in promoting economic growth and, by implication, in reducing poverty.[6] To respond to the world's continuing development challenges, the provision of foreign assistance, accompanied by increasing policy coherence, will consequently remain of central importance for today's and future generations.

Charting the way forward

DAC members acknowledge a strong moral imperative to respond to the extreme poverty and human suffering that exist in the world, as well as a strong self-interest in fostering increased prosperity, stability and security in developing countries.[7] As a concrete expression of this, tax payers in DAC member countries regularly provide well in excess of USD 50 billion each year in grants, concessional loans and technical assistance for both developing and transition countries, more than 95% of estimated total foreign assistance from all governments. In addition, developing and transition countries receive financing from the private sector in industrialised countries, most notably through foreign direct investment or grants from private philanthropic foundations and non-governmental organisations (NGOs).

A common vision has been taking shape over the last decade on how best to provide foreign assistance. There is now a wide measure of agreement that, in countries with a sound macro-economic framework and functioning institutions, aid is most likely to deliver sustainable results if it is provided in support of partner country-owned strategies for development. The foundations for this paradigm were laid out in the DAC's 1996 report *Shaping the 21st Century: The Contribution of Development Co-operation*[8] (see Box 1.1). This report also helped to usher in an era of greater concern by many DAC members on achieving development results, rather than focussing on inputs and individual activities. Since 1996, the DAC, the United Nations system and the development community as a whole have been active in giving substance to this vision for development and in making it operational. Work has also been proceeding to determine the types of approaches needed to support development in countries with poor policy and governance environments.

The adoption of the Millennium Declaration[9] by 189 nations at the United Nations General Assembly in September 2000 was significant as it refined and gave greater

Box 1.1. **Shaping the 21st Century: The Contribution of Development Co-operation**

The DAC's 1996 report *Shaping the 21st Century: The Contribution of Development Co-operation* described a framework for providing development co-operation based on four pillars:

1. A **shared vision** for development, defined by a set of measurable goals of economic well-being, social development and environmental sustainability to be pursued country by country. These goals included, most famously, the target of halving by 2015 the proportion of people living on less than USD 1 a day.
2. A concept of **partnership**, with basic changes to be given effect through compacts that allocate responsibility, reinforce local ownership, strengthen local capacities and foster participation and self reliance.
3. An emphasis on required **qualitative foundations** in developing countries, including democratic accountability, the protection of human rights and the rule of law, which are essential for the attainment of the more measurable goals.
4. The need for **coherence** between aid policies and other policies which impact on developing countries.

credibility to the vision for development sketched out in the *Shaping the 21st Century* strategy. In this declaration, developing as well as developed countries endorsed a partnership to create an environment which is conducive to development and the elimination of poverty. The declaration included a set of inter-related goals and targets – the Millennium Development Goals (MDGs) (see Table 1.1) – that incorporate and expand on the goals adopted in *Shaping the 21st Century* strategy.

In recent years, DAC members have been working through the commitment made in the *Shaping the 21st Century* report "... to change how [they] think and how [they] operate, in a far more co-ordinated effort than [they] have known until now". A key component of this

Table 1.1. **Millennium Development Goals (MDGs)**

	Goals and Targets from the Millennium Declaration
Goal 1:	**Eradicate extreme poverty and hunger**
Target 1:	Halve, between 1990 and 2015, the proportion of people whose income is less than one dollar a day.
Target 2:	Halve, between 1990 and 2015, the proportion of people who suffer from hunger.
Goal 2:	**Achieve universal primary education**
Target 3:	Ensure that, by 2015, children everywhere, boys and girls alike, will be able to complete a full course of primary schooling.
Goal 3:	**Promote gender equality and empower women**
Target 4:	Eliminate gender disparity in primary and secondary education preferably by 2005 and to all levels of education no later than 2015.
Goal 4:	**Reduce child mortality**
Target 5:	Reduce by two-thirds, between 1990 and 2015, the under-five mortality rate.
Goal 5:	**Improve maternal health**
Target 6:	Reduce by three-quarters, between 1990 and 2015, the maternal mortality ratio.
Goal 6:	**Combat HIV/AIDS, malaria and other diseases**
Target 7:	Have halted by 2015 and begun to reverse the spread of HIV/AIDS.
Target 8:	Have halted by 2015 and begun to reverse the incidence of malaria and other major diseases.
Goal 7:	**Ensure environmental sustainability**
Target 9:	Integrate the principles of sustainable development into country policies and programmes and reverse the loss of environmental resources.
Target 10:	Halve, by 2015, the proportion of people without sustainable access to safe drinking water and basic sanitation.
Target 11:	By 2020, to have achieved a significant improvement in the lives of at least 100 million slum dwellers.
Goal 8:	**Develop a global partnership for development**
Target 12:	Develop further an open, rule-based, predictable, non-discriminatory trading and financial system . Includes a commitment to good governance, development, and poverty reduction – both nationally and internationally.
Target 13:	Address the special needs of the least developed countries. Includes: tariff and quota free access for least developed countries' exports; enhanced programme of debt relief for HIPC and cancellation of official bilateral debt; and more generous ODA for countries committed to poverty reduction.
Target 14:	Address the special needs of landlocked countries and small island developing States. (through the Programme of Action for the Sustainable Development of Small Island Developing States and the outcome of the twenty-second special session of the General Assembly).
Target 15:	Deal comprehensively with the debt problems of developing countries through national and international measures in order to make debt sustainable in the long-term.
Target 16:	In co-operation with developing countries, develop and implement strategies for decent and productive work for youth.
Target 17:	In co-operation with pharmaceutical companies, provide access to affordable, essential drugs in developing countries.
Target 18:	In co-operation with the private sector, make available the benefits of new technologies, especially information and communications.

was the release of *The DAC Guidelines: Poverty Reduction* in 2001.[10] These point out that the principles underpinning the *Shaping the 21st Century* vision – partnership, ownership, partner country leadership, broad-based participation, development effectiveness and accountability – have far-reaching implications for the way development agencies conduct business. Agencies have become accountable to partner countries as well as to their own publics for their actions and commitments. According to these guidelines, agencies now need to work in a closer and more co-ordinated way with a wider range of development partners and to act as facilitators, rather than prime movers, of development. Where the conditions for partnership exist, DAC members should also tailor their assistance to partner country priorities and needs. Doing this has been facilitated by the recent emergence in most low-income countries of Poverty Reduction Strategy Papers (PRSPs). These documents, prepared by partner governments through participatory processes involving civil society and other development partners, have provided the basis of all World Bank and International Monetary Fund (IMF) concessional lending since 1999, as well as for debt relief under the Heavily Indebted Poor Countries (HIPC) Initiative.

Other important work carried out within the DAC included the establishment in 2000 of a Task Force on Donor Practices. The aim of this group, which involved multilateral donors and selected developing countries as well, was to help strengthen partner-country ownership of development processes by identifying and documenting donor practices which could cost effectively reduce the burden on the capacities of partner countries to manage aid and lower the transaction costs involved. The Task Force's work led to the release of a set of good practice papers.[11] It also provided a major input into international efforts to promote harmonisation of donors' operational policies, procedures and practices with those of partner country systems which culminated in the release of the *Rome Declaration on Harmonisation*,[12] agreed at a High-level Forum in 2003. As a result of these processes, a common understanding has been reached on a set of principles in the domains of country ownership, donor harmonisation and alignment (see Box 1.2).

Box 1.2. **Principles for country ownership, donor harmonisation and alignment**

Work involving the DAC has helped foster general agreement within the development community on principles for donors in the domains of country ownership, donor harmonisation and alignment. According to these principles, development agencies should:

- Rely on and support partner countries' own priorities, objectives, and results. This implies alignment with the national strategy (a sound poverty reduction strategy or equivalent, with national linkage to the Millennium Development Goals as applicable) and use of reliable national systems and procedures (including the government's budget, reporting cycle and monitoring timetable).
- Co-ordinate with other development agencies under partner country leadership and promote joint action whenever possible (including through delegated co-operation – *i.e.* one donor acting on behalf of another).
- Strengthen partner countries' own institutions, systems and capabilities to plan and implement projects and programmes, report on results and evaluate their development processes and outcomes, avoiding parallel donor-driven mechanisms.

Several ministerial meetings and major summits in recent years have also taken further forward the commitment to an outcome-focused and broad-ranging partnership to promote international development. The most significant of these was the International Conference on Financing for Development held in Monterrey in 2002.

- At the **United Nations International Conference on Financing for Development** in Monterrey in 2002, developed and developing countries agreed on a compact for eradicating poverty, achieving sustained economic growth and promoting sustainable development. At this conference, a commitment was made to a new partnership between developed and developing countries so that internationally agreed development goals can be achieved, including the goals contained in the Millennium Declaration. In the Monterrey Consensus, countries committed themselves to pursuing sound policies, good governance at all levels and the rule of law. They also committed themselves to mobilising domestic resources, attracting international flows, promoting international trade as an engine for development, increasing international financial and technical co-operation for development, sustainable debt financing and external debt relief and enhancing the coherence and consistency of the international monetary, financial and trading systems.
- The **World Summit on Sustainable Development** in Johannesburg in 2002 confirmed that significant progress had already been achieved towards a global consensus and partnership on a common path towards a world that respects and implements a vision of sustainable development. It noted that the ever-increasing gap between the developed and the developing worlds poses a major threat to global prosperity, security and stability. The Plan of Implementation agreed at the summit identified eradicating poverty as the greatest global challenge facing the world and an indispensable requirement for sustainable development, particularly for developing countries. It was consequently concluded that concerted and concrete measures were required by all concerned parties to enable developing countries to achieve their development goals.
- The Fourth **World Trade Organisation (WTO) Ministerial Conference** in Doha in 2001 launched a new round of multilateral trade negotiations. Because of their focus on issues of importance for developing countries, such as improving market access for agricultural products, this round is known as the Doha Development Agenda. The main task of the WTO Fifth Ministerial Conference in Cancún in 2003 was to take stock of progress in negotiations and other work that was underway. This meeting resulted in an *impasse* but consultations continue with the objective of identifying opportunities for advancing negotiations further.

Significant momentum has been generated through the consensus reached by the *Shaping the 21st Century* report, the Millennium Declaration and the Monterrey Consensus on development priorities, resource needs and increased access to external financing. This momentum, combined with the HIPC Initiative and development of national Poverty Reduction Strategies, as well as the general agreement on the objectives and ideal approaches for providing foreign assistance, marks a turning point in the history of development co-operation and establishes solid foundations for moving forward.

However, there is no room for complacency since the development challenges that remain are substantial. Data assembled by the OECD show that for every goal and target included in the Millennium Declaration, there are encouraging signs of progress in some parts of the world as well as worrying evidence of stagnation and even reversal in others.[13] The least-developed countries,[14] particularly those in sub-Saharan Africa, are facing serious difficulties in their efforts to meet the Millennium Development Goals. It is critical, therefore, that individually and collectively DAC member countries' foreign assistance programmes are well managed, carefully targeted and complementary so as to enhance their effectiveness and improve impact.

Policy coherence for development

Important as foreign assistance is, in a highly integrated world there are many domains where the policies of donor governments can complement or frustrate development efforts in other countries. For example, domestic agricultural subsidies in industrialised countries can have trade-distorting effects, environmental and sanitary restrictions on imports can act as non-tariff barriers and immigration policies can result in developing countries losing health workers and other professionals who may have been trained through foreign assistance programmes. On the positive side, industrialised country policies can foster trade and investment and facilitate the sharing of technology. All of this highlights the importance of governments following through on their commitments to promote international development by taking the development dimension into account when formulating policies in a diverse range of areas.[15] Otherwise, the impact of foreign assistance may simply be to offset the costs imposed on other countries by a lack of coherence in the policies of donor governments. Conscious of the implications for developed and developing countries alike of a more integrated world, Sweden recently adopted legislation that encourages a whole-of-government approach to promoting international development (see below).

An example: Sweden

The Swedish Parliament adopted legislation in December 2003 that makes contributing to equitable and sustainable development throughout the world a goal for all areas of Swedish policy. *Shared responsibility: Sweden's policy for global development* (ref.: 2002/03:122) consequently lays a solid foundation for decision making that promotes international development. The legislation emphasises the importance of close collaboration with actors in all sectors of society including local authorities, civil society institutions, the private business sector and trade unions. Significantly, trade, agriculture, environment, security, migration and economic policy are included as examples of areas in which policies can and should promote global development. Development co-operation itself is included as one aspect of Sweden's broader policy. It is expected that the new policy will result in some changes in the organisation and management of the Swedish development co-operation agency.

Experience across DAC member countries suggests that enhancing policy coherence for development[16] can be a challenging process due to competing national interests. Although full policy coherence for development may not be a feasible objective, it is critical that government decision making takes place with full awareness of the potential impact and implications of decisions on developing countries. Work within the DAC, building on more general work undertaken at the OECD,[17] has highlighted some institutional approaches that can facilitate policy coherence, including:

- **High-level political commitment:** A clear official statement on the global poverty reduction objective, reflecting a firm foundation for efforts by the government to ensure that developing countries' concerns are taken into account in the formulation of policies.

- **Co-ordination mechanisms across government:** Formal and informal inter-ministerial co-ordination processes at political and officials levels, allowing for a screening of policies and decisions *vis-à-vis* poverty reduction. It is important that development agencies themselves participate in these processes and are not represented by another agency or minister who may have a different perspective on issues.
- **Analytical capacity:** Staff with the training, experience and time to assess broader policy issues in terms of their actual or potential effects on developing countries and poverty reduction. These staff may be housed in a dedicated policy coherence unit within the development agency (see below).

An example: the Netherlands

To help promote policy coherence for development, the Netherlands established in 2002 a small Policy Coherence Unit, headed at director level, within the Directorate-General for Development Co-operation of its Ministry of Foreign Affairs. The unit has two main functions: *i)* contributing to policy formulation in non-development areas and *ii)* tackling concrete cases of policy incoherence. Because many non-aid policies impacting on developing countries fall within the purview of the European Union, the Unit engages actively in existing European Union co-ordination mechanisms within the Netherlands as well as works to build coalitions with like-minded European Union Member States. The Unit's approach to tackling incoherence is more opportunistic, seizing windows of opportunity for change. For example, in 2002, the Unit took advantage of the mid-term review of the European Union's Common Agricultural Policy and negotiations within the WTO on the Doha Development Agenda to prepare a report on improving coherence between agriculture, trade and development, particularly in relation to the three highly supported commodities of cotton, rice and sugar. The resulting *Memorandum on Coherence between Agricultural and Development Policy* was signed by both the Minister for Agriculture, Nature Management and Fisheries and the Minister for Development Co-operation, approved at cabinet level and sent to the Parliament.

From comparative DAC experience, some lessons can be highlighted related to enhancing policy coherence for development. The range of issues, actors and responses involved means that no single policy-making system can guarantee greater policy coherence in all contexts. Variable approaches should consequently be expected and, in their specific national context, may be just as effective in promoting policy coherence. Not surprisingly, the degree of policy coherence tends to diminish where a policy area is domestically sensitive and when there are strong domestic interest groups and government agencies with other primary interests involved. Sometimes, positive measures have been adopted but not necessarily in order to promote policy coherence for development. For example, the pressure to reform the European Union's Common Agricultural Policy has mainly been promoted by net contributors to the programme, which raises the question of whether a lack of policy coherence for development provides sufficient grounds for changing policies. This demonstrates the usefulness of development agencies pursuing strategic alliances with other stakeholders so as to promote reforms that contribute to enhancing policy coherence for development.

Notes

1. World Bank (2003), *World Development Indicators*, World Bank, Washington DC. It should be noted that data are not published for all developing countries.
2. Princeton Survey Research Associates (2003), *Global Poll: Multinational Survey of Opinion Leaders 2002*. Washington DC. The survey included 2 600 opinion leaders in 48 countries.
3. United Nations Population Division (2003), *World Population Prospects: The 2002 Revision*, New York. Figures quoted are "Medium variant" projections.
4. In DAC terminology, "developing countries and territories" means those on Part I of the DAC List of Aid Recipients while "transition countries and territories" means those on Part II of the List (see Annex A.3 for further details).
5. In this report, the terms "development co-operation", "foreign assistance" and "aid" are used interchangeably and refer to both official development assistance (ODA) and official aid.
6. McGillivray, M. (2003), *Aid Effectiveness and Selectivity: Integrating Multiple Objectives into Aid Allocations*, World Institute for Development Economics Research Discussion Paper No. 2003/71, Helsinki.
7. OECD (1996), *Shaping the 21st Century: The Contribution of Development Co-operation*, OECD, Paris,
8. Available at: *www.oecd.org/dataoecd/23/35/2508761.pdf*.
9. Available at: *www.un.org/millennium/declaration/ares552e.pdf*. The General Assembly has requested that the United Nations Secretary-General prepare an annual report on progress achieved by the United Nations system and member states towards implementing the Millennium Declaration. This information is published on the Internet at: *www.un.org/millenniumgoals/*.
10. Available at: *www.oecd.org/dataoecd/47/14/2672735.pdf*.
11. OECD (2003), *DAC Guidelines and Reference Series: Harmonising Donor Practices for Effective Aid Delivery*, OECD, Paris. Available at *www.oecd.org/dataoecd/0/48/20896122.pdf*.
12. Available at *www1.worldbank.org/harmonization/romehlf/Documents/RomeDeclaration.pdf*.
13. OECD (2004), "Progress Towards the Millennium Development Goals", *The DAC Journal, Vol. 5, No. 1*, OECD, Paris, pp. 51-70.
14. The term "least-developed countries" describes the world's poorest countries according to a United Nations classification based on income, economic diversification, social development and population criteria.
15. Among other commitments, developed countries have set themselves the objective of assuring that the entire range of relevant policies are consistent with, and do not undermine, development objectives. OECD (1996), *Shaping the 21st Century: The Contribution of Development Co-operation*, OECD, Paris. See also: OECD Action for a Shared Development Agenda – Final Communiqué, Ministerial Meeting 2002.
16. It is useful to distinguish between policy *consistency*, *i.e.* ensuring that development co-operation policies are not internally contradictory, and policy *coherence*, which implies pursuing development objectives through mutually reinforcing aid and non-aid policies.
17. OECD (1996), *Building Policy Coherence: Tools and Tensions*, Public Management Occasional Papers, No. 12, OECD, Paris.

ISBN 92-64-00761-X
Managing Aid: Practices of DAC Member Countries

Chapter 2

The Legal and Political Foundations for Development Co-operation

Just over half of DAC member countries have passed legislation which establishes the basis for, and the main objectives of, their development co-operation programme and over two-thirds have developed policy statements which, while they do not carry the force of law, also set out the priorities and approaches of the development programme. Having a clear legal or policy basis for development co-operation, together with political representation at cabinet level, is critical if development objectives are to be regarded as a key component of government approaches in all major policy areas and if they are to take priority. Although public support for development co-operation is high within DAC member countries, understanding of development issues is fairly limited. Given the importance of the public contribution to development co-operation, improving public understanding may be critical if commitments to increase levels of development assistance and to promote greater policy coherence are to be met.

Legislative basis

To a large extent, the legislative basis for development co-operation programmes reflects the legal traditions of each DAC member country. It is striking that while 12 member countries (see Annex A.1), particularly those with codified legal systems (including Spain, see below), have extensive and detailed legislation to guide their foreign assistance programmes, other DAC member countries have no specific legislation at all, with overall policies and strategies being set by government and spending authority being obtained through appropriations legislation. In a few DAC member countries, general legislation sets the main lines of the development co-operation programme but then delegates to the government or the responsible minister authority to implement programmes within the limits defined. A well-developed legislative basis has the advantages of transparency and of clarifying responsibilities among the various government entities that may be involved, as well as establishing development objectives as the main thrust of development co-operation for the whole system. On the other hand, countries with a less formalised legal basis may have more flexibility to act and this could be an advantage when trying to build coalitions between development agencies and other government entities whose policies and actions have an impact on development prospects in developing countries.

An example: Spain

The Spanish Parliament passed a major new law in 1998 to up-date and consolidate the legislative basis for Spain's development co-operation programme. *Law 23/1998, dated 7 July, on International Co-operation in Matters of Development* contains six chapters. Chapter I defines Spanish policy on international co-operation in matters of development. Chapter II outlines planning, instruments and forms of Spanish policy on international co-operation. Chapter III establishes the institutions responsible for formulating and implementing Spanish policy on international co-operation. Chapter IV addresses resources issues, Chapter V personnel issues and Chapter VI participation by NGOs and other civil society partners. The law refers to the Spanish Agency for International Co-operation as the body to manage Spanish policy in this domain. That agency's statutes – covering its role and responsibilities, aims and functions, management bodies, basic organisational structure, human resources policies and arrangements in respect of assets, economic and financial matters and labour contracts – were approved in *Royal Decree 3432/2000, dated 15 December*.

Political context

From a development perspective, the goals and targets of the Millennium Declaration have established medium-term objectives for foreign assistance at the international level. However, achieving development objectives may be only one reason for providing foreign assistance. Many DAC members acknowledge that development co-operation is an integral

 MANAGING AID: PRACTICES OF DAC MEMBER COUNTRIES – ISBN 92-64-00761-X – © OECD 2005

part of their foreign relations; some explicitly refer to development co-operation as an instrument for pursuing their national interests. The view of a former deputy administrator of the United States Agency for International Development (USAID) is that "most governments also pursue other goals with their aid, including diplomatic, commercial and national cultural goals".[1] The Simons Committee's report on Australia's foreign assistance found that the aid programme had been "struggling to satisfy a triple mandate, emphasising foreign policy and commercial benefits to Australia as well as development benefits to developing countries".[2] The United Kingdom's *International Development Act 2002* made it unlawful to provide aid for purposes other than the reduction of poverty, such as the previous practice of promoting commercial interests by tying aid to the purchase of British goods and services.

Striking an appropriate balance between development objectives and other goals pursued through foreign assistance programmes is ultimately a political choice which each DAC member country makes. This choice is made, however, within the boundaries of the formal DAC definition of official development assistance (ODA), agreed to by all DAC members, that the main objective of ODA is the promotion of economic development and the welfare of the partner country. Additionally, sufficient weight needs to be given to development concerns because achieving development results and maintaining public support for aid require that foreign assistance does have an impact in terms of achieving development objectives. International initiatives are helping to restrict the possibility of using foreign assistance for non-development purposes. For example, the recommendation adopted by the DAC in 2001 to untie most categories of ODA to the least-developed countries[3] has reduced opportunities for using foreign assistance to promote commercial interests.

General policy statements

Irrespective of the legislative basis, DAC member countries often find it useful to prepare an overarching general policy statement for their foreign assistance that outlines its main purpose and objectives. For example, 20 DAC member countries have an overriding policy objective guiding their development co-operation programme with poverty reduction featuring significantly in the overall objective for at least 16 members (see Annex A.1 for an outline of DAC member countries policy objectives and statements). These policy statements may take the form of a government White Paper and should ideally be endorsed by all ministers responsible for activities that impact on development prospects in developing countries. Since such policies are often debated with or take account of inputs from civil society, the consultative process through which they are prepared may be as important as the document itself, if this helps to build public awareness of and support for the development co-operation programme. General policy statements can also provide a unity of purpose when a country has several agencies charged with implementing its foreign assistance, as is the case in Germany (see below). Such policy statements may also contain information that does not lend itself to being set in legislation, for example ambitions regarding future levels of ODA as a share of gross national income (GNI). In some cases, policy statements relate exclusively to foreign assistance while others form part of broader government statements on international development, foreign relations or national security.

For example: Germany

The German government released in 2001 its *Programme of Action 2015 for Poverty Reduction*, which sets out the concrete steps the various German ministries and agencies will take to contribute to halving the proportion of the world population living in extreme poverty by 2015. The programme, produced with broad involvement of civil society and the private sector, situates poverty reduction as an important part of the government's overall policy, as well as being the overarching goal of Germany's development policy. The programme sets out 10 priority areas for action under which some 75 specific actions are listed. The 10 priority areas are: *i)* boosting economic activity and active participation of the poor, *ii)* giving effect to the right to food and implementing agrarian reform, *iii)* creating fair trade opportunities for developing countries, *iv)* reducing debt and financing development, *v)* providing basic social services and strengthening social protection, *vi)* ensuring access to essential resources and fostering an intact environment, *vii)* realising human rights and respecting core labour standards, *viii)* promoting gender equality, *ix)* strengthening good governance, and *x)* resolving conflicts peacefully and fostering human security and disarmament.

Ministerial arrangements

The national political environment plays a decisive role in explaining the number and variety of ministerial arrangements for development co-operation found in DAC member countries. Objectively, an ideal system would have clear leadership and most DAC member countries do have an identifiable political leader of their development agency. This may be a Minister of Development Co-operation or the Minister of Foreign Affairs with responsibilities that go beyond development co-operation to include foreign and sometimes trade relations as well. Nevertheless, the complex nature of development co-operation means that other ministers may also have responsibility for certain key aspects of their country's development co-operation programme. For example, contributions to international financial institutions such as the World Bank may be the responsibility of the Treasurer or the Minister of Economy. Humanitarian assistance may be implemented separately from the rest of the development co-operation programme and be under the responsibility of a different minister. In the final analysis, only a few DAC members have a single minister responsible for almost all aspects of their country's foreign assistance programme.

As regards the seniority of the minister with main responsibility for development co-operation, in only a few DAC member countries is development co-operation the minister's sole responsibility and this person sits in the cabinet of ministers (*i.e.* the inner circle of government). In many other cases, either the minister sits in cabinet but has a wide range of responsibilities or the minister is solely responsible for development co-operation but does not have a seat in cabinet. Neither of these situations are ideal from a development perspective. In the first case, the minister can defend development issues at the highest levels but cannot devote their full attention to development issues. In the second case, there is a risk that development issues may receive little attention at the highest level of government or that development issues are championed in cabinet by a more senior minister who otherwise has little contact with the development co-operation programme.

In countries where several ministers are involved in the development co-operation programme, it is important that some mechanism exists to co-ordinate activities and promote synergies. In some cases, a formal co-ordination mechanism has been established (including France, see below). The membership, meeting schedule and mandates of such committees varies. Among the key factors that appear to influence the impact of these committees are the level of authority of the committee, its membership, the periodicity of formal and secretariat meetings, the mandate and the range of issues addressed.

An example: France

France established the Inter-Ministerial Committee for International Co-operation and Development (CICID) in 1998 with a role that includes promoting cross ministry co-ordination. It is presided over by the Prime Minister and its members include the Minister for Foreign Affairs, the Minister for Economic Affairs and Finance and the Minister for Co-operation, as well as other ministers who have responsibilities related to France's development co-operation programme. The specific aims of CICID are to: *i)* designate the countries included in the Priority Zone for Partnerships (ZSP); *ii)* establish guidelines for the objectives and instruments of international co-operation and development assistance policy; *iii)* ensure coherence in the geographical and sectoral priorities for the different components of French co-operation; and *iv)* ensure the continuous monitoring and evaluation of aid relative to targets set. CICID normally meets at least once a year. In between these meetings, the committee may meet at official or senior official levels. The Ministry of Foreign Affairs and the Ministry of the Economy, Finance and Industry act as a co-secretariat for the committee.

Parliamentary oversight

Parliamentarians, as the elected representatives of the taxpayers who fund development co-operation programmes, are responsible for and can play an important role in monitoring the management and implementation of foreign assistance programmes. Parliamentarians may become involved during plenary sessions of the parliament, such as during question time, or in meetings or hearings of parliamentary committees. In some DAC members such as the United Kingdom (see below), a specific committee or sub-committee has been established that focuses exclusively on international development and related issues.

An example: the United Kingdom

International development has been scrutinised by a committee or sub-committee of the United Kingdom Parliament since 1967, sometimes as part of a broader mandate to monitor foreign policy issues. The creation of the Department for International Development in 1997 triggered the establishment of the current International Development Committee with the role of examining the department's expenditure, policy and administration. Since then, the 11 person committee has prepared reports and called for evidence on a variety of subjects, including most recently: strategic export control; migration and development; and development assistance and the occupied Palestinian territories. The committee may take evidence from whomever it pleases in government or from civil society. The government may publish responses to the reports issued by the committee. The United Kingdom Parliament also has a long-standing informal All-Party Parliamentary Group on Overseas Development, a 20-member group that aims to keep abreast of all matters concerning international development, notably in its economic, social, political and humanitarian dimensions.

Parliaments are quite active in some DAC member countries and a considerable time may be spent by ministers and civil servants in responding to their requests for information or briefings. In these countries, parliamentarians' participation may extend to an active involvement in setting overall policies and taking major decisions. However, in many other countries, the role of the parliament is comparatively modest. The existence of a specific committee dealing with development issues or a unified budget that covers most foreign assistance expenditure appear to be two important factors influencing the level of parliamentary involvement in development co-operation.

Public support for development co-operation

The public in DAC member countries are key stakeholders in foreign assistance programmes. Not only do they contribute to these programmes through their taxes and by electing the politicians who monitor aid policies, management and implementation, they also stand to benefit from the increased prosperity and security that will flow from greater economic growth and less poverty in developing and transition countries. At the same time, in many DAC member countries, the public's understanding of development issues is fairly shallow and support for foreign assistance, though strong, is based upon the erroneous assumption that it will mostly be spent on humanitarian crises. People also tend to overestimate considerably their government's aid effort.[4] As with other major public policy areas, the public have a right to be aware of, and to understand better, issues related to international development and foreign assistance. Some DAC member countries see this as being of critical importance. In Switzerland, for example, the *Federal Law on International Development Co-operation and Humanitarian Aid* obliges the government to provide public education on development issues. Other DAC member governments do not consider it to be their role to educate the public, or preclude their development agencies from doing this by law.

Development education

Improving awareness and understanding of development issues is important because it enables the public to engage better in debates on development policy, helps to build support for foreign assistance programmes and can promote policy reforms and improvements. The public in DAC member countries appear predisposed to learning more about development issues because their support for helping developing countries has remained consistently high for almost two decades. Better educated, young and urban-dwelling individuals tend to be stronger supporters, a finding that could be instructive for targeting awareness raising activities.[5]

Improving public understanding will be particularly important for achieving the Millennium Development Goals. These call for increased volumes of aid and greater development coherence in policies in donor governments, objectives which may require strong political will and sustained political support if difficult political trade offs are to be made that favour international development. With greater understanding of issues, the public, and their elected representatives, should become more convinced that difficult political choices may be necessary but that these are justified by the longer-term benefits that will accrue.

An important aspect of the work of development agencies is consequently to inform the public about development issues in general and the national aid programme in particular. DAC member countries typically spend less than 1% of their ODA on information and development education[6] although some DAC members have been increasing their development education budget in recent years. However, for most people, the media remain the primary source of information about developing countries and development issues. In many DAC member countries, NGOs can also be a significant source of information and may be more effective than government development agencies or other official channels in promoting awareness of development issues.

Many DAC member countries take a systematic and long-term approach to promoting public awareness using a variety of methods (see below). These include the publication of annual reports and the availability and accessibility of key policy documents, working through schools and with youth and including development issues in the curricula of certain subjects, making information and educational resource material available through the Internet,[7] organising national forums where government policy can be presented and debated with the public and working with NGOs and faith-based structures to hold public information sessions and debates. In many cases, communications have focused on "inputs", such as aid levels and debt forgiveness, rather than on the results or impact of foreign assistance efforts. One way development agencies could improve the impact of their public awareness activities is to link international development to more broadly understood issues such as health, the environment and defence. Another would be to focus on desirable development results by using the Millennium Development Goals more.

An example: Finland

The Finnish Ministry of Foreign Affairs has demonstrated motivation and innovation in its development education programme. It works with the National Board of Education to support development education programmes in schools. Programmes have included the development of inter-active web-based materials, quizzes, teacher training programmes, seminars and workshops. National campaigns, such as one on Africa in 2002, have included festivals and exhibitions and reached significant numbers of visitors. The ministry has financed a publication that shows development issues through comic strips entitled *Comics with an Attitude: A Guide to the use of Comics in Development Information.* Ministers travel throughout the country to inform people about Finnish development co-operation. European Union information offices in Finland have also been proposed as a way of disseminating materials on development co-operation.

Monitoring public opinion

Opinion surveys show that public support for development assistance is high within DAC member countries and has remained fairly stable over time, a significant result given that most people tend to think that aid levels are higher than they actually are. Europeans in particular appear increasingly supportive of development assistance: in 2002, 86% of them believed development co-operation to be either "very" or "rather" important (compared to 76% in 1998). A further indication of public support is the increasing amounts donated by the public to development and humanitarian NGOs.[8]

Public support for foreign assistance can exist alongside concern about levels of public spending. For example, in the United States a 1995 opinion poll found that the majority of respondents felt the government was spending too much on foreign assistance and yet 80% of respondents agreed with the principle that the United States should help people overseas who are in genuine need. In Italy, high levels of support for development assistance co-exist with an emphasis on the need for it to be more effectively used. Moreover, high levels of support sometimes co-exist with limited understanding about development, poverty issues and the nature of official development assistance programmes.

Many development agencies take steps to keep up to date with public opinion and use a variety of methods to do this. Sweden and Norway carry out annual surveys of public opinion although for most other DAC member countries these are found to be too costly and so tend to be less frequent even though they generate a wide range of valuable information. More focused or issue-specific surveys may be conducted as a supplement to national opinion polls carried out on other topics. Regular surveys of different types are valuable as they can be used to monitor trends in public opinion over time and also to establish links between public opinion and changes in government policy. A small number of DAC member countries have yet to carry out research or surveys to establish levels of public awareness and understanding of development issues while others have no established system for regular surveys.

Recently, DAC members, the United Nations Economic Commission for Europe (UNECE) and the OECD have been working to improve the reliability and comparability of data collected through public opinion surveys so as to facilitate deeper analysis of attitudes and trends across DAC member countries. This includes a set of common questions that could be included in broader, nationally representative surveys on development co-operation.

Notes

1. Lancaster, C. (1999), *Aid to Africa: So much to do, so little done*, University of Chicago Press, Chicago.
2. The Simons Report (1997), *One Clear Objective: Poverty Reduction through Sustainable Development. Report of the Committee of Review*, Canberra.
3. *Available at www1.oecd.org/media/release/dac_recommendation.pdf.*
4. OECD (2004), *Mobilising Public Opinion Against Global Poverty*, Policy Insights No. 2, OECD, Paris.
5. OECD (2003), *Public Opinion and the Fight against Poverty*, OECD, Paris.
6. *Ibid.*
7. See, for example, AusAID's *Global Education* website *www.ausaid.gov.au/globaled/default.cfm* and the site of the New Zealand Global Education Centre *www.globaled.nz*, an NGO which receives financial support from NZAID.
8. OECD (2003), *Public Opinion and the Fight against Poverty*, OECD, Paris.

ISBN 92-64-00761-X
Managing Aid : Practices of DAC Member Countries

Chapter 3

DAC Member Countries' Development Co-operation at the Dawn of the 21st Century

DAC member countries' development co-operation programmes vary in many ways including their size, the types of aid instruments used, the number of activities supported, sources of funds, allocation of funds, main partner countries and sectoral focus. This variation is due to a range of factors including differing political or strategic choices, each country's comparative advantage, as well as historical, cultural, geo-political, strategic and development interests. The main impact of this variety in development programmes is on partner countries where donor country development policy and practices affect the degree to which local ownership and genuine partnership is feasible. An increasing emphasis on donor co-ordination, as well as on aid harmonisation and alignment (see Chapter 8), should contribute to improved aid effectiveness and reduced transaction costs on partner countries.

Aid to developing and transition countries

In 2003, DAC member countries provided USD 69.0 billion of net ODA to developing countries, 0.25% of their combined GNI (see Figure 3.1). ODA consists of grants and concessional loans for mainly development or welfare purposes from the government sector of a donor country to a developing country or a multilateral agency active in development. Debt forgiveness has become an increasingly important component of ODA, rising steadily as a percentage of ODA since 2000. By 2006, ODA could rise to nearly USD 88 billion (at 2003 prices and exchange rates) if pledges made at or around the time of the United Nations International Conference on Financing for Development in Monterrey in 2002 are met.[1]

Flows to countries in transition or to agencies primarily active in countries in transition are known as official aid.[2] DAC member countries provided more than USD 7 billion of net official aid to transition countries in 2003, with the largest donors being France (USD 2.0 billion), the United States (USD 1.5 billion) and Germany (USD 1.2 billion).

More than two-thirds of total DAC foreign assistance is provided bilaterally, mostly as grants, with the largest recipients being the Democratic Republic of Congo, China and India (see Figure 3.2). Aid to large countries can have an important catalytic effect through the transfer of ideas and good practice, even if in volume terms this aid is modest in relation to the size of their economies. And, as the crisis in South-East Asia in 1997 showed, development gains may not be sustainable if a country's financial and management systems are weak. In such circumstances, a continuing engagement may be necessary to help improve the sustainability of progress achieved. In the poorest counties, on the other hand, ODA remains an important source of public sector funding because these countries simply do not yet have access to sufficient amounts of other sources of financing to help them develop – their domestic revenue base is still too weak and private finance is limited and sometimes non-existent. Donors supply 40% or more of public resources in at least 30 developing countries, including Bolivia, Madagascar, Nepal and Tanzania.[3] To a large extent, increasing prosperity in the least-developed countries will depend on the continued availability of ODA, while these countries build up their capacity to create and mobilise domestic resources and to promote private investment.

Some characteristics of individual foreign assistance programmes

When viewed individually, there is a noticeable degree of variety in DAC member countries' development co-operation programmes, to a certain degree due to different political or strategic choices made by each DAC member country as well as their comparative advantage (see Annex A.1 for a basic profile of each DAC member country's programme). The number and choice of main partner countries varies, often reflecting a range of historical, cultural, geo-political, strategic as well as development interests. Some DAC members have a wide selection of aid instruments at their disposal whereas some do not extend loans, provide general budget support or send volunteers, to mention three

Figure 3.1. **Net Official Development Assistance in 2003 – Amounts**

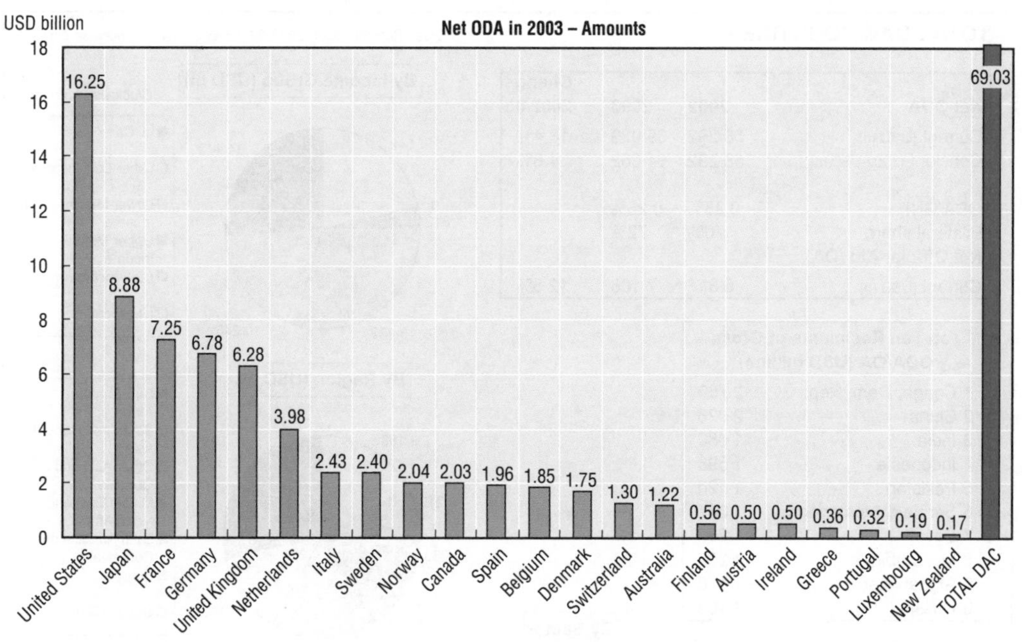

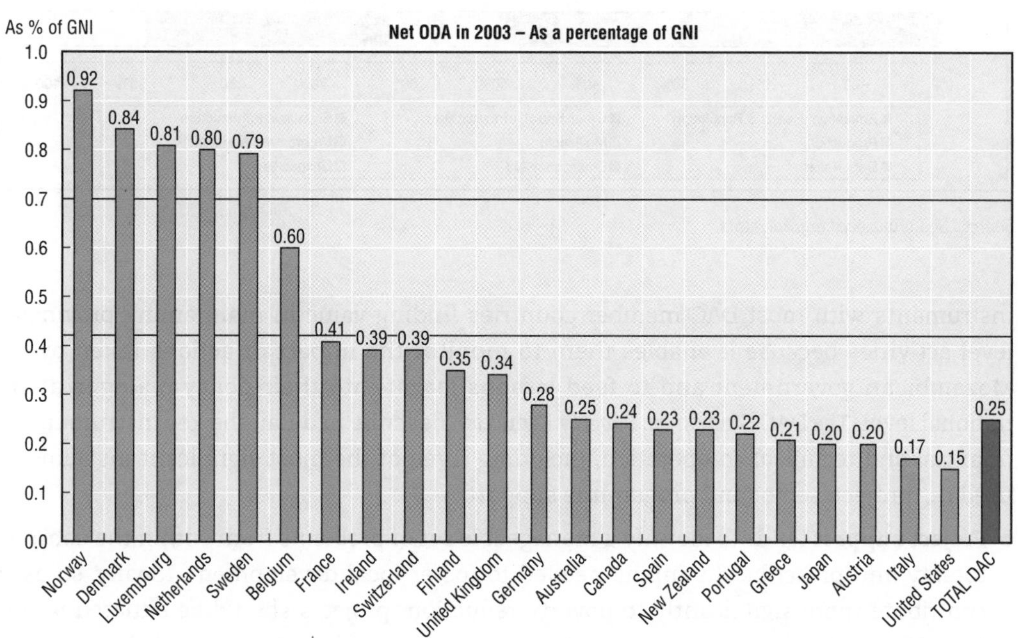

possibilities. The share of multilateral ODA varies from around one-quarter to nearly three-quarters of their total net ODA. Few DAC member countries are members of all the regional development banks and many have become more selective regarding the United Nations agencies to which they make voluntary contributions.

DAC member countries use a variety of aid instruments in their main partner countries, the choice and combination of which normally flows from country-level analysis. In Mozambique, for example, DAC members employ a wide range of aid

Figure 3.2. **DAC member countries' foreign assistance at a glance**

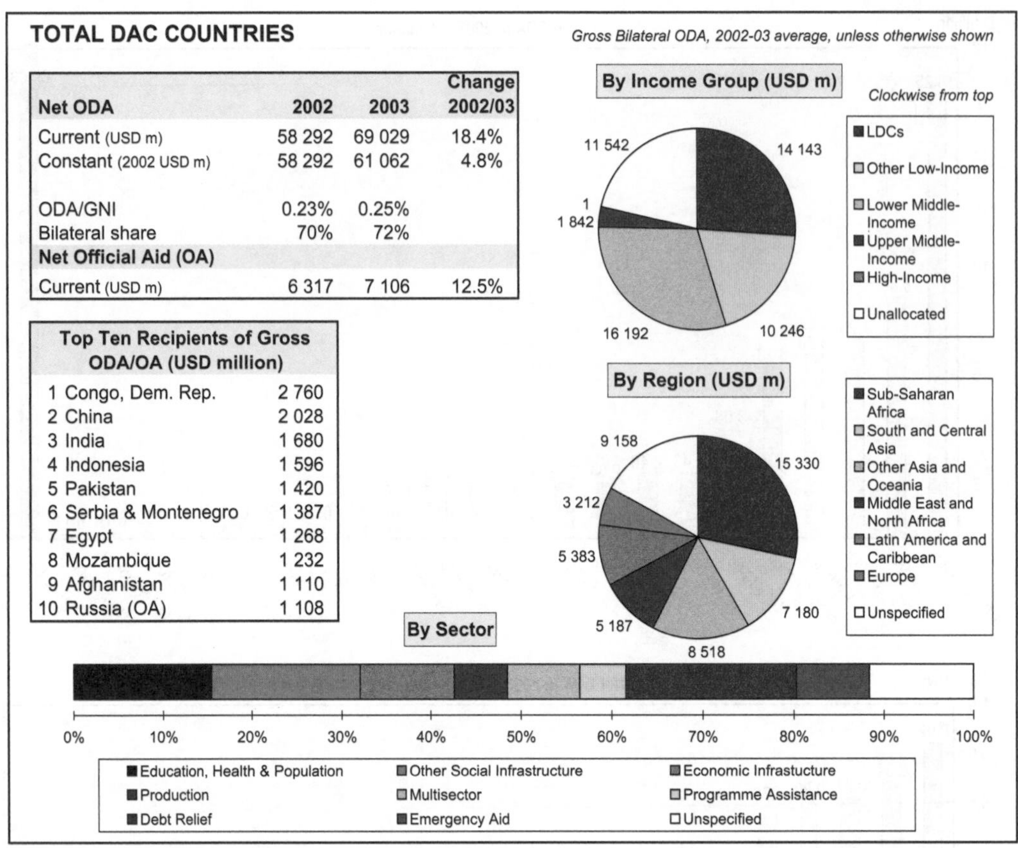

Source: See *www.oecd.org/dac/stats.*

instruments with most DAC member countries finding value in maintaining provincial-level activities because it enables them to monitor the impact of actions taken by the Mozambican government and to feed lessons learnt into their policy dialogue at the national level. *The DAC Guidelines: Poverty Reduction* describe in detail the key instruments of financial and technical co-operation, including three of the most significant instruments used *i.e.* project, sector and programme support:

- **Project support** tends to identify a manageable set of problems from within the complex totality and prescribe the inputs needed to foster local development. Ideally, so as to contribute more significantly to poverty reduction, projects should be situated within the broader development framework, address the multiple concerns of the poor and strengthen the capacities of the poor to achieve sustainable livelihoods.[4]
- **Sector support** or Sector-Wide Approaches (SWAps) contribute, under partner government leadership, towards a single sector policy and expenditure programme and should, where possible, use common management and reporting procedures to disburse and account for all funds. Sector programmes imply a different approach to aid management calling for greater modesty, an acceptance of a slow process of change, and partnership building.
- **Programme aid** consists of financial contributions, not linked to specific project activities, extended to a partner country for general development purposes, such as

 MANAGING AID: PRACTICES OF DAC MEMBER COUNTRIES – ISBN 92-64-00761-X –

balance of payment support or general budget support. It is often associated with the promotion of policy reforms at the macroeconomic level and/or in specific sectors.

The size of bilateral foreign assistance programmes "managed" annually by DAC member countries also varies noticeably. The concept of "managed bilateral foreign assistance" gives an indication of the amount of money actively managed by DAC member countries' development agencies. It includes all gross bilateral ODA and all gross bilateral official aid with the exception of debt forgiveness, imputed student costs, domestic refugee costs and official aid grants to overseas territories. In 2002, it ranged from less than USD 100 million to more than USD 13 billion, with countries falling into four broad categories:

- **Seven smaller donors** (managing bilateral foreign assistance programmes of less than USD 300 million): Austria, Finland, Greece, Ireland, Luxembourg, New Zealand and Portugal.
- **Nine medium-sized donnors** (managing bilateral foreign assistance programmes of between USD 500 million and USD 1 500 million): Australia, Belgium, Canada, Denmark, Italy, Norway, Spain, Sweden and Switzerland.
- **Four larger donors** (managing bilateral foreign assistance programmes of between USD 2 billion and USD 4 billion): France, Germany, the Netherlands and the United Kingdom.
- **Two large donors** (managing bilateral foreign assistance programmes of more than USD 9 billion): Japan and the United States.

The collective impact of foreign assistance programmes

When viewed collectively, there is a noticeable degree of dispersion in the foreign assistance provided by DAC member countries. Foreign assistance is provided by DAC member countries through a large number of government agencies – in a few countries more than eight agencies – to a total of 186 developing or transition countries. These activities are delivered by a wide range of intermediaries including partner government institutions at national, provincial and local levels, multilateral agencies, global funds, NGOs and other civil society institutions, private contracting firms, individual consultants and volunteers. The assistance may take the form of training, technical advice, scholarships for tertiary studies, provision of goods such as medicines and food, construction, maintenance or repair of infrastructure, direct payments into foreign governments' budgets or debt relief. During the period 1999 to 2001, DAC members alone reported an average of 35 225 new development activities[5] a year to the OECD's Creditor Reporting System, with an average cost of USD 1.5 million per activity.

The very large number of activities supported by DAC members imposes high transaction costs on partner countries, as well as on donors themselves, and reduces the collective impact of foreign assistance. A typical developing country received aid from around 15 bilateral donors (as well as 10 multilateral agencies) in 2000[6] and an issue for the donor community as a whole is whether a more efficient matching of donors with partner countries' needs can be promoted, building on each donor's comparative advantage. European Union Member States have had a treaty obligation since 1992 to co-ordinate their development co-operation policies and to consult each other on their aid programmes.[7] So far, however, these efforts have not resulted in the number of aid activities funded being reduced to more manageable levels. The general agreement on the overall objectives and approaches for development co-operation should provide a good basis for greater collaboration among donors, including expanding opportunities for donors to work or provide funds through other donors. The issue of different and more efficient ways of delivering foreign assistance is becoming more pressing as new donors continue to emerge (see Box 3.1).

Box 3.1. **Non-DAC donors**

When originally established in 1960, the DAC had 10 member countries but this number has now more than doubled over the subsequent four decades. Greece is the most recent member of the DAC, having joined in 1999. Other OECD members have ambitions to join the DAC in the coming years. With a total net ODA volume of USD 279 million in 2002, Korea already has a significant aid programme although at 0.06%, its ODA/GNI ratio remains low by comparative DAC standards. Some non-OECD countries and economies are also active and major players in development co-operation, including China, Chinese Taipei, Kuwait, Saudi Arabia and the United Arab Emirates.

Since their accession to the European Union on 1 May 2004, the 10 new member states from central Europe and the Mediterranean have also become more significant donors. These countries now contribute to funding the European Communities' aid programmes and participate in their management. Alongside this significant increase in each of these countries' multilateral assistance, some are working to build up their institutional capacities to manage and implement more substantial and effective bilateral programmes. The Czech Republic, for example, provided USD 45 million of ODA and USD 9 million of official aid in 2002. In recent years, it has re-inforced capacity within its Ministry of Foreign Affairs to co-ordinate the 11 ministries that implement its bilateral aid as well as set up a small centre that could be the embryo of an implementing agency with a wide range of responsibilities.

Very few countries in fact have the means to implement a substantial and effective development co-operation programme in all developing countries around the world. For most donors, therefore, some degree of selectivity will be necessary in terms of main partner countries, specific sectors or aid instruments if their activities are to have the critical mass to be effective and their aid is to have a sustained impact. The development co-operation provided by new and emerging donors is a welcome addition to global financing for development and is often an endorsement, from first-hand experience, of the positive contribution that foreign assistance can make. The value of this aid may, however, be diminished if these donors follow the path of joining the large number of bilateral donors already operating in some well-aided "good performing" developing countries, such as Mozambique, with bilateral programmes of a few million dollars each. Current DAC members can be of assistance to other donors by helping them identify where their experience and special expertise can be used to maximum advantage. DAC members can also set a useful example by demonstrating how some more efficient forms of bilateral development co-operation can be implemented, such as delegating delivery of bilateral development assistance to another donor or acting through silent partnerships. A further issue that merits consideration, by DAC and non-DAC donors alike, is the appropriate balance between providing aid bilaterally and multilaterally and the potential gains, in terms of greater efficiency and reducing burdens on partner countries, from channelling more aid through multilateral agencies. Given this expanding importance and role of non-OECD and non-DAC donors, the DAC is currently considering a range of options to facilitate informal co-operation and to manage growing interest in participating in the Committee.

Mechanisms for donor co-ordination

DAC member countries consider co-ordination to be a central and critical issue and that promoting good co-ordination among donors will help improve the effectiveness of foreign assistance and reduce transaction costs on partner countries. Alongside other initiatives for donor harmonisation, there are some key and long-standing formal mechanisms for dialogue between donors. In addition, there are a number of co-ordination mechanisms for donors and partner countries at the field level which are becoming increasingly important.

The OECD's Development Assistance Committee

The major bilateral donors work together in the DAC to increase the effectiveness of their common effort to support development. Through this work, the DAC plays an important policy co-ordination role among its members. The DAC undertakes four principal types of activities:

- It adopts authoritative policy guidance (see Box 3.2 for details of DAC reference material).
- It conducts periodic critical peer reviews of members' development co-operation policies and programmes.
- It provides a forum for dialogue to exchange experience and build international consensus on policy and management issues of interest to members.
- It publishes statistics and reports on aid and other resources flows to developing and transition countries.

The European Union

European Union Member States are mandated under the provisions of the 1993 Maastricht Treaty to co-ordinate their policies on development co-operation and to consult each other on their aid programmes. The objective for European Union Member States is to achieve greater co-ordination, coherence and complimentarity of their aid programmes. Currently, 15 of the 25 European Union Member States are also members of the DAC.

Strategic Partnership with Africa

The World Bank's Strategic Partnership with Africa (SPA) was established in 1987 and has been one of the most important fora for the co-ordination of aid to sub-Saharan Africa. The agenda of the SPA has evolved beyond financing to include the developmental context of economic reform with the formation of working groups on particular themes to support this. The SPA is also committed to ensuring that all aid supports country-led national poverty reduction strategies, to greater efforts to co-ordinate and streamline requirements at the country level, and to building stronger capacity in African governments.

Country level co-ordination mechanisms

These may include Poverty Reduction Strategy (PRS) monitoring groups set up by partner countries to monitor implementation and impact of the PRS, thematic or sectoral donor co-ordination groups, and United Nations roundtables as well as the formal World Bank Consultative Group (CG) meetings.

Box 3.2. **DAC reference material**

OECD (1992), *Development Assistance Manual:* DAC Principles for Effective Aid.

OECD (1992-1995), *DAC Guidelines on Aid and Environment*, Nos. 1-9.

OECD (1995), *Donor Assistance to Capacity Development in Environment.*

OECD (1995), *Participatory Development and Good Governance.*

OECD (1995), *DAC Orientations for Development Co-operation in Support of Private Sector Development.*

OECD (1998), *Conflict, Peace and Development Co-operation on the Threshold of the 21st Century.*

OECD (1998), *DAC Sourcebook on Concepts and Approaches Linked to Gender Equality.*

OECD (1999), *DAC Guidelines for Gender Equality and Women's Empowerment in Development Co-operation.*

OECD (2000), *Effective Practices in Conducting a Joint Multi-Donor Evaluation.*

OECD (2001), *DAC Recommendation on Untying Official Development Assistance to the Least Developed Countries.*

OECD (2001), *Evaluation Feedback for Effective Learning and Accountability.*

OECD (2001), *The DAC Guidelines: Helping Prevent Violent Conflict.*

OECD (2001), *The DAC Guidelines: Poverty Reduction.*

OECD (2001), *The DAC Guidelines: Strategies for Sustainable Development.*

OECD (2001), *The DAC Guidelines: Strengthening Trade Capacity for Development.*

OECD (2001), "Conflict Prevention and Development Co-operation Papers" in *The DAC Journal*, Vol. 2, No. 3.

OECD (2002), *Gender Equality in Sector Wide Approaches.*

OECD (n.d.), Gender Equality Tipsheets.

OECD (2003), *DAC Guidelines and Reference Series: Harmonising Donor Practices for Effective Aid Delivery.*

OECD/World Health Organization (2003), *DAC Guidelines and Reference Series: Poverty and Health.*

OECD (2003), *DAC Guidelines and Reference Series: A Development Co-operation Lens on Terrorism prevention. Key Entry Points for Action.*

World Bank Consultative Group meetings

The principle aims of Consultative Group meetings are to promote policy dialogue between donors and an individual partner country as well as to mobilise resources in support of its development. One of the primary functions of these meetings has been the pledging of commitments by donors to fill a country's financing requirements. Discussions have, in recent years, centred on both sectoral planning and issues relating to governance and participatory development. CG meetings have increasingly been organised in-country to enable broader local participation from members of parliament, civil society, NGOs and the private sector.

Notes

1. The bulk of the increase in ODA is expected to come from five DAC members: France, Germany, Italy, the United Kingdom and the United States. For further information, see OECD (2004), "Progress Towards the Millennium Development Goals", *The DAC Journal, Vol. 5, No. 1*, OECD, Paris, pp. 51-70.
2. See Annex A.3 for further information on statistical concepts.
3. World Bank (2003), *World Development Report 2004: Making Services Work for the Poor*, World Bank, Washington DC, p. 203.
4. Information on the management of projects and programmes is provided in Annex A.5.
5. A development activity can take many forms. It can be a project or a programme, a cash transfer or delivery of goods, a training course or research project, a debt relief operation or a contribution to a NGO.
6. Acharya, A., A. Fuzzo de Lima, and M. Moore (2004), *Aid proliferation: How responsible are the donors?*, Institute of Development Studies Working Paper 214, Brighton.
7. See Article 180 of the Consolidated Version of the Treaty Establishing the European Community.

ISBN 92-64-00761-X
Managing Aid : Practices of DAC Member Countries

Chapter 4

Sources and Allocation of Funds

An important issue for many DAC member countries is the different sources of funds used to finance their development co-operation programme. The lack of one consolidated budget for development co-operation can create difficulties in monitoring and reporting development-related expenditure. Increasing the predictability of development budgets could also facilitate better planning and management. Decisions about the allocation of development funds are influenced by multiple factors but are increasingly related to concerns with improving effectiveness and impacting on poverty reduction.

Sources of foreign assistance funds

Appropriations

DAC member countries primarily fund their foreign assistance programmes through annual appropriations voted by their national Parliaments on the basis of proposals made by the government. Such budgets have the force of law and are sometimes used to define the main features of the foreign assistance programme. Normally these budgets are sufficiently general in nature to allow governments, the responsible minister or senior officials some flexibility to adjust allocations to fit evolving circumstances or unpredictable events, including emergency situations and humanitarian crises. However, in some countries where the legislature operates fairly independently of the government, parliaments give more precise indications in terms of geographic allocations, aid levels for particular countries or regions, or specific uses. This may reduce the efficiency and effectiveness of foreign assistance programmes as it forces aid managers to concentrate on adjusting existing programmes and allocating new resources to comply with the various requirements set by parliament.

Few DAC member countries have a single budget which finances all their ODA and official aid activities. There are several reasons for this. Some aid does not require a transfer of funds and so does not need to be appropriated, such as the forgiveness of non-performing loans or, for European Union Member States, the *pro rata* share of disbursements made by the European Commission financed directly from its own resources. Other ODA-eligible expenditures may not be made or managed by the development agency/Ministry of Foreign Affairs, including sustenance costs for refugees during their first year in a donor country or the additional costs incurred by armed forces when carrying out some development-related activities. Finally, appropriated funds may be supplemented from other sources, such as sub-national authorities. The Netherlands provides an example of how foreign assistance can be grouped into one overall budgetary framework (see below).

Even when a single ministry or development agency in a DAC member country is responsible for managing the vast majority of the foreign assistance programme, appropriations for foreign assistance expenditures may be made to other ministries as well. Core contributions to multilateral agencies in particular are often made directly by the relevant ministry rather than the development agency/Ministry of Foreign Affairs. For example, the Ministry of Finance may pay contributions to international financial institutions and the Ministry of Health may pay core contributions to the World Health Organization (WHO), even if the development agency also makes additional payments to support specific activities. In DAC member countries where several ministries are involved in implementing foreign assistance activities, there may be no "aid budget" at all. Each ministry funds aid-related activities from its own regular budget allocation and activities are compiled at the end of the year to determine expenditures on aid.

An example: the Netherlands

The Homogeneous Budget for International Co-operation (HGIS) was introduced by the Netherlands' government in 1995 in order to ensure that all foreign assistance is regrouped into one overall planning framework. The HGIS is based on the five foreign policy priorities: international order; peace, security and stability; European integration; sustainable poverty reduction; and bilateral relations. The table below indicates the relative budgetary weight of these different categories and, in particular, the percentage of ODA subsumed in each. The HGIS is a very useful tool because it gives an overview of all expenditure by the various ministries involved in development co-operation (including ODA that does not consist of expenditure in developing countries such as debt relief and domestic refugee costs). It also helps to make the distinction between activities that are consistent with the ODA definition and those that are not.

Table 4.1. **The Homogeneous Budget for International Co-operation (HGIS)**

	Total HGIS in € 1 000	*Of which:* ODA in € 1 000	Total HGIS in %	*Of which:* ODA in %
1. International order	**142 387**	**17 951**	**3**	**0**
2. Peace, security and stability	**477 193**	**239 155**	**9**	**5**
Of which:				
Humanitarian aid	*168 586*	*164 101*	*3*	*3*
Good governance, human rights and peacebuilding	*42 027*	*11 654*	*1*	*0*
3. European integration	**36 440**	**0**	**1**	**0**
4. Sustainable poverty reduction	**3 433 365**	**3 156 838**	**65**	**60**
A. Bilateral development co-operation	1 277 001	1 197 462	24	23
B. Multilateral development co-operation	1 013 234	874 913	19	17
Of which:				
European Union	*423 440*	*299 368*	*8*	*6*
United Nations	*305 806*	*298 533*	*6*	*6*
International financial institutions	*283 988*	*277 012*	*5*	*5*
C. Private development co-operation	1 143 130	1 084 463	22	21
Of which:				
NGOs	*745 600*	*745 146*	*14*	*14*
Research and international education	*137 192*	*131 317*	*3*	*2*
Private sector	*260 338*	*208 000*	*5*	*4*
5. Dutch bilateral relations	**499 231**	**200 845**	**9**	**4**
Of which:				
Asylum, migration and consular services	*202 447*	*194 420*	*4*	*4*
6. Other	**682 268**	**196 032**	**13**	**4**
TOTAL	**5 270 884**	**3 810 821**	**100**	**72**

Source: Netherlands Ministry of Foreign Affairs (2004).

The variety of sources of funds for foreign assistance activities has two (unfortunate) consequences. It may make it more difficult for parliamentarians to monitor and influence foreign assistance programmes because a variety of appropriations made may need to be examined, including some appropriations that are not obviously development related. It also means that governments may not manage and so cannot directly control all expenditures which are eligible for reporting as ODA. This can introduce a degree of chance into whether and when countries reach quantitative objectives set for ODA, such as ODA/GNI targets.

One perennial question about managing foreign assistance funds is how to reconcile the long-term nature of development co-operation, calling for multi-year planning horizons, with the normal practice of aid appropriations lapsing each year. In many DAC member countries, general government procedures require that funds appropriated in a given fiscal year be disbursed within that year or, as a minimum, committed within that year and spent soon afterwards. As a consequence, aid managers in some countries operate under considerable pressure to commit and disburse funds rapidly, promoting undue emphasis on the financial inputs of development activities, rather than desired outcomes and actual results.

Related to the appropriation of funds is the issue of disbursements of those funds. It tends to be easier to elaborate and authorise development activities than to implement them because numerous problems can intervene which delay activities significantly or even result in them being impossible to implement. For example, activity managers may find it difficult to recruit staff, legal clearances may be slow in coming through or technical problems may arise. Political decisions may also be taken by donors in response to major changes in circumstances in partner countries, for example delaying or cancelling general budget support payments or contributions to sector programmes or cancelling all government-to-government activities. "Pipelines" of committed but unspent funds can accumulate. Unless the development agency as a whole, or specific programme areas, have the flexibility to redirect funds to other activities or to carry unspent funds forward (see below), the point may be reached where questions are raised about why more funds need to be made available. Pipeline analysis may help agencies identify generic issues that are contributing to the accumulation of unspent funds.

An example: New Zealand

The 1994 *Fiscal Responsibility Act* obliges the New Zealand government to present rolling three-year projections for each budget item, including the aid budget, providing a degree of predictability in budget allocations which is beneficial for ensuring continuity in aid planning and management. In addition, NZAID can overspend its annual budget allocation by up to 10% or carry forward 20% of its annual budget to the next fiscal year, thus reducing the pressure on aid managers to spend money within an externally determined time frame and irrespective of the evolving realities in developing countries.

Other sources of funds

In addition to funds from sub-national authorities, aid budgets appropriated by national parliaments may be supplemented in a variety of other ways. Debt forgiveness, for example, is increasing as a proportion of ODA (see below). The World Bank and the regional development banks derive a substantial share of their lending from international capital markets and some DAC member countries whose development co-operation system includes banking institutions, such as France, Germany and Japan, also on-lend borrowings from international capital markets to developing and transition countries. The repayment of principal (amortization) and payment of interest from earlier lending is another source of funds. In general, this money is returned to the Treasury or the central government budget, although in a few countries these funds may be re-used for new development activities.

An example: Italy

Italy has adopted a flexible approach to debt relief. For example, Italy goes beyond the HIPC initiative to include lower middle-income countries in its debt relief agreements. Italian law allows both the cancellation of ODA-related debt as well as up to 100% of commercial debt. Debt relief is conditional on criteria related to good governance, refusal of war, and commitment to poverty reduction, social and human development. Italy is flexible in its requirements on the traceability of released funds according to the partner country's overall fiduciary environment and capacity to absorb the burden of strict financial controls. In some countries, resources released by debt cancellation operations are placed in a local fund, managed jointly by Italy and the local authorities, with strict control exerted over expenses as well as certification that resources released are used to fund poverty reduction activities. However, in partner countries such as Mozambique, where a high level of trust exists between the donor community and the government, debt cancellation is carried out under a set of minimum requirements, in order to limit the administrative burden on the partner government.

Money raised through lotteries and assets seized in drug trafficking cases (see below) are perhaps less obvious means some DAC member countries also use to fund development activities.

An example: Belgium

Through the *Belgian Survival Fund*, net profits from the Belgian National Lottery are used to finance development activities in some of the poorest countries. The fund was originally set up by law in 1983 as the *Survival Fund for the Third World* and was a response to public concerns about the magnitude of drought-inflicted mortalities in Ethiopia and other parts of sub-Saharan Africa at the time. It had an initial endowment of EUR 248 million. A new law was promulgated in 1999 that included a further allocation of EUR 250 million, to be paid in annual instalments of a minimum of EUR 18.6 million. Programmes financed by the *Belgian Survival Fund* favour an integrated approach and aim to improve the food and nutritional security of families and local communities in rural and semi-urban environments. Projects are implemented jointly with NGOs or multilateral agencies (especially IFAD, UNDP, UNICEF and WHO). Between 1984 and 2002, the fund financed approximately 125 projects with a total value of EUR 287 million.

An example: Luxembourg

The 1988 *United Nations Convention against Illicit Traffic in Narcotic Drugs and Psychotropic Substances* invites signatories to provide funds derived from assets seized in drug trafficking cases – including funds seized in related money-laundering operations – to the United Nations for its work in this field. Of the 168 parties to this convention, Luxembourg has to date been the only signatory to apply this provision. Monies collected by Luxembourg are first paid into an *Anti-Drug Trafficking Fund*. Allocations of these funds are then decided by an inter-ministerial steering committee comprising representatives from the Ministries of Finance (as President), Foreign Affairs, Health and Justice. Since the fund's creation in 1993, approval has been given for projects worth more than EUR 11 million, principally in priority countries for Luxembourg's development co-operation programme or through the United Nations Office on Drugs and Crime. Activities funded through the United Nations have included training drug control officials in Argentina, Bolivia, Chile and Peru and alternative development programmes aimed at eliminating economic dependency on illicit drug production in Bolivia, Laos and Vietnam.

New sources of funds

Realising that achieving the Millennium Development Goals will require substantial extra funds for aid – estimates have indicated that at least USD 50 billion a year in extra aid is likely to be needed[1] – DAC members have been exploring avenues other than traditional ODA to finance development. The most important options being considered are:

- **Global taxes** on currency transactions, energy use or drug sales.
- **Voluntary private sector contributions** through donations, global lotteries, premium bonds or global funds.
- **Financial engineering** including "frontloading" aid through the proposed International Finance Facility,[2] a focussed use of additional Special Drawing Rights (SDRs) issued by the IMF and public guarantees.

Each of these options has advantages as well as economic and political drawbacks. With renewed political will, enhanced support from public opinion and changes in domestic attitudes in some DAC member countries, some of these options might succeed in providing additional aid. To a large degree, variations on a few of these options could also be implemented by DAC member countries on a unilateral basis. It nonetheless remains the case that the most straightforward way to increase aid is through additional appropriations by national parliaments.

Allocation of funds

One of the most difficult to understand aspects of development co-operation is how decisions are made about the distribution of foreign assistance funds, both the choice between bilateral and multilateral channels and the breakdown within each of those channels. In most DAC member countries, radical changes to these distribution patterns are rare, with established commitments tending to continue and changes generally occurring by making small adjustments regularly. At the same time, many DAC member countries are assessing their engagement in particular multilateral agencies and main partner countries more critically than in the past and may be more ready to leave multilateral agencies that are considered to be under performing or to phase out government-to-government programmes in countries with a poor record of respecting human rights and democracy. The end of the Cold War and increased concerns about the effectiveness of aid may be promoting a more strategic and focussed approach.

The share of multilateral assistance provided by DAC member countries is typically around one-quarter to one-third of total ODA, although there are some notable exceptions. A few countries have a policy of providing a certain share of their aid multilaterally. Multilateral assistance takes the form of capital subscriptions, which governments pay as part of their membership, and discretionary contributions to funds managed by multilateral agencies, especially the United Nations agencies. Capital subscriptions are fixed and normally do not require any further decisions, providing membership of the institution is not called into question.

DAC member countries need to make important decisions about the distribution of their voluntary multilateral contributions and bilateral assistance: its geographic focus, the number and choice of main partner countries and which sectors to focus on. Guidance on these choices may be contained in the legislation underpinning the aid programme or an over-arching policy statement. For some DAC member countries, the choice of main partners may reflect strong historical and political ties with certain countries or groups of countries or be linked to their geographic proximity to the donor country.

Partner country selection and allocations

DAC member countries fund development activities in a large number of partner countries, often in excess of 100, through the variety of funding mechanisms at their disposal. These activities can include, for example, NGO co-financing schemes, humanitarian assistance and specific themes such as gender, HIV/AIDS, democracy and good governance or private sector development. In some cases, there is a noticeable difference between the main recipients of a DAC member country's foreign assistance and their designated main partner countries and donors may only devote a small share of their bilateral aid to their main partner countries.

Several DAC member countries are working to build stronger partnerships with a more limited number of main partner countries for their government-to-government programmes. These moves towards increased focus may arise in the context of the creation of a new development programme or funding mechanism, a policy of greater decentralisation of responsibility to field missions or the objective of concentrating on a more limited number of countries so as to improve effectiveness. The prospect of a major expansion, or contraction, in aid can spark reflections within a development agency about why the foreign assistance programme is the way it is and these findings can help guide future decision making on main partners and appropriate allocation levels.

Limiting the number of countries in which agencies are operational is a challenge and decisions to focus on a more limited number of main partner countries only rarely result in a donor withdrawing rapidly and totally from a country. Only government-to-government activities tend to be affected and on-going activities may be allowed to run their full course. Denmark, for example, recently decided to phase out its co-operation programme in Bhutan, as a positive consequence of that country's rapid economic, political and social development, with activities to be wound down over a ten-year period. In the meantime, Denmark is establishing a new education sector programme in Bhutan.[3]

To help donors improve the effectiveness of aid allocations, the OECD organised an expert's seminar in 2003[4] which addressed the issue of country selectivity and allocations and provided information on how the Netherlands and the United States have been approaching the issue (see Box 4.1). Participants recognised that questions of country selectivity are ultimately highly political choices but that the use of good analytical models could usefully inform these processes. There are risks, however. On the one hand, too much complexity in the underlying analyses could cause allocation models to be ignored. On the other hand, if greater simplicity led to some important variables being left out, the results may be considered irrelevant and so also be ignored. An appropriate balance consequently needs to be struck. A further issue for the donor community as a whole was raised at the seminar: if all donors use a similar set of country-allocation criteria, they risk ending up providing foreign assistance to the same subset of partner countries (the "good performers"). This could lead both to problems of diminishing or even negative returns in

Box 4.1. **OECD Expert Seminar on Aid Effectiveness and Selectivity: Integrating Multiple Objectives into Aid Allocations**

The most important finding from this seminar, which was attended by representatives of development agencies, NGOs and researches from OECD and developing countries, was that there is a strong and growing convergence of views on how to make cross-country aid allocations more effective in reducing poverty. The main criteria to use are:

- The level of poverty (as proxied by average *per capita* income), concentrating ODA heavily on the lowest income countries.
- The incidence of poverty (as proxied by population).
- The development performance of partners.

Some important differences of view remain on the margin, however, including how much weight to give to population and to development performance, respectively, and how best to measure the latter.

A number of DAC member countries, including the Netherlands and the United States, are using these findings to influence decisions on country allocations. The purpose in doing this is not to deny political decision makers the final decisions, but to inform them of the allocations suggested by these criteria and weightings. In other words, the starting point for decision making on allocations becomes the results of this quantitative approach, rather than the previous years' level or *ad hoc* preferences.

In **the Netherlands**, both selection of main partner countries for government-to-government programmes and the determination of the amount of aid for each country are highly political processes, involving cabinet ministers and the parliament, but evidence from aid effectiveness studies has become a significant selectivity element in recent years. The Dutch use a series of criteria to derive their assessments:

- For the **selection of countries** during the latter half of 2003 the procedure was modified. The selection of partner countries is based not only on the current situation, but also on long-term prospects. The main criteria in the process remain poverty (eligibility for funding from the World Bank's International Development Association [IDA]), good governance and social policies. Other criteria are the need for aid, the added value provided by Dutch development cooperation and foreign policy considerations. This shift has resulted in a single list of 36 partner countries (including Afghanistan) with which the Netherlands will enter into long-term development relationships.
- The determination of **allocation levels** among selected countries is based on both performance and needs. The performance indicators are: social and economic policies, governance (using the World Bank's country policy and institutional assessment exercise) and human rights as well as an assessment of the on-going aid programme in the country. Need is assessed using three per capita indicators: GNP, ODA and debt. These scores are added and then a 50% bonus is given to least-developed countries and to sub-Saharan African countries. The final score is then applied to the available budget to give an allocation per capita, which is multiplied by the square root of the country's population so as to introduce a small country bias. Finally, allocations below EUR 10 million are disregarded, to eliminate unworkably small programmes. In late 2004, however, the system was under revision.

The **United States** is using a set of clear, concrete and objective criteria to determine which countries will be eligible for funding from its new Millennium Challenge Account. A poverty reduction focus will be promoted in the first two years by limiting eligibility to

Box 4.1. **OECD Expert Seminar on Aid Effectiveness and Selectivity: Integrating Multiple Objectives into Aid Allocations** *(cont.)*

countries meeting criteria for concessional funding from the World Bank. From the third year, the threshold will be increased to include lower middle-income countries. There are 16 performance indicators in three policy areas: governing justly, investing in people and promoting economic reform. To qualify for funding, partner countries must score above the median on half of the indicators in each of the three policy areas (and not be excluded from receiving foreign assistance from the United States government). The 16 indicators are:

- **Governing justly:** *i)* civil liberties, *ii)* civil rights, *iii)* voice and accountability, *iv)* government effectiveness, v) rule of law and *vi)* control of corruption.
- **Investing in people:** *i)* country credit rating, *ii)* one year consumer price inflation, *iii)* fiscal policy, *iv)* trade policy, *v)* regulatory quality and *vi)* days to start a business.
- **Promoting economic reform:** *i)* public expenditures on health/GDP, *ii)* immunization rates for DPT3 and measles, *iii)* public primary education spending/GDP and *iv)* primary education completion rate.

the selected subset of countries as well as under funding and the risk of increasing poverty and instability in other countries. Participants at the seminar concluded that each donor should consider what other donors are already doing in main or potential new partner countries. Aid needs and donors' capacities should be viewed in a matrix at sector, national and international levels. Co-ordination, both within and across countries, is crucial.

Sectoral focus

The selection of sectors in which DAC member countries are operational in their main partner countries remains a critical aspect of the development of a bilateral government-to-government programme. Several DAC member countries limit, or are increasingly limiting, the number of sectors in which they operate in each of their main partner countries. Denmark, for example, aims to work in a maximum of four sectors per main partner country and Finland and the Netherlands in a maximum of three sectors. This approach could give each donor the critical mass to be more effective in each sector.

Consultations with the partner country government and the sectoral priorities outlined in their national Poverty Reduction Strategy should guide the sector operations of donors. In several partner countries, however, many DAC members can be found concentrated in the same sectors. The field visit to Mozambique, for example, found that of the 19 DAC member countries operational there, 14 have a priority focus on the health sector, 12 are focused on rural development/agriculture, 11 are focused on education, and 9 on good governance. Seven DAC member countries focussed on three of these four sectors. At the same time, the Mozambican government could not find sufficient support for fisheries, a potentially important sector for Mozambique's development. In partner countries where many development agencies are operational, a greater degree of partner government-led donor co-ordination may be needed to prevent duplication and to ensure that all important sectors are adequately covered.

Notes

1. United Nations (2003), *Implementation of the United Nations Millennium Declaration: Report of the Secretary-General*. New York. Ref. A/58/323.
2. The International Finance Facility would provide up to an additional USD 50 billion a year in aid between now and 2015 by transforming current pledges for additional ODA into legally-binding long-term commitments and using these to issue AAA-rated bonds that donor governments would repay in the years following 2015. This mechanism would increase the amount of aid available in the short-term but donor governments could not include these extra amounts in their ODA until they started to repay the bonds, *i.e.* after 2015.
3. Royal Danish Ministry of Foreign Affairs (2003), *A World of Difference*, Copenhagen.
4. OECD (2003), *Aid Effectiveness and Selectivity: Integrating Multiple Objectives into Aid Allocations*. OECD, Paris.

ISBN 92-64-00761-X
Managing Aid: Practices of DAC Member Countries

Chapter 5

The Overall Shape of DAC Member Countries' Development Co-operation Systems

There are notable and important differences in the way that DAC member countries structure themselves to manage and implement their development co-operation programmes. These include the degree of involvement of the foreign affairs ministry, the degree of institutional dispersion and representation in partner countries and relations with headquarters. There appears to be little correlation between the size of the bilateral foreign assistance programme managed and the approaches adopted. The structure of development co-operation programmes is highly dynamic: many DAC member country programmes go through regular organisational change prompted by factors such as changes in leadership, focus or size of the programme. Regardless of the organisational structure, the main concern should be with developing operational structures that improve the effectiveness of aid management and contribute to attaining objectives efficiently and effectively.

The shape of development co-operation systems

One important reason for the variations in structures found across DAC member countries is that aid programmes remain rooted in their different national political environments, systems of government and civil service practices, including human resources policies. Within some countries, choices may be excluded that are options in others. For example, the Irish Constitution limits the number of government ministers to 15, which has an impact on whether Ireland can establish a separate department for development co-operation with its own minister. In the Swedish approach to government, ministries oversee a number of agencies that implement the laws passed by parliament. This explains the existence of an implementing agency for development co-operation separate from the Ministry of Foreign Affairs, a structure that is consequently likely to continue. Similarly, general civil service reforms within countries can have a profound impact on aid programmes, as has notably been the case when results-based management systems have been introduced in some countries as government-wide initiatives. Understanding development co-operation systems requires an awareness of those domains where countries have flexibility to adapt their structure and approach and those where the national context imposes limitations or requires extended processes before changes can be introduced.

In recent years, there have been some significant restructurings and major changes in the shape of development co-operation systems. In 2004, Austria established a new implementing agency separate from its Ministry of Foreign Affairs while Norway folded many of the functions of its implementing agency back into its foreign ministry. Reviews of the development co-operation divisions in the Ministry of Foreign Affairs in Ireland and New Zealand led to Ireland deciding to reinforce its existing structure but to New Zealand deciding to establish a new development agency as a semi-autonomous body of its Ministry of Foreign Affairs and Trade. The United States has established the Millennium Challenge Corporation to administer the substantial new foreign assistance money pledged for developing countries that rule justly, invest in their people and encourage economic freedom. This adds another agency to the range of institutions already delivering the United States' foreign assistance. (See also Box 5.1.)

Specific features of DAC member countries' development co-operation systems

Involvement of the Ministry of Foreign Affairs

As foreign assistance implies working with the people, institutions and governments of other countries, there is an inextricable link between development co-operation and foreign relations. This results in ministries of foreign affairs being implicated to some degree in all DAC member countries' development co-operation systems (see Box 5.2), if not at headquarters at least in the field. In some countries, a development co-operation division may exist within the ministry of foreign affairs or the ministry may have main

Box 5.1. **Restructuring DAC member countries' development co-operation systems**

The organisational structures adopted by DAC member countries for their foreign assistance are dynamic and often complex. Major reforms and restructurings occur regularly – such as amalgamating previously separate bodies, creating new entities or re-organising the internal structure of development agencies. But what prompts these events?

- A change of government:
  - ❖ In **Australia**, the government elected in 1996 commissioned an independent review of Australia's overseas aid programme which produced a detailed report entitled *One clear objective: Poverty reduction through sustainable development*. The review reaffirmed the value of maintaining management of the aid programme in a single autonomous development agency but led to a number of changes including the establishment of an independent ministerial committee and the creation of an Office of Review and Evaluation to provide more frequent and transparent reporting on aid outcomes.
  - ❖ In **New Zealand**, the government elected in 2000 commissioned an independent review of the official development assistance programme, the results of which were published in *Towards Excellence in Aid Delivery*. This process led to the creation, in 2002, of the New Zealand Agency for International Development (NZAID) as a semi-autonomous body within the Ministry of Foreign Affairs.
- A change of leadership:
  - ❖ In **Japan**, the new President of the Japan International Co-operation Agency (JICA) is instigating major institutional reforms aimed at strengthening its overseas aid programmes by shifting more staff from headquarters to missions abroad.
  - ❖ In **Norway**, the new Minister of International Development, appointed in 2002, commissioned an evaluation of Norwegian development policy administration and this led, in 2004, to the transfer of some responsibilities from the Norwegian Agency for Development Co-operation (NORAD) to the Ministry of Foreign Affairs.
  - ❖ The appointment of a new Permanent Secretary of the **United Kingdom**'s Department for International Development (DFID) has led to some major restructuring including within the department's Policy Division, which has moved from several single-discipline departments in such areas as education and health to multi-disciplinary teams focussed on key issues, for example aid effectiveness and poverty reduction in difficult environments.
- A decision to provide extra resources for foreign assistance:
  - ❖ In the wake of its decision to increase its ODA to 0.7% of GNI by the end of 2007, the Government of **Ireland** appointed in 2001 a committee of independent experts to undertake a comprehensive review of Irish aid policy and management. This led to the integration of two agencies into the Ministry of Foreign Affairs and the establishment of a new high-level oversight and ministerial advisory body.
  - ❖ In 2002, the President of the **United States** announced the creation of a new Millennium Challenge Account which is expected to provide an additional USD 5 billion of foreign assistance annually by 2006. A process of consultations and reflections followed to determine how best to administer these funds with the decision taken to create a new Millennium Challenge Corporation.

Box 5.1. **Restructuring DAC member countries' development co-operation systems** *(cont.)*

- Major external events:
  - **Sweden**'s Ministry of Foreign Affairs underwent a major re-organisation in 1996, following its accession to the European Union in 1995. The new structure was designed to enable Sweden to respond more effectively to the wider range of issues that the ministry would be called on to address.
- Concerns to improve aid effectiveness:
  - The **Austrian** Development Agency (ADA) was established in 2004 as the implementing agent for bilateral assistance. ADA has the scope to recruit more staff, technical and administrative, and to enhance the timeliness and quality of Austrian co-operation efforts.
  - The Institute for **Portuguese** Development Support (IPAD) was created in 2003 through the merger of the Portuguese Co-operation Institute (ICP) and the Portuguese Development Support Agency (APAD). This created one main body within the Ministry of Foreign Affairs for the formulation and implementation of development co-operation policies. The objective behind this move was to improve the quality and efficiency of Portugal's foreign assistance programme.

responsibility for a specific aspect of the aid programme, such as humanitarian assistance, the promotion of democracy and good governance or contributions to some multilateral agencies. In countries where a number of government entities are involved in delivering foreign assistance, the ministry of foreign affairs may take on a leadership or a co-ordinating role. Another possibility sometimes found is an organisation with a large degree of autonomy managing the development co-operation programme but falling under the political responsibility of the minister of foreign affairs.

Irrespective of the organisational structure at headquarters, the links between development programmes and broader foreign relations come out clearly in partner countries where the ambassador and other foreign service diplomats may play important roles. The ambassador represents the donor country at the highest levels and has the opportunity to influence debates in areas of key importance for achieving development goals, such as up-holding democratic practices, promoting good governance and respecting human rights and the rule of law. In many countries, the ambassador will help formulate or comment on the donor's country assistance strategy and the ambassador's agreement may be needed before any activity can go ahead. Some ambassadors also have a fund at their disposal to support small developmentally relevant activities identified in the field. It is consequently preferable that ambassadors and diplomats stationed in developing or transition countries have a good grounding in development issues which may be obtained through training or previous development-related experience, so that their work reinforces and builds on the development co-operation programme. While diplomats can cultivate an interest in development issues themselves, they may be more likely to have had relevant training or experience if they come from a country where the foreign assistance programme is closely associated with the ministry of foreign affairs.

Degree of institutional dispersion

The degree of institutional dispersion within foreign assistance programmes is another dimension where significant differences of approach are found across DAC member countries. In only a few countries – Denmark, Finland, the Netherlands and New Zealand – is all or almost all foreign assistance managed or co-ordinated by the same institution and where it is meaningful to equate the development agency with the countries' development co-operation programme. For many countries, a small and arguably manageable degree of dispersion occurs. This can result from some contributions to multilateral agencies, especially the international financial institutions, being provided and managed by other government departments, as is the case in Ireland and the United Kingdom. It may also be because small specialised institutions, such as the Australian Centre for International Agricultural Research (ACIAR) or Canada's International Development Research Centre (IDRC), form part of the foreign assistance programme. Another configuration is found in Austria, Luxembourg, Norway and Sweden where implementation is entrusted to a separate executing agency.

In most other DAC member countries, the degree of institutional dispersion is such that formal mechanisms may be required to bring the different elements together to ensure that efforts are complementary and that possible synergies are being exploited. This may not be an easy task when governments at national, regional and local levels are involved, when some of the institutions are large and have multiple objectives aside from promoting development, when the ministries being co-ordinated are larger and politically more powerful or when the institutions are located in different cities. When one ministry has responsibility for co-ordinating the activities of others, the co-ordinating ministry needs to have the authority to fulfil its role successfully, such as by having responsibility for approving projects or for deciding on funding for activities.

Many DAC member countries are rising to this challenge and strengthening the co-ordination authority of key ministries or implementing new approaches (for example in Japan and the United States, see below). Aside from formal structures, informal meetings and communications between staff of different institutions is a major and complementary aspect of co-ordination that should be encouraged by senior managers. In some countries, inter-departmental committees may also be formed either on a semi-permanent basis or in response to important issues that emerge.

An example: Japan

To co-ordinate the many official agencies working within the Japanese development co-operation system, Japan has put in place an extensive network of management mechanisms. In addition to ministerial-level meetings of the eight economic co-operation ministries, instruments of co-ordination have been set up at almost every administrative level in Tokyo. These include inter-ministerial meetings of ODA directors-general and bureau meetings of ODA division directors to address major ODA issues and negotiate proposals for inter-ministerial meetings. In addition, there are a number of meetings of technical experts on issues such as technical co-operation, ODA evaluation and financial co-operation.

An example: the United States

The United States has the largest foreign assistance programme in the DAC and uses a variety of institutions to deliver its assistance. Co-ordination among these different institutions is consequently important if the United States is to maximise the overall impact of its activities. At a policy level, co-ordination was promoted in the 2002 *National Security Strategy* which clearly situated development as a cornerstone of the United States national security and emphasised the strategic value of development co-operation along side defence and diplomacy. This vision was taken forward in the first joint Department of State/USAID *Strategic Plan* for 2004-09 which sets out four strategic objectives for these two agencies under the responsibility of the Secretary of State. These objectives, to be pursued by both agencies at corporate and sub-corporate levels, including missions abroad, are: *i)* achieving peace and security, *ii)* advancing sustainable development and global interests, *iii)* promoting international understanding, and *iv)* strengthening diplomatic and programme capabilities. To oversee implementation of the *Strategic Plan*, a Joint Management Council and a Joint Policy Council have been established, each comprising senior officials from both agencies. In addition, contacts and exchanges between the two agencies are being encouraged through such initiatives as joint training programmes and formal staff interchanges.

Box 5.2. **Involvement of the Ministry of Foreign Affairs in the management of foreign assistance programmes**

Across DAC member countries, different patterns of involvement by the Ministry of Foreign Affairs can be found:

- The ministry has a **pre-eminent role** and is responsible for managing the vast majority of the foreign assistance programme:
  - **Denmark:** Danish foreign assistance is managed by the Ministry of Foreign Affairs' "South Group".
  - **Finland:** Finnish foreign assistance is managed by the Department for Development Policy in the Ministry for Foreign Affairs.
  - **Ireland:** Irish foreign assistance is mostly managed by the Development Co-operation Directorate (DCD) in the Department of Foreign Affairs.
  - **The Netherlands:** Dutch foreign assistance is managed by the Directorate-General for International Co-operation (DGIS) in the Ministry of Foreign Affairs.
- A variation on this theme is to give a pre-eminent role to an agency that operates somewhat independently of the ministry of foreign affairs:
  - **Australia:** The Australian Agency for International Development (AusAID) is an administratively autonomous agency within the portfolio of the Ministry for Foreign Affairs and Trade.
  - **New Zealand:** The New Zealand Agency for International Development is a semi-autonomous body within the Ministry of Foreign Affairs and Trade.
  - **Switzerland:** Swiss foreign assistance is mainly the responsibility of the Swiss Agency for Development Co-operation (SDC) in the Federal Department of Foreign Affairs. However, a specific aspect of the Swiss programme is the substantial assistance also provided by Political Department IV of the Federal Foreign Ministry and by the State Secretariat for Economic Affairs (SECO).

Box 5.2. **Involvement of the Ministry of Foreign Affairs in the management of foreign assistance programmes** *(cont.)*

- A further variation is to give a pre-eminent role to a ministry or agency completely separate from the ministry of foreign affairs:
  - **Canada:** The Canadian International Development Agency (CIDA) is separate from the Department of Foreign Affairs and International Trade and reports to parliament through the Minister for International Co-operation.
  - **The United Kingdom:** The Department for International Development is separate from the Foreign and Commonwealth Office and reports to parliament through the Secretary of State for International Development.
- The ministry of foreign affairs can also have **overall responsibility** for foreign assistance while bilateral activities are implemented by a separate executing agency:
  - **Austria:** The Department for Development and Co-operation with Eastern Europe of the Foreign Ministry has overall responsibility for Austrian foreign assistance. Bilateral projects are implemented by the Austrian Development Agency.
  - **Belgium:** The Directorate-General for Development Co-operation (DGDC) of the Federal Department of Foreign Affairs, Foreign Trade and Development Co-operation has overall responsibility for Belgian federal foreign assistance. Activities are implemented by the Belgian Technical Co-operation (BTC) organisation. A specific feature of Belgium's programme is the active but separate engagements by the Flemish and Walloon regional governments.
  - **Luxembourg:** The Ministry of Foreign Affairs has overall responsibility for Luxembourg's foreign assistance, which is delivered through Lux-Development, a separate executing agency.
  - **Norway:** The Ministry of Foreign Affairs has overall responsibility for Norwegian foreign assistance, some of which is delivered through the Norwegian Agency for Development Co-operation, an agency under the Ministry of Foreign Affairs.
  - **Sweden:** The Global Development Department of the Ministry of Foreign Affairs has overall responsibility for Swedish foreign assistance, which is delivered through the Swedish International Development Co-operation Agency (Sida).
- There are several variations on this theme, such as sharing overall responsibility, giving overall responsibility to a different ministry or having a variety of executing agencies:
  - **France:** The main actors in the French system of foreign assistance are the Directorate-General for International Co-operation and Development (DGCID) in the Ministry of Foreign Affairs and the Treasury in the Ministry of Economic Affairs, Finance and Industry. The French Development Agency (AFD) is the principal executing agency for France's bilateral activities.
  - **Germany:** The Ministry of Economic Co-operation and Development (BMZ) is in charge of planning and implementing the German government's development co-operation. It is separate from the Federal Foreign Office and reports to the parliament through the Federal Minister for Economic Co-operation and Development. Development policy is implemented through numerous organisations including: the KfW Development Bank and its subsidiary the German Investment and Development Corporation (DEG) for financial co-operation, the GTZ Agency is commissioned to implement German technical co-operation, Capacity Building International (InWEnt)* for training, and the German Development Service (DED) for "volunteer" development workers. The Federal Foreign Office is in charge of humanitarian assistance implemented by the organisations mentioned above.

Box 5.2. **Involvement of the Ministry of Foreign Affairs in the management of foreign assistance programmes** *(cont.)*

- **Japan:** The Economic Co-operation Bureau in the Ministry of Foreign Affairs plays a central role but various government entities deliver Japanese foreign assistance, most notably the Japan International Co-operation Agency and the Japan Bank for International Co-operation (JBIC).

- In the remaining DAC member countries, the ministry of foreign affairs is an **important player** and may sometimes have a special co-ordinating role:
  - **Greece:** The Hellenic International Development Co-operation Department ("Hellenic Aid") within the Ministry of Foreign Affairs has a central and co-ordinating role in relation to Greece's bilateral foreign assistance, which is implemented through 12 other ministries and government agencies.
  - **Italy:** Among the various ministries and local government bodies providing foreign assistance, the Directorate-General for Development Co-operation (DGCS) in the Ministry of Foreign Affairs plays a leading role in relation to the bilateral programme.
  - **Portugal:** Foreign assistance is implemented by nearly 20 government ministries and agencies and over 300 municipalities. The Ministry of Foreign Affairs has overall responsibility for Portuguese foreign assistance, with its Institute for Portuguese Development Support playing a co-ordinating role.
  - **Spain:** The State Secretariat for International Co-operation and Latin America (SECIPI) within the Ministry of Foreign Affairs, and its executing agency the Spanish Agency for International Co-operation (AECI), are key players in Spain's foreign assistance system which also includes the Ministry of Economy and various autonomous regions and municipalities.
  - **The United States:** In addition to USAID, United States' foreign assistance is delivered by a range of other federal institutions including the Department of State, the Department of the Treasury, the Department of Health and Human Services, the Millennium Challenge Corporation and the Peace Corps. The Secretary of State is responsible at the cabinet level for the activities of the Department of State and USAID and chairs the Millennium Challenge Corporation's Board of Directors.

* InWEnt was established in 2002 through the merger of the Carl Duisberg Society (CDG) and the German Foundation for International Development (DSE).

Representation in partner countries and relations with headquarters

While DAC member countries' bilateral foreign assistance is mostly delivered in partner countries, its overall management takes place in the headquarters. Representation in the field is consequently critical for bridging the gap between headquarters and partner countries, especially if the effectiveness of foreign assistance is to be improved by aligning donors' policies, procedures and practices with those of partner countries. DAC member countries' representation takes a variety of forms as was found in Mozambique. Of the 19 DAC member countries represented there, only eight field missions are integral parts of the embassy/high commission. In each of these cases, the foreign affairs ministry has a pre-eminent role in managing or co-ordinating the development co-operation programme and the overall structure of the country's development co-operation system does not include a separate executing agency. With the remaining 11 countries, the field mission is in separate premises, the executing agency for the development co-operation programme is housed separately from the embassy or the embassy is located in another country.

MANAGING AID: PRACTICES OF DAC MEMBER COUNTRIES – ISBN 92-64-00761-X – © OECD 2005

Whatever the configuration in the field, staff based at headquarters, be they senior managers, desk officers or sectoral experts, provide back-up for the staff located in the field and visit partner countries regularly.

Staffing patterns in partner countries also vary widely with many, but not all, DAC member countries able to post development co-operation staff to their main partner countries. In some instances, where the programme managed is comparatively small, there may be a single person on posting from headquarters who may fulfil other responsibilities as well. Larger programmes require larger staffs and some field missions may have more than a hundred professional staff. In a few cases, especially in countries that are not main partners or where the development agency does not have the means or the legal authority to send people on posting from headquarters to the field, management of the programme is entrusted to someone already stationed at the embassy, usually a foreign service diplomat but possibly staff in the commercial office, which can generate confusion regarding the prime motives behind the foreign assistance programme. In a few other cases, a person is recruited locally on a fixed-term contract to manage the foreign assistance programme. This has the advantage of ensuring that an experienced and capable person manages the programme but the disadvantage of not helping to build-up and maintain a group of experienced development co-operation professionals in the country's development co-operation system. Most DAC member countries also hire staff locally for their field missions who increasingly are being called on to fill professional and sometimes managerial-level positions.

No matter what configuration is found in the field, staff in both headquarters and the field play important roles in formulating and implementing DAC member countries' bilateral projects and programmes which should be broadly in line with each country's overall policies and approaches. At the same time, there is considerable difference between countries in terms of the specific responsibilities of the field mission and the degree of delegated authority to their representatives in the field. To some extent, this may be dependent on the number and development experience of the people in the field managing the programme. The field visit to Mozambique found that half the DAC member countries have fairly centralised systems where field missions implement decisions made by headquarters, with little or no flexibility to change programmes or funding. At the other end of the spectrum, some field missions design and implement programmes, subject to headquarters' general approval, and make funding changes within the limits of the country framework prepared through an iterative process involving staff both at headquarters and in the field. In a few countries such as Denmark (see below), the move towards greater decentralisation took place only recently or is in the process of being implemented. The field visit to Mozambique also found that, for the most part, these decentralisation processes are resulting in changes in work patterns at the field mission, in particular less routine reporting to headquarters, and are being implemented without a notable change in overall staffing levels at the field mission. An up-grading in communications equipment, especially access to video conferencing facilities, may be introduced to support decentralisation.

An example: Denmark

With the objective of improving the effectiveness of its foreign assistance, Denmark has been further decentralising responsibility to its missions in main partner countries. This has had implications across its whole development co-operation system. Missions are now clearly designated as the focal point for country programmes and are responsible for monitoring and managing the programme, in accordance with the Annual Business Contract negotiated between the ambassador and headquarters. Missions are responsible for identifying, preparing and implementing activities, while the role of the Technical Advisory Services in headquarters is now limited to appraisals and reviews. The responsibility and number of staff in the geographic departments in headquarters have been reduced, with their main roles now including finalisation of country strategy papers and heading high-level consultations with partner governments. A new Quality Assurance Department has been created in headquarters to monitor the Annual Business Contracts, help build up the capacity of staff in the field and conduct performance reviews. Denmark has also developed a "model" staffing complement for a mission which requires posting more staff to partner countries and greater reliance on locally recruited staff. The "model" is *i)* the ambassador and/or deputy head of mission, *ii)* one Danish and one locally recruited professional for each main sector in the country programme, *iii)* a Danish macro-economist, *iv)* one Danish and one locally recruited professional for institutional reform, and *v)* a Danish financial manager. For a typical country programme with three priority sectors, this "model" implies a total professional staff complement of 12, of which eight are on posting from Copenhagen.

Foreign assistance provided by sub-national authorities

In some DAC member countries, there has been a trend in recent years towards an increasing engagement by sub-national authorities – regions, districts, provinces and municipalities – in financing and implementing foreign assistance activities. This form of development assistance, sometimes referred to as decentralised co-operation or twinning, is most developed in Austria, Belgium, Canada, France, Germany, Italy, Portugal and Spain (see examples below). In some countries, including France, Italy and Spain, the involvement of sub-national authorities is guided by a legislative framework enacted by the national government or a policy established by the national development agency.

An example: Portugal

Twenty-two districts and over 300 municipalities in Portugal are engaged in foreign assistance activities. These often take place in Portuguese-speaking countries such as Cape Verde where inter-municipal co-operation is an important component of Portugal's development co-operation effort. In part building on the links created through the Cape Verdian community living in Portugal, many of the 17 Cape Verdian municipalities have direct relationships with Portuguese cities covering such fields as education, culture, local institution building, conservation of heritage sites and social welfare. This type of co-operation is generally much appreciated by the Cape Verdian municipalities because it can provide a quick means of financing local projects such as the building of libraries, sports centres or schools. In most cases, particularly when there is an urgent need for financing, municipalities contact their partner cities in Portugal directly without passing through the Cape Verdian government or the Portuguese embassy in Praia.

An example: Spain

The regional government of Valencia has a significant budget for its development co-operation programme which was formally established in 1999. The Valencia Department for International Co-operation manages the region's entire aid programme. In 2002, the Valencia Committee for Humanitarian and Emergency Aid was established to improve co-ordination among the various stakeholders in Valencia. With the growing amount of resources available in the region, particularly for natural disasters, the purpose was to create one single channel for resources. The Committee, comprising representatives of local authorities, two banks, NGOs, the Valencia Solidarity Fund and the Valencia Federation of Municipalities, meets within 48 hours of a crisis and takes a decision for immediate intervention in collaboration with the Spanish Agency for International Co-operation. It then sends a delegation to identify the areas most affected and to discuss with local counterparts and Spanish organisations.

A number of arguments are given to support the involvement of sub-national authorities in foreign assistance activities. First, it raises a nation's aid level because taxes raised by sub-national authorities can be mobilised for development co-operation activities. In Spain, for example, some 15% of its ODA is funded by sub-national authorities. Secondly, there is a view that sub-national authorities enable citizens to engage more easily in development-related activities and so promote greater public awareness and understanding of development issues. Finally, the twinning of similar institutions at different levels of government is seen as appropriate because it can favour exchanges, as part of long-term relationships, of specialisations, competencies and skills.

On the other hand, some shortcomings have been identified with this form of foreign assistance.* It is challenging for partner countries to deal with a large number of donors and new or non-traditional actors render co-ordination and local ownership of development efforts more difficult. From a staffing perspective, many sub-national authorities are ill-equipped both in terms of staff numbers and professional competence. Monitoring and evaluation mechanisms are rare and, when they do exist, are comparatively weak. Reporting on activities, which would facilitate co-ordination, is often poorly organised. DAC member countries are increasingly aware of the shortcomings associated with actions by sub-national authorities and are responding accordingly. In France, for example, local government authorities are working to implement a number of reforms to improve their performance including establishing a database to collect information on their various activities, identifying good practices for this form of development co-operation and developing common tools in such areas as monitoring and evaluation.

* Desmet, A. and P. Develtere (2002), *Sub-national Authorities and Development Co-operation in the OECD-DAC member countries,* Hoger instituut voor de arbeid, Leuven.

ISBN 92-64-00761-X
Managing Aid: Practices of DAC Member Countries
© OECD 2005

Chapter 6

Managing Development Agencies: Internal Structures and Systems

As development co-operation has increased in its complexity over the years, addressing a wider range of interlinked issues managed across a number of government departments or ministries, the issue of the most appropriate internal structure for development agencies has become both increasingly pertinent and increasingly difficult to address. Among the key challenges for DAC member countries' internal structures and systems are: the need for greater co-ordination, the increasing need for specialist expertise and technical support, changing priorities and the emergence of a number of cross-cutting issues to be mainstreamed across the organisation.

Organisational design

When the first DAC member countries were establishing their development co-operation systems in the 1960s, it was typical and perhaps appropriate to adopt a compartmentalised approach to managing foreign assistance, with individual organisational units operating with a high degree of autonomy. Contributions to multilateral agencies and humanitarian assistance would be managed by specific organisational units, sometimes not located in the development agency. Strong regional departments at headquarters would manage bilateral programmes, with desk officers for main partner countries and representatives stationed in the field whose role may mainly have been to relay information between headquarters and the partner country. Specialist expertise was only needed in a limited range of areas, for example infrastructure, health and education. Few cross-cutting issues were addressed and the idea of mainstreaming was still in its infancy.

In the intervening decades, development co-operation has become a more complex field and organisational structures have needed to adapt, both to cover a wider range of issues and so that individual organisational units can work in more co-ordinated and complementary ways. The emergence of PRSs, for example, necessitates greater co-ordination between organisational units responsible for international financial institutions and those managing government-to-government programmes. Bilateral activities may now be implemented through earmarked contributions to multilateral agencies (so-called "multi-bi" assistance). Moves to partnership approaches to delivering foreign assistance have led some DAC member countries to move the focal point for their bilateral programmes to large offices in each main partner country, sometimes to the point of leaving only a skeleton staff in regional departments in headquarters. Short-term humanitarian assistance is increasingly provided with a view to evolving towards medium-term recovery programmes and possibly longer-term development partnerships. A variety of issues, including gender and HIV/AIDS, are now mainstreamed in development programmes, requiring specialist staff in these areas to work with and through their colleagues implementing bilateral and multilateral programmes, NGO co-financing schemes and humanitarian assistance.

As a result, whereas at one time it was common across DAC member countries to structure agencies on geographic rather functional lines, the complexities of reducing poverty have lead many agencies to adopt some form of hybrid structure, giving a pre-eminent role to geographic and multilateral departments but backing their activities up with substantial sectoral and technical support supplied as required (see below). This reflects increased attention to country programming to guide efforts in partner countries and shifts in some DAC members from project assistance to more programme aid, and activities planned and provided on a sectoral basis.

MANAGING AID: PRACTICES OF DAC MEMBER COUNTRIES – ISBN 92-64-00761-X – © OECD 2005

Figure 6.1. **Australian Agency for International Development (AusAID) simplified organisational structure**

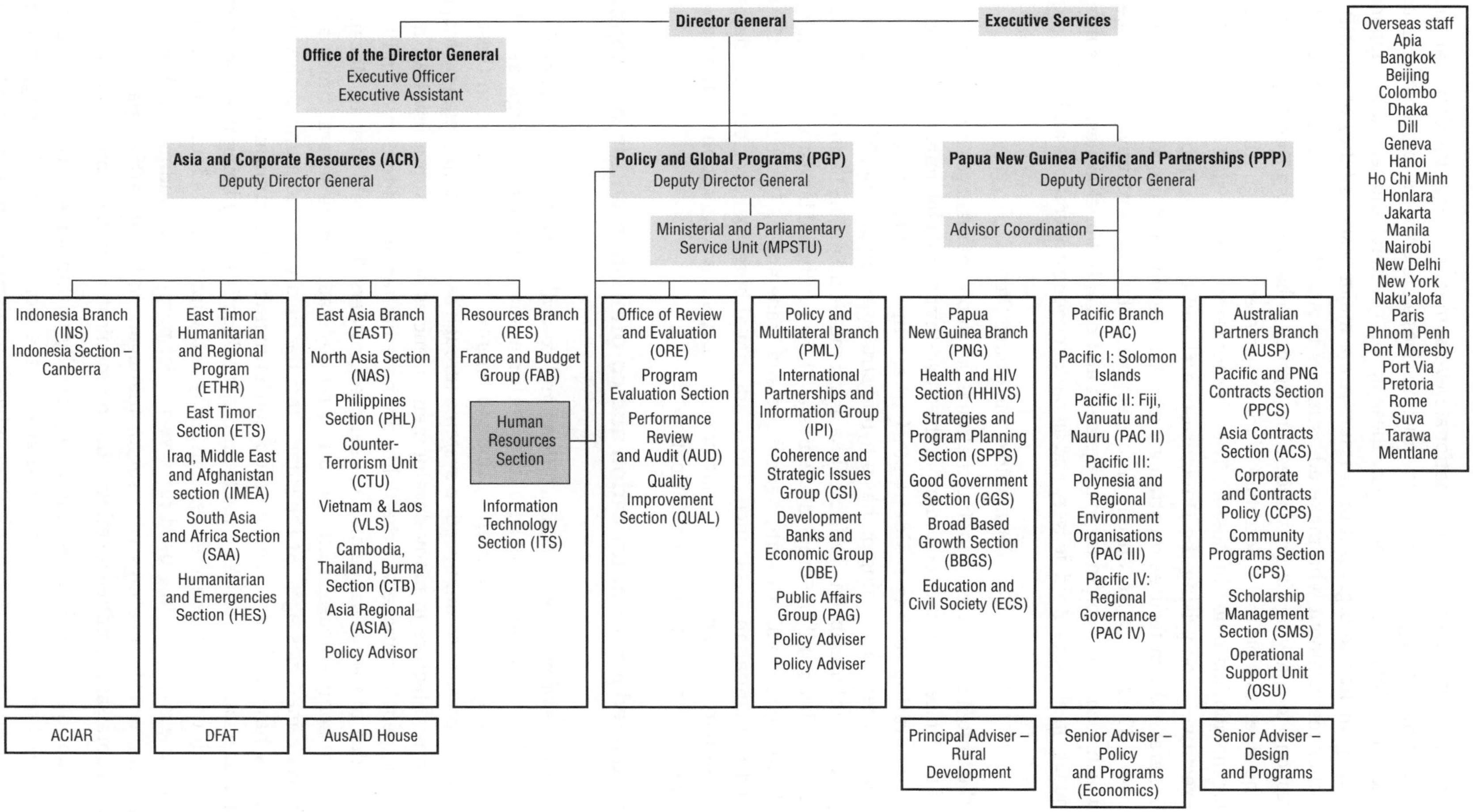

Director General

Executive Services

Office of the Director General
Executive Officer
Executive Assistant

Asia and Corporate Resources (ACR)
Deputy Director General

Policy and Global Programs (PGP)
Deputy Director General

Ministerial and Parliamentary Service Unit (MPSTU)

Papua New Guinea Pacific and Partnerships (PPP)
Deputy Director General

Advisor Coordination

Indonesia Branch (INS)
Indonesia Section – Canberra

East Timor Humanitarian and Regional Program (ETHR)
East Timor Section (ETS)
Iraq, Middle East and Afghanistan section (IMEA)
South Asia and Africa Section (SAA)
Humanitarian and Emergencies Section (HES)

East Asia Branch (EAST)
North Asia Section (NAS)
Philippines Section (PHL)
Counter-Terrorism Unit (CTU)
Vietnam & Laos (VLS)
Cambodia, Thailand, Burma Section (CTB)
Asia Regional (ASIA)
Policy Advisor

Resources Branch (RES)
France and Budget Group (FAB)
Human Resources Section
Information Technology Section (ITS)

Office of Review and Evaluation (ORE)
Program Evaluation Section
Performance Review and Audit (AUD)
Quality Improvement Section (QUAL)

Policy and Multilateral Branch (PML)
International Partnerships and Information Group (IPI)
Coherence and Strategic Issues Group (CSI)
Development Banks and Economic Group (DBE)
Public Affairs Group (PAG)
Policy Adviser
Policy Adviser

Papua New Guinea Branch (PNG)
Health and HIV Section (HHIVS)
Strategies and Program Planning Section (SPPS)
Good Government Section (GGS)
Broad Based Growth Section (BBGS)
Education and Civil Society (ECS)

Pacific Branch (PAC)
Pacific I: Solomon Islands
Pacific II: Fiji, Vanuatu and Nauru (PAC II)
Pacific III: Polynesia and Regional Environment Organisations (PAC III)
Pacific IV: Regional Governance (PAC IV)

Australian Partners Branch (AUSP)
Pacific and PNG Contracts Section (PPCS)
Asia Contracts Section (ACS)
Corporate and Contracts Policy (CCPS)
Community Programs Section (CPS)
Scholarship Management Section (SMS)
Operational Support Unit (OSU)

ACIAR

DFAT

AusAID House

Principal Adviser – Rural Development

Senior Adviser – Policy and Programs (Economics)

Senior Adviser – Design and Programs

Overseas staff
Apia
Bangkok
Beijing
Colombo
Dhaka
Dill
Geneva
Hanoi
Ho Chi Minh
Honlara
Jakarta
Manila
Nairobi
New Delhi
New York
Naku'alofa
Paris
Phnom Penh
Pont Moresby
Port Via
Pretoria
Rome
Suva
Tarawa
Mentlane

Source: AusAID (as of April 2004).

An example: Australia

The Australian Agency for International Development manages the vast majority of Australia's foreign assistance. Its structure gives a pre-eminent role to geographic and multilateral sections but backs these up with sectoral and technical support. Management and organisational issues are a major responsibility of AusAID's senior management who make adjustments to AusAID's structure regularly to respond to changing circumstances. The agency is headed by a Director-General, who is responsible to the Secretary of the Department of Foreign Affairs and Trade for the administration of AusAID. The Director-General is assisted by the AusAID Executive – comprising the Director-General and the three Deputy Directors-General – which focuses on strategic direction setting and broad management issues. The AusAID Executive is in turn supported by three Executive Committees which focus on: *i)* corporate management and organisational issues, *ii)* ensuring quality in all areas of aid delivery and *iii)* partner country operations and strategies.

An example: the United States

The United States Agency for International Development manages more than half of the United States' ODA and more than two-thirds of its bilateral development co-operation. It has resident staff in around 70 partner countries. The headquarters in Washington has a hybrid structure comprising 10 bureaux. Four geographic bureaux for: *i)* Africa, *ii)* Asia and the Near East, *iii)* Latin America and the Caribbean and *iv)* Europe and Eurasia. Three functional bureaux for: *i)* Global Health, *ii)* Economic Growth, Agriculture and Trade and *iii)* Democracy, Conflict and Humanitarian Assistance. Three additional bureaux cover certain major headquarters functions: *i)* Management, *ii)* Legislative and Public Affairs and *iii)* Policy and Programme Co-ordination.

The increased need for communication and co-ordination within development agencies

The issue of internal communications and co-ordination throughout development agencies has become critical for the better management of foreign assistance. Development agencies have been working to improve their performance in these areas. Worldwide access to communication systems through satellite-based e-mail messaging is now a normal feature in many development agencies although in a few DAC member countries, people stationed in the field only have limited access to e-mail and Intranet services due to their reliance on local service providers. The field visit to Mozambique found that some embassies still need to ring up headquarters several times a day to download e-mail messages. At the same time, the field visit also found that a few DAC members have moved to using video conferencing for communications between headquarters and field offices. This technology, which is mostly being used by countries with a high degree of delegated responsibility and with their headquarters located in a similar time zone, is being used for a variety of purposes including: interviewing job applicants, weekly meetings with senior managers in headquarters, participating in project appraisal committee meetings and communicating with regional offices.

Promoting internal co-ordination, especially within large development agencies with several thousand staff stationed around the world, can be challenging, perhaps more challenging than communication between ministries in smaller countries. Formal co-ordination mechanisms are one method of facilitating this, such as the establishment of task teams which bring together people from different organisational units to work or reflect collaboratively on key issues. Due to the fact that people in development agencies may be located in different locations in different time zones, these task teams may be "virtual" relying on Intranet and e-mail systems to communicate. Informal meetings and communications between staff are another aspect of co-ordination. These can be promoted through a variety of means including training courses, workshops and meetings bringing together people working on related issues or in neighbouring countries.

Specialised units and technical expertise

Development agencies need access to technical expertise in a range of areas to support and maintain high quality in the activities they fund. Such expertise may be highly specific, such as in health and HIV/AIDS, or be more generic and needed across the programme, such as expertise in evaluation. There are a number of challenges facing development agencies regarding technical expertise. These include whether technical staff should be field-based or located centrally in headquarters and the challenge of recruiting and retaining a critical mass of up-to-date expertise in a variety of specialist areas.

In order to address this need for in-house expertise, some agencies establish technical or specialised units within the development agency. Denmark, Ireland, Spain and Sweden, for example, have such technical units staffed by people with expertise in key sectoral areas for their foreign assistance programme. In other DAC member countries, technical staff may be based within regional departments and attached to specific country desks. Larger development agencies may employ specialist staff both in headquarters and offices in main partner countries, where there may be both home-based and locally-recruited experts. Smaller development agencies may not have the means to employ experts in each key sector of their programmes in each main partner country. In this case, technical staff may cover a range of sectors or cover the same sector but in a number of partner countries.

In many DAC member countries, there is an inadequate number of technical staff in certain key areas or sectors. One response that some DAC member countries have adopted is to recruit technical staff on fixed-term contracts or on a consultancy basis. This helps development agencies ensure that the technical expertise they use is regularly refreshed but may also lead to a significant turnover of staff and a consequential loss of institutional memory. Another approach is to negotiate multi-year contracts with research bodies or academic institutions which enable staff in development agencies to call down specialist expertise as required in a range of areas. This expertise may not necessarily be limited to sectoral expertise and can cover such other areas as programme support, research or evaluation.

Cross-cutting issues

Certain cross-cutting issues are fundamental to the achievement of overall development objectives. Issues such as poverty reduction and gender equality are cross-cutting in that they are critical to the outcome and impact of all aspects of the foreign assistance programme and cannot be pursued as stand-alone activities or managed as sectors. Most DAC member countries have identified three or four key cross-cutting issues or themes as being central for their foreign assistance programme. Across DAC member countries, the cross-cutting issues most frequently pursued are capacity development, conflict prevention, democracy, gender equality, good governance, environment, human rights and poverty reduction. Several countries, including Canada, Denmark, Ireland and the United Kingdom, consider and pursue HIV/AIDS as a cross-cutting issue.

As with specific sectoral areas, development agencies may need expertise in the management of cross-cutting issues, if these are to be addressed comprehensively within their foreign assistance programme. Many DAC member countries have established specialised units or identified in-house experts to take key cross-cutting issues forward. A specific challenge resulting from this approach has been the tendency for responsibility for issues to be left entirely to experts or technical units, which can undermine the extent to which issues are adequately addressed within the programme. A more appropriate approach would be to have both technical expertise available and for all staff to be trained in and responsible for pursuing cross-cutting issues, as a key aspect of their work.

Staff training is therefore key to the management of cross-cutting issues. Training programmes should include staff in both management and policy areas, both at headquarters and in the field, and need to encompass a range of skills appropriate for staff in different positions. It also needs to go beyond raising awareness to include analytic skills, advocacy skills, monitoring and evaluation. Various tools have been developed by development agencies and the DAC to support members' efforts to address cross-cutting issues. For example, the DAC Network on Gender Equality has developed a series of *Gender Equality Tipsheets** that provide essential information on how and why gender equality is a crucial dimension in all development activities. The Tipsheets cover a wide range of development-related sectors and issues, ranging from finance to evaluation to governance. Annex A.4 of this report provides guidance for staff in development agencies on mainstreaming cross-cutting issues.

In order to maintain consistency across programmes, development agencies need to ensure that NGOs, contractors, consultancies and other implementing partners are also addressing cross-cutting issues in their policy development and operational activities. Ireland, for example, has set up a short-term funding mechanism for NGOs to build their institutional capacity to mainstream HIV/AIDS.

Two different approaches can be taken to addressing cross-cutting issues. These may be *integrated* into a development programme so that the issue is built into the agency's existing conceptual framework and policies and programmes are *adapted* to take the cross-cutting issue into consideration. By contrast, the *mainstreaming* of a cross-cutting issue goes beyond integration and aims to ensure that analytical process, development policies, development planning and activities reflect the importance of the issue. The programme is, to an extent, *transformed* by the cross-cutting issue so that all decisions are informed by and take full account of the issue.

The key success factors for mainstreaming a cross-cutting issue (see Box 6.1) show that mainstreaming (rather than integrating) requires a considerable investment on the part of development agencies. This investment also means that it is not feasible for development agencies to mainstream multiple cross-cutting issues. A realistic approach would be the identification of one or two issues that reflect overall policy objectives that would be fully mainstreamed into all aspects of the programme. An additional two or three cross-cutting issues could then possibly be integrated across the programme. Although not to the same degree, the integration of issues into polices and procedures would require resources, expertise and commitment as well.

* The *Tipsheets* are available at: *www.oecd.org/dac/gender*.

Box 6.1. **Key success factors for mainstreaming cross-cutting issues**

A number of key success factors have been identified by different member countries for mainstreaming cross-cutting issues which show that a mainstreaming approach requires a significant investment on the part of development agencies. These success factors are:

- Evidence of institutional commitment through explicit policy and the allocation of resources.
- Senior management commitment and leadership.
- The importance of the issue being reflected in policies and procedures.
- The training of staff in a wide range of relevant and related skills.
- Ensuring that the issue is the responsibility of all staff, as well as receiving specialised technical support.
- Development of relevant monitoring indicators.

ISBN 92-64-00761-X
Managing Aid: Practices of DAC Member Countries

Chapter 7

Managing Human Resources for Development Co-operation

Effective development co-operation depends on the appropriate deployment of skilled and experienced personnel who have a strong understanding of development, especially at the field level. While there is growing interest in how development agencies manage their human resources, there is little comparable data available due to significant variation in influencing factors such as the nature of DAC members' development programmes, their organisational structure, policies on recruitment and contracting out and employment conditions. Managing human resources effectively is a challenge for most DAC member countries, with long-standing issues combining with new ones to create a complex management issue. For example, DAC member countries may face such difficulties as staffing cuts, inadequate staffing levels, the imminent retirement of significant numbers of senior staff, changing skill needs and the rapid turnover of staff. A single approach to addressing these and other human resource issues does not exist but, given the emphasis on partnership, local ownership, results-based approaches and evolution in aid modalities, it is clear that the management of human resources for development co-operation needs to be given higher priority than has been done to date, based on better understanding of the personnel and skills profile needed as well as longer-term human resource planning.

The human resource "system"

Approaches for staffing development agencies vary significantly among DAC member countries and are influenced by a number of factors including the organisational structure of aid management, the size and nature of the programme and government-wide policies on employment. Where a development agency is autonomous of the ministry of foreign affairs, as in the case of Australia, Canada, the United Kingdom or the United States, for example, human resources may be managed independently of the ministry of foreign affairs and the agency is usually staffed by specialists in development co-operation. These staff may be employed as permanent civil servants or on short or medium-term contracts.

Where the ministry of foreign affairs is responsible for managing the majority of the development co-operation programme as in Denmark, Finland, Ireland or the Netherlands, human resource management for development is not usually treated separately from management for the ministry of foreign affairs or the civil service in general. In this case, development co-operation directorates and indeed overseas missions may be staffed by generalist career diplomatic staff that may have no specialist background in development co-operation, nor skills in organisation and contract management. Career diplomats are expected to service different functions over their career and are valued for their generalist skills and adaptability. To support career diplomats, specialist technical staff may be recruited to staff technical units but are often employed only on a contractual basis. Employment terms and conditions as well as the number of staff may be determined by overall government policy on human resource management.

In member countries with a separate implementing agency there can be other human resource challenges. In some cases, agency staff are unable to be posted to the field as all field-based posts are reserved for diplomatic staff. Or, both the ministry and the agency may have field-based representation, sometimes located in separate offices, which can cause some confusion or overlap and generate an additional management layer for partner countries.

Planning human resources

Developing a detailed understanding of the number, skill mix and location of staff managing development assistance is essential for effective human resource planning in the area of development co-operation. Some member countries have carried out analysis of staffing or skills profile but these have rarely been government-wide or included contracted staff and consultants. In most countries, a variety of ministries and directorates are involved in different aspects of development co-operation. This, together with the employment, by some countries, of significant numbers of contracted staff and consultants, means that few countries are able to give a comprehensive picture of the number, skills and background, or institutional location of staff involved in managing different aspects of their development co-operation.

 MANAGING AID: PRACTICES OF DAC MEMBER COUNTRIES – ISBN 92-64-00761-X – © OECD 2005

Improving the planning of human resources for development co-operation is becoming increasingly important for many DAC member countries due to the challenges of a dynamic global environment. Such planning is, in many cases, highly political, influenced by overall budgetary constraints, and requires an adequate lead in time if it is to be effective. Some of the issues that need to be considered as part of the planning approach are discussed below.

The need for a critical mass of development co-operation expertise

One challenge that has arisen for some DAC member countries, particularly those with an integrated ministry of foreign affairs, is that of creating and retaining a critical mass of development co-operation expertise. As mentioned above, development co-operation directorates may be staffed by rotating career diplomats with limited specialist and technical expertise. This may not cause any difficulties for those programmes with a significant administrative component such as large scholarships programmes. However, most development co-operation work is distinct from the representational and political work that is the main business of foreign affairs ministries. Effective development co-operation increasingly requires skilled specialists in poverty reduction efforts which demand social, economic and cultural knowledge of grass roots issues, developing country governance reforms and results-based and outcome-oriented implementation of development projects and programmes. Moreover, an understanding of the realities and challenges of development co-operation at the field level is important for policy development and decision-making at headquarters while increasing decentralisation requires more experienced and senior staff in the field.

In countries where development specialists are employed on short or medium-term contracts they may lack incentives to remain within the system. Ideally, a working environment should be created which encourages both short-term staff and permanent specialists to remain and contribute to the development of institutional capacity and operational expertise. This could include, for example, developing a career track for development specialists within the ministry of foreign affairs, reviewing the contractual basis of specialist staff, lengthening contracts and making employment conditions as attractive as possible, emphasising staff development or introducing a performance-based management system. Although constraints may exist to the implementation of such strategies due to government-wide human resource policies, the discussion and exploration of different ways of meeting staff needs for development is critical.

Skill mix and staff development

The recognition of the increasing range of skills required in development co-operation – particularly at the field level – has led several DAC member countries to review and redefine their skill profiles (see below). Many countries are now placing greater emphasis on the need for development staff to have, in addition to sound technical knowledge, effective analytical skills, strategic thinking ability, cultural receptivity, language skills, and negotiation skills. Rewards and incentives may play a role in improving staff performance in these areas and some member countries are increasingly discussing the importance of incentives in the context of change management. Non-monetary incentives may include choice of job assignments or overseas postings, giving staff greater visibility, access to special training or sponsored research. Changing skills profile and the introduction of incentives carry implications for human resource policies in the areas of recruitment, performance management, training policies and in some cases for working modalities. While review and pro-active management of human resources for development is essential, such changes need to be carefully managed to avoid staff insecurities, disillusionment and the unplanned loss of staff.

An example: Australia

The AusAID Strategic Plan anticipated the need to identify the skills, knowledge and attributes AusAID would require in the following five years. A skills analysis was carried out and used to inform recruitment policies, performance management, learning and development approaches and overseas posting requirements. A Capability Framework identifies the skill and knowledge sets required reflecting different levels of proficiency. The Framework was designed to facilitate staff performance appraisal, guide the setting of short and medium-term goals, identify tasks to enhance performance in key skill and knowledge areas relevant to the tasks or career aspirations of the individual. Options identified for meeting critical skill needs include a refocusing of current skills, knowledge and attributes, on-going coaching and other targeted development opportunities, bulk recruitment exercises, specific recruitment exercises and the targeting of people with the right profile. The need to retain staff with key capabilities is highlighted.

One way of addressing changing skills requirements, in addition to recruitment, is through training and staff development programmes. These are essential both for current and recently recruited staff particularly in light of evolving aid modalities and partnership approaches. Emphasis on training and staff development also creates an incentive for staff to remain within an organisation. Some countries are, for example, increasing the emphasis within current training on issues such as programme aid and risk assessment. Within Sweden, Sida devotes significant resources to developing staff and fostering a process of continuous learning within the organisation (see below).

An example: Sweden

Sida has identified five types of skills necessary to create a learning environment – strategic, professional, learning, relational and functional. These are summarised in a "skills star". In addition, the roles and responsibilities of Sida's managers and staff have been analysed and documented. Sida's Management Policy defines the main task of managers as creating the conditions necessary for staff to develop, implement and follow-up on operations. The manager is seen as having six roles: explorer, communicator, coach, agent of change, creator of learning opportunities and decision maker, and there is a quality assurance process for ensuring that managers fulfil their ascribed roles.

Recruitment and equal opportunities policy

Several DAC member countries face the loss of a significant number of senior staff in the coming years through retirement. A number of countries have introduced specific strategies to respond to this imminent human resource challenge. Some countries are actively recruiting younger staff or have introduced a junior professional programme. Others are recognising that without career development opportunities, there is little incentive for staff employed on a contractual basis to remain with the organisation over the long-term.

A few DAC member countries emphasise equality within human resource management and monitor carefully the gender breakdown of personnel as well as ethnic diversity or employment of people with special needs. In some countries, women are almost equally employed with men within the lower or middle levels but may be in a smaller proportion at senior levels. While equality issues would usually fall under the remit of broader government employment policy, some member countries take pro-active steps to promote equality specifically among staff working in development co-operation. The employment and management of people living with HIV or AIDS is an aspect of this and is addressed in a later section.

Contracting out

One way that DAC member countries complement their human resource capacities is through contracting out such activities as technical support, research, evaluation or the management of a specific development initiative. To contract out effectively, the development agency needs to identify the nature of activities that can be contracted out and to ensure that there is sufficient capacity within the administration to manage the work of contracted staff and consultants. Staff employed on short- or medium-term contracts may provide invaluable specialist expertise while not forming part of the permanent staffing complement, and they may be contracted to work in headquarters or in the field. In some cases the number of contracted staff may exceed the number of permanent staff due to greater financial flexibility for the recruitment of contracted staff or consultants using programme funds (*i.e.* funds that could otherwise be used to fund development activities) to pay their salaries.

While contracted organisations, staff and consultants fill technical and specialist needs, they may not contribute to the development of corporate memory or adequate lesson learning. Where technical experts are employed on short or medium-term contracts rather than as permanent staff, the lack of a career stream and promotion prospects can lead to frustrations and high turnover further contributing to a lack of continuity.

The Public Management Services of the OECD has produced a set of guidelines which identify key success factors for achieving the benefits of contracting out (see Box 7.1). While not designed exclusively for development agencies, several factors are of particular relevance for aid managers:

- Service requirements should be specified in terms of outcomes and outputs, not inputs. This means that specifying *what* the activity is, not *how* the activity is to be performed. Operational flexibility is essential for the contractor to be innovative in performing the activity, and thereby securing efficiency gains. These outcomes or outputs should be specified as fully as possible, and include appropriate service quality measures.
- Contracting out an activity does not diminish, in any way, the responsibility of the organisation for the performance of the service. This is especially relevant when that service is being provided to a third party.
- The organisation should regularly and formally monitor the performance of the contractor to ensure that the performance standards stated in the contract are fulfilled. When performance information originates from the contractor, it should be audited to ensure its accuracy.

- Competitive supplier markets are key to achieving the benefits of contracting out. The government should foster competitive markets by recognising that its contracting out practices can play a major role in the development of markets for the relevant services.
- Organisations that contract out activities need to maintain their knowledge of the market and their technical knowledge of the activity. This is imperative in order to be able to communicate with the contractor on equal terms, and to be in a position to effectively tender the activity again. This is especially relevant in the case of contracting out complex activities.

Box 7.1. **Best Practice Guidelines for Contracting Out Government Services**

At the 1996 meeting of the OECD's Public Management Committee, a series of *Best Practice Guidelines for Contracting Out Government Services* were approved. The purpose of these guidelines is not to identify which activities should be contracted out, but rather to identify best practices for evaluating whether government services should be contracted out and how the process can best be managed once the decision to contact out has been made.

Under eight headings, these guidelines identify the key success factors for achieving the benefits of contracting out.

1. Secure top management involvement and encourage re-engineering.
2. Focus on staff issues.
3. Specify service requirements in terms of outcomes or outputs.
4. Monitor performance and foster co-operative relationships.
5. Ensure valid comparisons.
6. Foster competitive markets; and develop and maintain the necessary skills.

Staff mobility and decentralisation

The trend towards increased dialogue in the field with the partner government and other donors, and greater decentralisation of responsibility to field missions, points to a need for experienced and capable development staff in the field. Most DAC member country systems allow staff from headquarters to be posted to the field and then take the knowledge and experience they have gained back to headquarters, or another developing country, at the end of their posting. However, in a few DAC member countries with fairly centralised management approaches, no system exists for rotating staff between headquarters and the field. In these cases, management of the development co-operation programme may be assigned to diplomats stationed in the country – who may lack the requisite management skills to handle development co-operation in the isolated conditions found in the field – or to staff recruited locally on fixed-term contracts. Neither approach supports the building up of development expertise within the country's development co-operation system or greater decentralisation of responsibility to the field. The lack of a rotation system consequently appears to limit the scope for these countries' development co-operation systems to evolve in the same direction as those of many other DAC member countries.

Among those agencies that are decentralising both staff and responsibility to the field, personnel issues have been highlighted as a major challenge. For example, an issue to be addressed is the extent to which increasing decentralisation leads to streamlining of human resources at headquarters. If responsibility and decision-making are decentralised then certain administrative layers at headquarters may no longer be necessary requiring some re-organisation of personnel. If, however, most responsibility is retained by headquarters then there is a risk of duplication of tasks and overlapping responsibilities. This highlights the need for good communications between the field and headquarters. In order to facilitate this, some members are upgrading communications equipment, especially access to video conferencing facilities, but this approach may be too costly for other members who nonetheless need improved communications. As field-based staff numbers increase, partner countries may be faced with meeting and managing larger numbers of development agency staff whose roles and mandate are not always clear. In some countries, all major donors may have sector specialists present. As the aid harmonisation agenda moves forward, there may be some possibility for a greater rationalisation of specialist human resource needs between, as well as within, DAC member countries.

An example: Japan

Japan is strengthening the operations of its overseas offices through an approach called "field-oriented management". The Japan Bank for International Cooperation has delegated more authority to its field offices, especially regarding the management of ongoing projects for which loan agreements have already been signed. Specifically, the offices have been given the following responsibilities: overseeing of procurement procedures mainly conducted by partner countries and the approval of sub-projects. The Japan International Cooperation Agency has also been strengthening its capacity to support partner countries, by shifting more staff and delegating more authority to its overseas offices. By the end of 2006, JICA will have increased its overseas staff by almost 200 individuals, resulting in a headquarter to field ratio of about 1:1 (excluding local staff and experts/volunteers). JICA is also establishing six "Regional Assistance Offices" to strengthen operational activity and support improved effectiveness. It has also delegated more authority to overseas offices for programme/project identification, planning and implementation, and for evaluation.

Human resources at the field level

Staffing levels in Mozambique

In order to illustrate the significant variation in the way member countries approach human resource issues at the field level, an attempt was made to quantify the number of professional staff* used by DAC member countries to manage and implement their country programme for Mozambique. At one end of the scale, a few countries have a total of six or fewer professional staff while two countries have in excess of 75 (see Figure 7.1). Although the average number of professional staff is 21, most countries have between 10 and 15 people. One country currently has 40 long-term advisors stationed in Mozambique. Several countries reported they are phasing out their long-term advisors in the field, as

* For this exercise, the following categories of personnel are not included: volunteers, administrative assistants, secretaries, drivers, security guards, cleaners and gardeners.

Figure 7.1. **Programme size and staff numbers in Mozambique**

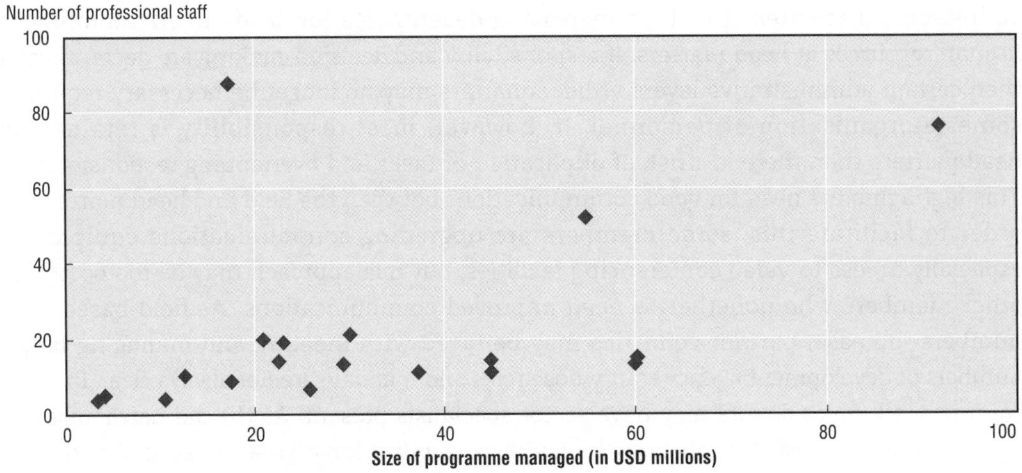

Number of professional staff

Size of programme managed (in USD millions)

Source: Information provided by DAC member countries.

part of a more general shift from project to programming modalities. A sentiment expressed by many DAC member country representatives interviewed in Mozambique was that the number of staff they have in the field is insufficient to enable them to participate in the full range of donor co-ordination mechanisms taking place and to keep abreast of developments in all of their main areas of focus. A few countries recognised that a consequence of this is that staff spend too much of their time attending meetings in Maputo and may become out of touch with the situation in more isolated and poorer parts of the country.

There were also clear differences in the number of staff in headquarters providing back-up for the staff located in Mozambique. In one case, four desk officers in headquarters work on the Mozambique programme alone whereas in another only two people are available for all activities in Africa. Most countries reported between one officer partially responsible to two full-time officers working on the Mozambique desk in headquarters. Many countries also indicated that sections in headquarters dealing with various thematic areas become involved in the Mozambique programme from time to time.

Relating the size of the programme managed to professional staff numbers in the field (*i.e.* taking no account of the back-up available in headquarters) provides a rough basis for comparing across DAC member countries. In nine countries, and irrespective of the size of the programme managed, one professional staff member manages on average between USD 0.7 million and USD 1.5 million per year (see Figure 7.2). In four countries, one professional staff member manages over USD 4 million a year while at the other end of the scale one professional staff member manages USD 0.2 million. Across the DAC member countries in Mozambique, each professional staff member manages on average around USD 1.5 million a year.

The increasing use of programme aid alongside other aid modalities may carry implications for the number and skill mix of staff based in partner countries. Field-based staff of some DAC member countries suggests there is a need for greater skills in such areas as interpersonal communication, negotiation, strategic thinking, analysis and research. Consensus appears to be lacking on whether the use of programme aid demands greater or

Figure 7.2. **Programme managed in Mozambique per professional staff member**

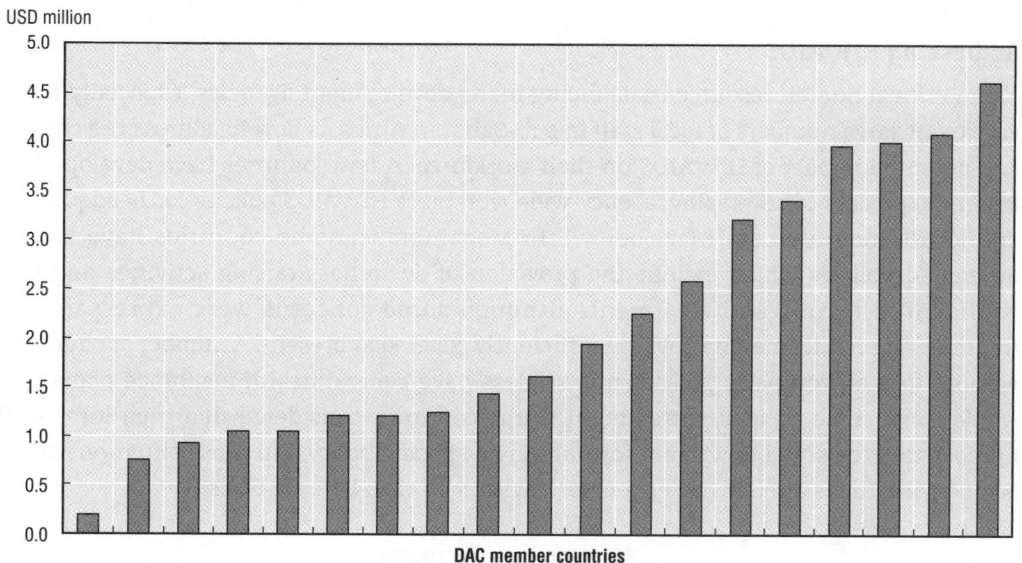

Source: Information provided by DAC member countries.

fewer numbers of staff but this in itself highlights the importance of flexibility and responsiveness to changing circumstances in the deployment of staff.

The employment of local staff

Most DAC member countries acknowledge that staff recruited locally for field offices (nationals of the partner country, nationals of the donor country and third-country nationals) add value to their field missions because they are often the custodians of the mission's institutional memory and bring local knowledge that international staff cannot gain easily. A central part of the decentralisation plans of a few countries is to rely increasingly on locally recruited staff to fulfil professional and sometimes managerial positions in the field mission. Although there is a significant advantage of recruiting local technical expertise, there is a risk of poaching experienced staff from government or local organisations. Many agencies have a policy against poaching but in practice it is difficult to avoid local staff taking up lucrative vacancies with development agencies. Some development agencies have also adopted English as a corporate language in order to facilitate communications between headquarters and field-based staff of various nationalities.

In Mozambique, the majority of DAC member countries indicated that no explicit policies have been put in place to foster long-term career development for locally employed staff; most of these mentioned that training is available, either in Mozambique or at headquarters. Two countries, on the other hand, do have policies in place with one offering permanent contracts complete with full training, a retirement package and the option to transfer to other field missions. A few countries maintain formal or informal policies to encourage local staff to eventually move back to broader Mozambican society while some others doubt whether this is a realistic proposition, given the substantial drop in salary that it would most likely imply. In the health sector, a growing number of counties have signed a Memorandum of Understanding with the Mozambican government stating that they will avoid recruiting local civil servants.

Addressing HIV/AIDS

A critical human resource issue facing many development agencies, especially those employing large numbers of local staff in sub-Saharan Africa, is how to address the current and potential impact of HIV/AIDS on their workforce. A few countries have developed, or are in the process of developing, agency-wide workplace HIV/AIDS policies for headquarters and locally recruited staff (see below). In Mozambique, some countries have locally developed policies which include the provision of awareness raising activities and free confidential testing and treatment, although some concerns were expressed that treatment for family members was insufficiently covered at present. A number of countries without formal workplace policies nonetheless have general health insurance plans that would cover some aspects of treatment. Some countries considered that their local staff numbers are too small to warrant formulating a specific policy and those situations could be and sometimes already have been dealt with on a case-by-case basis.

An example: Germany

Based on the GTZ agency-wide HIV/AIDS workplace policy (created in accordance with International Labour Organization recommendations), a set of guidelines has been drawn up for implementation within GTZ's programme in Mozambique. The Guidelines cover locally engaged staff and are based on the creation of a supportive work environment and non-discrimination. Local staff receive regular and updated training and information on HIV/AIDS prevention which is adapted according to the age and gender profile. A focal person is designated in each project to carry out information and training sessions on different aspects of HIV/AIDS. Information and reference materials are made available for staff and further consultation is available from a local NGO. GTZ covers the cost of post-exposure prophylaxis and treatment for staff, their partner (as long as they have been living together for one year) and all children up to 18 years of age. This includes treatment for opportunistic infections and access to anti-retroviral therapy as long as it is provided by a recognised physician. If a staff member is unable to continue in their current position due to ill health, GTZ will cover the cost of retraining and find an alternative position within the project. Provision is made for extended paid sick leave and payment to the next of kin in the case of death.

ISBN 92-64-00761-X
Managing Aid: Practices of DAC Member Countries

Chapter 8

Implementing Bilateral Programmes in Different Partner Country Contexts

Each developing country presents different and constantly changing opportunities and propensities for reducing poverty. In implementing their foreign assistance programmes, DAC member countries need to adapt their approach to the specific context in each partner country and make adjustments according to the local social and political conditions, the strength and capabilities of national institutions, the depth and breadth of poverty and its geographic and spatial character. While the differing realities in developing countries make generalisations about implementing bilateral programmes difficult, there is now a wide measure of agreement that a partnership approach should be adopted in countries where an appropriately supportive environment for fostering development exists. As part of this, member countries are making progress towards increasing the harmonisation and alignment of their development programmes though much more work is still to be done. Many country strategies, for example, have yet to provide greater predictability for partners on planned levels of assistance. In other circumstances, such as in the case of "difficult partnerships", different types of approaches will be required and development agencies may need to adjust their approach in line with changes occurring in the country concerned.

Implementing development partnerships

Good practice approaches

In partner countries with a sound macro-economic framework and functioning institutions, foreign assistance can be provided effectively through a partnership model that stresses rights and responsibilities for both external partners and developing countries. Much work has taken place in recent years to understand better the principles underpinning development partnerships and to identify good practices that support poverty reduction partnerships (see Box 8.1).

Alignment, harmonisation and streamlining

The use of national poverty reduction strategies as the framework for development co-operation is a key objective for the many DAC member countries that accept the validity of the Poverty Reduction Strategy approach and consider that these strategies provide a sound basis for stronger partnerships and improved donor co-ordination. A joint IMF/World Bank review[1] suggests, however, that while development agencies agree, in principle, to align the content of their programmes with the priorities set out in PRSs, many have yet to do so. The lack of prioritisation and limited detail of many PRSs creates some difficulties for alignment, although improvements in both the PRS process and content have been observed as partner countries have moved ahead with preparation and implementation. According to this review, the major achievements of the PRS process to date have included a growing sense of ownership among partner governments and civil society of their poverty reduction strategies, a more open dialogue within government and with some parts of civil society and a more prominent place for poverty reduction in policy debates.

In 2003, DAC members agreed in the *Rome Declaration on Harmonisation* to harmonise around partner country systems and – in consequence – with each other. But alignment with partner country systems and procedures may pose an even greater challenge for DAC member countries than does alignment with partner country development policies and priorities. Some progress is being made, however, and a range of harmonisation activities is taking place in various partner countries including the formation of government-donor working groups, the development of joint donor-government action plans for harmonisation and alignment and the preparation of joint multi-donor country assistance strategies.

Donors can also work together to simplify or streamline their administrative procedures and practices and thus reduce the burden on partner governments. Amongst other good practices (see Box 8.2), organising joint high-level meetings and joint monitoring teams can, for example, lower the burden of administering foreign assistance. Although for the time being, the practice of holding high-level bilateral meetings is continuing in Mozambique, the trend appears to be to hold consultations when they are most appropriate rather than annually. Moreover, with pooled-funding arrangements

Box 8.1. **Good practice approaches for supporting poverty reduction partnerships**

Working in partnership can require fundamental changes to the ways that development agencies interact with governments and civil society in partner countries and with each other. It may also call for important changes in the way they work at the partner country level. *The DAC Guidelines: Poverty Reduction* outline a number of practical ways of working in partnership:

- Use the partner country's poverty reduction strategy and the national budget as the general framework for development co-operation.
- Be sensitive to partner government leadership.
- Clarify the role and responsibilities of the different partners (government, bilateral agencies, international and regional financial institutions, United Nations agencies, civil society, labour and the private sector).
- Never work alone. Before undertaking discussions or actions, search out other partners (from the development community, government and civil society) who could participate.
- Invest in mechanisms for co-ordination (which should be country led and used for co-ordinating *ex ante* strategic planning and joint implementation), including working out the details of how, where and when to interact with other external and local partners.
- Promote and consolidate joint work (data collection, analyses, missions, evaluations, management and accountability of aid flows) and share information (data, analysis, policy and programming intentions) with other partners.
- Simplify and rationalise, where feasible, development agency administrative and financial requirements (for example, financial management and accountability, preparatory phases of the project cycle, and reporting and monitoring) and strengthen related partner government systems.
- Facilitate local mobilisation, participation, monitoring and assessment.
- Provide capacity development to strengthen government leadership of poverty reduction co-ordination and consultative processes and to enable civil society, including women's organisations and gender equality advocates, to engage effectively in the consultation process and to actively monitor and evaluate poverty reduction policies and programmes – while at the same time not undermining partner government authority or national democratic institutions.

attracting an increasing number of donors and larger amounts of ODA, there is an increasing tendency towards joint evaluations.

Moving beyond closer working and the streamlining of procedures, development agencies can enter into more formal co-operative relationships where one "lead" donor acts on behalf of one or more other "delegating" donors. The delegating donor, who may also be known as a silent partner, surrenders to a certain degree their distinct identity. However, the field visit to Mozambique found that field representatives of certain DAC member countries were ready to pursue silent partnerships but their headquarters were not yet ready to support these initiatives. The level and type of delegated co-operation can vary significantly from carrying out an initial activity on behalf of other donors to acting on

Box 8.2. **Good practices for donor-donor relationships**

Good practices for development agencies have been set out in the *DAC Guidelines and Reference Series: Harmonising Donor Practices for Effective Aid Delivery*. These include:

- Consult with partner governments on ways of reducing administrative burdens by joint working.
- Communicate coherently with partner governments resolving differences of view on policy to the minimum desired by the partner government to enable it to make informed choices. Donors and partner governments may achieve greater coherence through a lead donor representing all donors engaged in a sector or cross-cutting issue.
- Share information on relevant donor operations in a sector with other donors and the partner government.
- Standardise systems and simplify procedures using, where possible, the systems of partner countries.
- Develop common donor procedures in consultation with partner governments, to allow for the more active involvement of the partner government and joint development of country and donor systems.
- Share country-specific examples of common procedures, to enable the identification of lessons that can be applied more widely.

behalf of other donors in all phases of a project or programme cycle. In Bangladesh, for example, six bilateral development agencies and five other donors jointly support the Primary Education Sector Development Programme with the Asian Development Bank (AsDB) – as the lead agency – reporting back to the donors on a quarterly basis. In Mozambique and Zambia, DAC member countries are making significant efforts to align, harmonise and streamline behind government priorities and systems (see Box 8.3).

To facilitate development partnerships, alignment, harmonisation, and streamlining, some DAC member countries are moving towards further decentralisation of staff and responsibilities to field-based offices in order to increase understanding and responsiveness to local conditions and to encourage better dialogue. The knowledge and expertise of field-based staff is critical to informed decision-making on programme development and effective interactions with counterparts. This carries implications for human resources management, recruitment and staffing policies.

Management of development projects

As outlined earlier, despite an increased emphasis on programme-based approaches to development co-operation, support for development projects remains an important aid instrument for many DAC member countries. Even among those countries that favour the use of programme-based approaches, many find value in maintaining support for local-level activities (projects) because it enables them to monitor the impact of actions taken by the government and to feed lessons learnt into their policy dialogue at the national level.

There has been, however, a significant move away from stand-alone projects to support for projects situated within a broader development framework, which address the multiple concerns of the poor and strengthen the capacities of the poor to achieve

Box 8.3. **Joint donor work in Mozambique and Zambia**

Fifteen donors, known as the "G 15", are now providing direct budget support to the Government of Mozambique based on an *Aide Mémoire* they signed with the government. The G 15 meets together with the government every quarter to review revenue and expenditure priorities, budget execution and progress in implementing the PARPA (the national PRS). The programme is reviewed annually in March/April and provisional pledges for direct budget support are made for the following calendar year. Donors use common arrangements for the disbursement of funds through a simple mechanism that provides untied, un-earmarked financing. The Government of Mozambique is required to implement the poverty reduction programme, as set out in the PARPA and the Medium-Term Expenditure Framework (MTEF), and to stay on track with the macroeconomic programme set out in their Poverty Reduction and Growth Facility (PRGF) agreed with the IMF.

The harmonization programme in Zambia was initiated by seven donors – Denmark, Finland, Ireland, the Netherlands, Norway, Sweden and the United Kingdom – shortly after the High-level Forum on Harmonisation in Rome. In March 2003, the Government of the Republic of Zambia in collaboration with interested donors developed a common agreement on how to take the harmonisation agenda forward in Zambia. The resulting Framework for Harmonization in Practice builds, on the one hand, on the *Rome Declaration on Harmonization*, the work of the DAC and the Special Programme for Africa as well as, on the other hand, positive harmonization experiences in the health and education sectors in Zambia. International financial institutions, the European Commission and other bilateral donors are now working to extend harmonization efforts beyond the original seven-member group and the Zambian government has taken the lead on harmonization. In future, the overall approach will be guided by the following principles to which both government and donors subscribe:

- Leadership, co-ordination and guidance by the partner government.
- Commitment to civil service reform.
- Public financial management reform.
- Commitment to using the PRS as a basis for strategic planning and monitoring.
- Commitment to adoption of SWAps and possible move towards direct budget support.

Zambia also provides some examples of delegated co-operation and silent partnerships. Norway plans to provide support to Zambia's agricultural sector through a silent partnership with the Netherlands. The United Kingdom will provide support to CIDA's involvement in the education SWAp. Ireland, the Netherlands, Norway, Sweden and the United Kingdom are also considering providing support to Zambia's National AIDS Council, with Norway taking administrative responsibility on behalf of the other donors.

Source: www.aidharmonization.org.

sustainable livelihoods. Projects should also be managed in a manner that promotes greater leadership and ownership by partner countries and contributes to the harmonisation and alignment agenda. In Mozambique, for example, among several of the countries that work principally through projects, conscious efforts are being made to increase impact by concentrating on a smaller number of more substantial activities. This will also help reduce the transaction costs for Mozambique associated with managing a very large number of development activities.[2]

The use of project cycle management (PCM) approaches is now common practice among DAC member countries. PCM is the process that begins with the initial conception of a development intervention and concludes with post-completion evaluation. The process can be applied to both projects and programmes and focuses on potential beneficiaries, detailed assessment and application of the logical framework approach. These methods provide a structured, logical approach to the setting of priorities and in determining the intended results of an activity. (Annex A.5 describes the project cycle management approach in detail.)

Country strategies

The field visit to Mozambique found that most DAC member countries produce country strategies or detailed policy documents that set out the context, rationale, objectives and strategy for their programmes in main partner countries. These can provide a conceptual and practical framework for the development and implementation of co-operation programmes in partnership with the partner government. They may also enable a clear articulation of the needs of a partner country and of how the programme of a development agency may contribute to national poverty reduction and related objectives. The priorities and strategies identified in country strategy documents should apply to all agencies and departments involved in implementing different aspects of a country's development co-operation programme.

Working in partnership has led to an increasingly participatory process of country strategy development with a much greater degree of consultation with both government and civil society actors (see below). Partnership also means that the inclusion of firm budget commitments for the strategy period is valuable so as to enable partner governments to plan appropriately and invest in the future, rather than meeting short-term priorities. However, in Mozambique although all donors stated that their country strategy is in line with the PARPA (the Mozambican PRS covers the period 2001 to 2005), the duration of country strategies ranges from two to six years and is mostly determined by donors' own internal processes. This does not facilitate the management of foreign assistance from the partner's perspective.

An example: Denmark

Denmark developed its first co-operation strategy with Mozambique for the period 1995 to 1999 and in May 2000 published its second strategy covering 2000 to 2004. The strategy was developed in dialogue with the Mozambican authorities and placed emphasis on the empirical evidence of previous co-operation strategies, developments within the partner country and the prevailing situation in Mozambique at the time. The strategy covers the following areas:

- The political and economic situation.
- The Mozambican government's development strategy and priorities.
- The Mozambican government's poverty reduction strategy.
- The extent and distribution of donor activity.
- Donor co-ordination.
- Co-operation with NGOs.

 MANAGING AID: PRACTICES OF DAC MEMBER COUNTRIES – ISBN 92-64-00761-X – © OECD 2005

- Status of dialogue with public authorities.
- Overall goals of the Danish development co-operation programme.
- The poverty reduction strategy of the bilateral programme.
- The programme's fields of concentration.
- Implementing sector concentration.
- Cross-cutting themes.
- Co-operating with Danish business and industry, research institutions, NGOs and consultants.
- Control and auditing problems related to Danish co-operation efforts.
- The human resource base in Mozambique.
- Evaluation.
- Key social and economic indicators.
- Indicative planning figures for the period 2000 to 2004.

In principle, and in accordance with the partnership model, development agencies should increasingly use the partner country's poverty reduction strategy as the general framework for development co-operation. However, in some DAC member countries, political reality dictates the need for some type of country strategy. In these cases, as the poverty diagnosis and quality of PRSs improve, national poverty reduction strategies may be able to form the core of a much shorter country strategy document that fulfils these requirements in DAC member countries.

Local ownership

In the past, many developing country governments have lacked the capacity to co-ordinate development agencies and to ensure they operate according to partnership principles. This situation is changing, due to a greater sense of leadership and ownership by partner governments and, in part, also due to capacity development initiatives supported by donors. The New Partnership for Africa's Development (NEPAD) is an important initiative owned and led by African leaders to address current development challenges facing the African continent (see below). As an example of a developing country demonstrating leadership and developing guidelines for donors, India recently decided to limit its sources of government-to-government external assistance to six donors (see below).

An example: NEPAD

The New Partnership for Africa's Development is a strategic framework for Africa's renewal spearheaded by African leaders. NEPAD is a programme of the African Union designed to address the current challenges facing the African continent including escalating poverty and underdevelopment. The primary objectives are poverty eradication; to place African countries, both individually and collectively, on a path of sustainable growth and development; to halt the marginalisation of Africa in the globalisation process and enhance its full and beneficial integration into the global economy; and to accelerate the empowerment of women. The principles of NEPAD are: good governance; African ownership and leadership, as well as broad and deep participation by all sectors of society; anchoring the development of Africa on its resources and resourcefulness of its people; partnership between and amongst African peoples; acceleration of regional and continental integration; building the competitiveness of African countries and the continent; forging a new international partnership that changes the unequal relationship between Africa and the developed world; and ensuring that all partnerships with NEPAD are linked to the Millennium Development Goals and other agreed development goals and targets.

An example: India

In June 2003, the Government of India announced its intention to limit its dependence on foreign assistance by accepting further aid from only six donors: the European Commission, Japan, Germany, the Russian Federation, the United Kingdom and the United States. Twenty two other donors to India, including some making significant transfers relative to the size of their total foreign assistance programmes, will be excluded once existing programmes are completed. India also announced it would not accept any aid tied to the provision of goods and services from the donor. In addition, the Ministry of Finance announced its plans to develop new guidelines to govern future bilateral aid flows to India including annual meetings with donors at the beginning of each financial year to plan assistance packages.

Supporting development in difficult partnerships

"Difficult partnerships" arise in developing countries where development objectives play little role for governments compared to other objectives such as the prolongation of power or the accumulation of wealth. Political repression, corruption, violent conflict and the violation of human rights are characteristic of unresponsive regimes. In effect, governments do not have credible commitment to effective policies or their implementation and there is a lack of common development objectives with potential donors.

An important distinction may be drawn between difficult partnerships and those countries in which the government is making an effort to implement effective policies but where the capacity to do so is very weak. The partnership model may need adapting for "fragile states" or those emerging from conflict or at risk of instability. In these cases, foreign assistance may play a critical role in strengthening institutions, improving governance and accountability and promoting stability, and ultimately helping to prevent such states from failing and becoming difficult partners.

The commonly agreed partnership model and development approach can no longer apply in the case of difficult partnerships. However, there is increasing recognition within the DAC that complete disengagement by the donor community from difficult partnership countries carries implications for the 500 million mostly poor people who live in such countries, as well as for neighbouring countries and the international community. These implications can include the risk of complete state failure, conflict and regional destabilisation, greater suffering and deprivation of poor populations and little prospect of autonomous recovery.[3]

Given international interest in promoting international stability, recent work in the DAC has considered different approaches to engagement that are warranted for DAC member countries engaging in difficult partnership countries. No single model of engagement is appropriate for the wide range of countries that fall within the difficult partnership grouping. The characteristics of these countries vary significantly and development agencies need to carry out detailed social and political analyses jointly so as to understand better and agree upon the type of engagement model that is appropriate.

The experience of some DAC member countries demonstrates that it is possible to remain engaged in difficult partnership countries (see Box 8.4 for an example). The DAC has outlined a number of key strategies for development co-operation in these contexts:

- **Promote pro-poor change:** It is possible to support democratic institutions and the enabling environment for democracy in difficult partnerships. The strategy is directed more towards key change agents within and outside the state in order to expose key players to new ideas, promote debate and facilitate (or accelerate) change. Support for the development of capacity of civil society can also be critical with regard to its advocacy role, as can the role of the private sector. Medium-term measures may also be included such as the training of future leaders and the education of girls.
- **Maintain development activities in support of the poor:** There is consensus on the importance of addressing the delivery of services to the poor despite the challenges of working in difficult partnerships. The World Bank proposes the establishment of Independent Services Authorities to contract service delivery agents. However, host governments may not agree with these agencies and some evidence suggest that agencies can, over time, lose their independence. Many DAC member countries prefer to avoid long-term support to parallel service delivery channels. Development agencies can support the work of the private sector, international and national NGOs and faith-based groups which often play critical roles in service delivery in such countries because of the weaknesses of the public sector. Development agencies may also consider the possibility of working through sub-national or local government structures, as a way of keeping government involved and maintaining dialogue.
- **Adapt donor co-ordination and enhance policy coherence:** This is even more critical in difficult partnerships, even though not all donors may stay engaged. A lack of co-ordination can have serious impacts in a context of limited external resources, few entry points and significant need. Co-ordination strategies could include the identification of focal development agencies for certain tasks, policy analysis, support to the private sector and support to sector strengthening or to the political system. It may be that a focus of all foreign assistance on a limited number of priorities, rather than a division of labour, is appropriate. Effective co-ordination requires:
  - Building common criteria for assessment.
  - Greater sharing of analysis.
  - Agreement on conditions for engagement.
  - Tasking focal or lead agencies.
  - Building on the comparative advantage of both bilateral and multilateral agencies.

Box 8.4. CIDA's country development framework for Haiti

Given the history of conflict and recurring crises in Haiti and its poor performance, CIDA determined in 2003 that the development context in Haiti warranted an approach that was based on the DAC's difficult partnership model. CIDA consequently developed a vision of long-term strategic engagement with Haiti that would involve making necessary resources available to support advances, limiting the effects of setbacks and creating incentives to include the population's most disadvantaged groups in evolutional processes in as broad a manner as possible. The key elements of the approach are:

- **Local ownership:** Promoting local ownership will be a gradual process at first, involving establishing partnerships with local stakeholders that have already begun to take charge of their development and fostering the development of a critical mass of stakeholders involved in development actions and capable of finding solutions to the country's problems.
- **Improved donor co-ordination:** In Haiti, co-ordination can be provided by neither government nor civil society organisations in the short or medium term. A co-ordination strategy focused on establishing and maintaining a climate of trust among government, civil society and the international community and encouraging more transparent information and policy dialogue is critical.
- **The concept of stronger partnerships:** In Haiti, partnerships can only be built through progressive alliances with groups or institutions that can manage change and work together towards a common development goal. These alliances constitute a risk in the short-term, as they are likely to experience setbacks or failures. It will be necessary to maintain an alternative scenario, to ensure that engagement is maintained.
- **A results-based approach:** Programme results will be defined according to the specific context in Haiti. Results will need to be modest, modifiable in scope and progressively verifiable over time. They must be defined not only in terms of positive change but also in terms of what has already been achieved, *i.e.* preventing negative change. The identification and monitoring of risk factors will be an integral part of monitoring.
- **Greater coherence:** The high degree of consistency between Canadian foreign policy and development co-operation programmes in Haiti will have to be expanded to include all Canadian departments and agencies working in Haiti.

Source: CIDA (2003), Haiti: Country Development Programming Framework, CIDA.

Notes

1. World Bank/International Monetary Fund (2002), *A Review of the Poverty Reduction Strategy Paper Approach,* World Bank, Washington DC.
2. On average, there were 845 new development activities started in Mozambique each year between 1999 and 2001.
3. World Bank (2002), *World Bank Group Work in Low-Income Countries Under Stress: A Task Force Report,* World Bank, Washington DC.

ISBN 92-64-00761-X
Managing Aid: Practices of DAC Member Countries

Chapter 9

Humanitarian Assistance, NGO Co-financing Schemes and Other Forms of Bilateral Assistance

As well as delivering foreign assistance through country programmes adapted to the specific context in each partner country, development agencies provide bilateral assistance through a range of other mechanisms that are typically managed with substantial involvement of staff in headquarters and for which there may be a special and separate budget. These mechanisms include regional programmes, humanitarian assistance, programmes in such functional areas as private sector development or promoting good governance and NGO co-financing schemes. They may complement on-going activities in main partner countries or be implemented in developing countries where no other programme activities are occurring. In this latter case, these mechanisms expand the geographical reach of a foreign assistance programme but may do so at the risk of dispersing and diluting a donor's development co-operation efforts. Other significant issues that need to be addressed during the design and implementation of such programmes include their consistency with overall development priorities, their compatibility with the partnership model, the extent to which they increase local ownership, as well as ensuring effective monitoring and evaluation. Humanitarian programmes create particular challenges including the development of a strategic approach to this form of aid, ensuring humanitarian concerns remain the driving factors rather than foreign policy or political objectives and the trade-off with using resources for longer-term development purposes.

Regional programmes

The regional programming of foreign assistance can be a useful instrument for addressing a range of development issues not bound by national borders. Development of the Southern Africa region, for example, is critically influenced by the economic situation in South Africa, the up-grading of regional transport infrastructure and immigration policies. In the Pacific, the over exploitation of renewable natural resources, especially fish, carries implications for the livelihoods of many small island communities. More generally, increased travel, migration and trade in food and animals across borders has made regions more vulnerable to the cross-border spread of communicable diseases.

Such regional dimensions of development issues must be addressed primarily by national governments working closely together to develop joint regional policies and responses. Development agencies can play a supportive role by fostering collective action and strengthening partner governments' capacity to address regional issues.

A second approach development agencies can take to addressing regional issues is to provide funding to and support the capacity development of regional organisations and groupings. Collectively, DAC member countries support a variety of regional groupings including the Southern African Development Community (SADC), Asia-Pacific Economic Co-operation (APEC) (see below) and the South Asia Association for Regional Co-operation (SAARC).*

An example: New Zealand

New Zealand is an active member of regional organisations and groupings in the Asia-Pacific region and is engaged in a range of activities to assist developing countries in the region integrate into the global economy. For example, New Zealand has provided significant leadership within APEC in efforts to address the causes of the Asian financial crisis, supporting initiatives aimed at strengthening financial and corporate governance and supporting capacity development activities provided through APEC's Economic and Technical Co-operation programme. New Zealand has also funded participation by officials from countries in the Mekong region in courses on trade policy at the Mekong Institute.

Finally, DAC members can also design and implement foreign assistance programmes on a regional basis. This occurs particularly in the areas of agriculture, conflict, environment, health and HIV/AIDS. In some cases, the need to address regional dimensions of issues, such as HIV/AIDS and conflict, has become a priority in order to improve the effectiveness and sustainability of bilateral programmes in partner countries in the region.

* DAC member countries also support regional development banks and regional multilateral organisations, such as the South Pacific Forum. These contributions are classified as multilateral assistance.

Canada, for example, supports a number of regional or pan-African programmes focusing mainly on health and agriculture (see below).

An example: Canada

Canada is funding a seven-year 35 million Canadian dollar project to minimise the transmission of HIV/AIDS in West Africa. It supports the efforts of health and community development workers concerned with high-risk groups along the chief migration routes of nine West African countries: Benin, Burkina Faso, Côte d'Ivoire, Ghana, Guinea, Mali, Niger, Senegal and Togo. The project addresses the management of sexually transmitted infections, community education for vulnerable groups, including drug vendors, and promotes health education, condom use, seeking treatment for infections as well as addressing problems of drug availability. It also focuses on the de-stigmatisation of high-risk groups and has succeeded in promoting understanding that HIV/AIDS is "everyone's business".

Centrally-managed programmes

A substantial component of the activities managed by development agencies are single issue or "functional" programmes, the most common of which are those focusing on the promotion of democracy and good governance, the environment, developmental food aid, private sector development, tertiary scholarships and volunteer programmes. For many DAC member countries, the largest single issue programme is emergency and humanitarian assistance – discussed in the next section. The key features of centrally-managed programmes are their design, management and funding directly from headquarters. Although normally focusing on a single development issue, if the issue is complex, as is the case with improving security, programmes may include activities to address broader related issues such as participation, ownership and gender equality. Centrally-managed programmes provide development agencies with additional funding flexibility and an alternative programming mechanism. The central management of these programmes means they may be a useful instrument for smaller and medium-sized donors in particular to expand their activities to partner countries where they do not have development staff stationed.

In some cases, it is the nature of the programme that determines the need for central design and management. Private sector development programmes, for example, may link firms and professional associations in the donor country with counterparts in partner countries and provide support, loans or guarantees for joint ventures. This is better facilitated centrally. On the other hand, recent changes to the way DAC member countries consider security issues, with an increased focus on security as a key aspect of poverty reduction and the achievement of the MDGs, could lead to an increase in single issue programmes focusing on particular aspects of security sector reform and good governance. Indeed, the Netherlands has recently developed a financing facility to improve the effectiveness of a more integrated approach to peace, security and development (see below).

An example: the Netherlands

The Netherlands recently created a Stability Fund to finance activities at the interface of peace keeping and peace building where traditional assessments of whether an activity can be classified as ODA can complicate a comprehensive and integrated approach to tackling security issues essential to poverty reduction and sustainable development. The aim of the Fund is to provide rapid and flexible support for activities required to promote peace, security and development in countries and regions where violent conflicts are threatening to erupt or have already broken out. It is intended to support the integrated foreign policy of the Netherlands in the field of peace, conflict and development, based on a multi-dimensional approach including stability analysis, conflict prevention, conflict mediation, peace keeping and peace building, including security sector reform and demobilisation and reintegration programmes. At the end of each financial year, an assessment is conducted to determine which activities are ODA eligible.

Tertiary scholarships are a particular type of programme often centrally managed. They support students from developing and transition countries to pursue higher-level studies often in the sponsoring country. Ideally, to maximise the development impact, students should pursue developmentally relevant courses and return to their home country on completion of their course to apply the knowledge and skills they have acquired. Scholarships programmes have, however, often been used as a foreign policy tool to promote good will between countries, languages and cultural knowledge. This can weaken the usefulness of such programmes as a development instrument. Some development agencies seeking to maximise the development impact of tertiary scholarship programmes are now placing greater emphasis on scholarships for studies within the partner country itself or countries within its region, or on shorter-term courses with clearly articulated development linkages. Few DAC members have commissioned formal assessments or evaluations of this long-standing and common form of foreign assistance. DAC members wishing to improve the development impact of their tertiary scholarship programme can, however, draw lessons from an assessment the Czech Republic recently carried out of its scholarship programme (see below).

An example: the Czech Republic

As with many DAC member countries, tertiary scholarships are a substantial and long-standing component of the Czech Republic's foreign assistance programme. Embassies abroad ask the local Ministry of Education to nominate applicants, most of who are normally accepted. Students typically study for six years in the Czech Republic, including one year of language training, and come from around 70 countries. The assessment found that although a proportion of places are allocated to least-developed countries, the quota is usually not filled. Students choose their area of study, many of which have little developmental relevance. Only about two-thirds of students completed their studies and, of these, it is estimated that between 20% and 50% failed to return to their home country upon completion. On the other hand, the estimated 13% to 33% of students who completed their courses and returned home were likely to have found good employment.

Volunteer programmes are another long-standing and common form of foreign assistance. A few DAC member countries, including Germany, Norway and the United States, have specialised agencies to implement volunteer programmes while some other countries, such as New Zealand and the United Kingdom, support NGOs that send volunteer workers to developing countries. In line with the evolving practice in development co-operation to focus on developing local capacity in partner countries, rather than supplying expatriate expertise, a number of changes can be noted in DAC member countries' practices regarding volunteer programmes. Finland has phased out its volunteer programme, after conducting an evaluation that found that its costs were high and its effectiveness difficult to determine. In 1998, Australia introduced a new "Youth Ambassadors for Development" programme, which places skilled young Australians on short-term assignments of between 3 and 12 months in developing countries throughout the Asia-Pacific region. Ireland, which formerly had a substantial volunteer programme managed by a specialised agency, launched a "Volunteer 21" initiative in 2004 to identify and promote contemporary approaches to volunteering such as short-term volunteering and using information technology to support virtual volunteering, including "e-mentoring".

To be consistent with the partnership model, centrally-managed programmes should be developed in consultation with partner governments and be consistent with their poverty reduction objectives. If activities are supported within a partner country where a bilateral programme is already being implemented, these should also be coherent with the donor's bilateral country strategy and developed in consultation with development and other staff based in the partner country. They should also avoid duplication and not exacerbate donor co-ordination problems. In all cases, but particularly in countries where no bilateral programme exists, adequate systems for monitoring and evaluating impact are essential.

Humanitarian action

Humanitarian action is the largest single issue programme of many DAC member countries although there is significant variation in the size and the approaches adopted to managing humanitarian programmes. In some countries, humanitarian assistance is managed within the ministry of foreign affairs by a special humanitarian department or desk. In other cases, larger departments managing a range of global issues have been established whose remit includes emergency and humanitarian assistance, in part as a result of increasing political attention on peace and security issues. Countries with a separate development agency may locate the emergency or humanitarian department within that agency, but have a significant amount of collaboration and discussion with counterparts in the ministry of foreign affairs. In some cases, and often when the humanitarian programme is a significant aspect of a country's foreign assistance, these departments are staffed by specialists and are able to respond rapidly to international events and requests for assistance, in some cases mobilising emergency response teams at very short notice (see below).

An example: Norway

Norway is a prominent actor in the humanitarian field and the share of emergency and humanitarian assistance in the Norwegian programme is significantly higher than the DAC average. Norwegian humanitarian assistance extends to many countries with a particular focus on countries affected by conflict. Activities are managed by a special and separate department within the Ministry of Foreign Affairs. Norway has a well established emergency preparedness system – NOREPS – which has established stand-by capacities, supplies emergency relief products and is linked to an emergency personnel roster – NORSTAFF – made up of 300 experienced professionals in 25 different job categories who can be mobilised at short notice.

Most DAC member countries channel a significant proportion of their humanitarian funding through national and international NGOs and the main international agencies: the United Nations High Commissioner for Refugees (UNHCR), the International Committee of the Red Cross (ICRC), the World Food Programme (WFP) and, for European Union Member States, the European Commission's Humanitarian Aid Office (ECHO). In the case of multilateral agencies, DAC member countries fund core contributions as well as provide multi-bi contributions in response to specific humanitarian crises. Levels of multi-bi contributions to humanitarian agencies are significantly higher than core contributions, reflecting the number and scale of humanitarian emergencies.

The growth in levels of humanitarian action has contributed to a growth in the number of implementing agencies and a need for more focus on co-ordination and impact. One noteworthy initiative is the United Nations Consolidated Appeals Process (CAP), launched in 1991, which provides a framework for stakeholders to analyse the context, assess needs and responses, agree on priorities, set goals and draw up a Common Humanitarian Action Plan (CHAP) to address them. The CAP has helped foster closer co-operation between governments, donors, development agencies and beneficiaries and, importantly, helped to raise funds including for "forgotten crises".

The growth in humanitarian action, the increased complexity of humanitarian crises and a growth in the numbers and types of organisation providing humanitarian assistance has also led to growing concerns about the potentially negative impact of poorly managed and unaccountable relief. Consequently, donors are placing greater emphasis on quality and accountability issues and focusing more on the achievement of results. A number of DAC member countries have, for example, developed specific strategies to guide humanitarian programmes setting out the criteria, mechanisms and policies for support and intervention. An increasingly strategic engagement with relevant external agencies is also taking place with some DAC member countries developing strategic partnership agreements with key international organisations and examining other ways of ensuring that their response to crises is timely and effective. Reviews of responses to particular emergencies are also increasingly being used to learn lessons and improve effectiveness.

A more strategic approach by DAC member countries can also be facilitated by the development of stronger links across government departments. A review of the country allocation of humanitarian funding may be beneficial in this context. Some countries fund activities in a very large number of partner countries while others strive for a regional focus so as to be consistent with the strategic direction of their overall programme. Italy, for example, has a strong focus in the Balkans while Australia's largest humanitarian programme has been in East Timor.

A major challenge for DAC member countries is the trade off between using foreign assistance for humanitarian purposes as opposed to long-term development co-operation. As demands for emergency relief and humanitarian assistance have risen, many countries are focusing on the management of the transition from emergency/humanitarian assistance to long-term development co-operation and taking an increasingly long-term view. Short-term strategies for relief are no longer viewed as an end in themselves, but part of a process of system and capacity development. Indeed, some DAC member countries allocate humanitarian funds to support capacity development for disaster or emergency preparedness in countries vulnerable to natural disasters.

In some instances, partner countries may graduate from receiving humanitarian aid to being a main partner country, as has been the case with East Timor (see below). However, the needs and expectations of partner countries that have received emergency and humanitarian support for reconstruction or post-conflict rehabilitation have to be balanced against the efforts of DAC member countries to focus their bilateral programmes on a limited number of main partner countries.

An example: Ireland

Ireland's support in East Timor demonstrates how a more strategic approach can facilitate the transition from emergency and humanitarian assistance to long-term development co-operation. Ireland's support moved from initial emergency and relief, to project-based interventions proposed by NGOs, to a multi-annual government-to-government strategy, whose key objective is assisting the East Timorese to achieve the vision set out in their National Development Plan. East Timor is now one of Ireland's seven programme countries and the management of the programme has been transferred from the Emergency and Recovery Section to the Programme Countries Section.

Box 9.1. **General principles and good practice for humanitarian assistance**

A group comprising the world's largest official humanitarian donors and a number of major organisations and experts in the field met in Stockholm in June 2003 and agreed on the following general principles (among others) to underpin good humanitarian action:

- Respect and promote the implementation of international humanitarian law, refugee law and human rights.
- While reaffirming the primary responsibility of states for the victims of humanitarian emergencies within their own borders, strive to ensure flexible and timely funding, on the basis of the collective obligation of striving to meet humanitarian needs.
- Allocate humanitarian funding in proportion to needs and on the basis of needs assessment.
- Request implementing organisations to ensure, to the greatest possible extent, adequate involvement of beneficiaries in the design, implementation, monitoring and evaluation of the humanitarian response.
- Strengthen the capacity of affected countries and local communities to prevent, prepare for, mitigate and respond to humanitarian crises with the goal of ensuring that governments and local communities are better able to meet their responsibilities and co-ordinate effectively with humanitarian partners.
- Provide humanitarian assistance in ways that are supportive of recovery and long-term development, striving to ensure support, where appropriate, to the maintenance and return of sustainable livelihoods and transitions from humanitarian relief to recovery and development activities.
- Support and promote the central and unique role of the United Nations in providing leaderships and co-ordination of international humanitarian action, the special role of the International Committee of the Red Cross, and the vital role of the United Nations, the International Red Cross and Red Crescent Movement in implementing humanitarian action.

As part of broader efforts to improve the management, quality, content and transparency of humanitarian programmes, a meeting of major actors in humanitarian assistance (including 19 DAC members) was held in Stockholm in June 2003. This led to the adoption of a set of *Principles and Good Practice of Humanitarian Donorship* (see Box 9.1), an *Implementation Plan for Good Humanitarian Donorship* and the establishment of an implementation group. The work of this group continues and includes a proposal to review the current OECD/DAC definition of official humanitarian assistance for reporting and statistical purposes. The Stockholm meeting identified the main objectives of humanitarian assistance as being to save lives, alleviate suffering and to maintain human dignity. Yet, in some DAC member countries, foreign policy and political objectives play a role in the allocation of humanitarian assistance. According to participants at the Stockholm meeting, humanitarian assistance should not be used as an instrument of foreign policy and more appropriate foreign policy instruments should be used to address factors such as the causes of conflict or instability.

Co-financing of NGOs and other civil society organisations

All DAC member countries provide foreign assistance funds to civil society organisations to support their development-related activities or to implement activities on behalf of development agencies. Most of this funding is directed towards national NGOs working in development but some DAC member countries fund other types of civil society organisations including political foundations, charitable foundations, faith-based organisations, community-based groups, trade unions and training and research organisations. Among these, some private foundations – most notably United States-based philanthropic foundations – have become major contributors of development assistance, mostly from private sources, and increasingly significant actors in development. Civil society groups in developing or transition countries are funded directly by only a limited number of DAC member countries but are able to partner groups in DAC member countries and so receive funding indirectly.

NGOs and other civil society organisations are generally considered to offer a number of operational alternatives to government development agencies. Their partnerships with local NGOs and community-based organisations may enable them to reach further into inaccessible regions and excluded communities, they tend to be effective at working with highly vulnerable groups, such as commercial sex workers who may fear government approaches, and their operations are often implemented by nationals of the partner country. Working through NGOs or civil society organisations may also be of particular relevance in the cases of poor performing countries, failed states or in conflict or post-conflict situations. Where governments are obliged to suspend development assistance, NGOs may provide an essential avenue for ongoing humanitarian support. NGOs are also perceived as providing a strong identity for DAC member countries, both at home and abroad, their activities are sometimes better known to the public than the operations of government development agencies and some civil society organisations are actively involved in development education.

The proportion of ODA channelled through NGOs varies significantly within the DAC as does the existence of formal policies to guide relationships with government donors. Some DAC member countries fund a large number of NGOs based on broad criteria (or no criteria at all) while others limit funding to larger or more formalised NGOs or according to certain well developed criteria.

 MANAGING AID: PRACTICES OF DAC MEMBER COUNTRIES – ISBN 92-64-00761-X – © OECD 2005

DAC member countries use a range of funding mechanisms for NGOs and in many cases combine the use of different mechanisms. In the case of countries that are able to make budget commitments on an annual basis only, NGOs operate within an uncertain environment working on development activities which are inevitably more long-term in nature. Recognising the difficulties this creates for NGOs, and as part of an increasingly strategic approach, some countries have moved to multi-annual funding for some NGOs – usually the larger and more long-standing organisations. In addition to such arrangements, NGOs may be able to access donors' issue-specific funding through specially designed funding schemes such as those for humanitarian assistance, reproductive health or governance, although some DAC member countries are trying to limit the number of different funding schemes to reduce management costs and increase efficiency. Many of these schemes operate on a co-financing basis, with the NGO also providing funds from other, usually charitable, sources.

In most DAC member countries, the geographical priorities of the government development programme do not apply to the activities of NGOs in receipt of government funding. This allows government programmes to reach beyond the geographic limits of its activities and to support interventions in a range of other countries, particularly for humanitarian purposes. However, this increases dispersion, is inconsistent with attempts to focus and reduces possible synergies between NGO activities and bilateral government-to-government programmes. Some countries have taken steps to encourage partner NGOs to focus activities in programme countries. They include the development of formal criteria to determine NGO activities and a greater level of funding for activities in main partner countries (see below).

An example: Austria

Austrian NGOs play a major role in Austria's development co-operation programme with more than 50% of the bilateral aid programme of the Ministry of Foreign Affairs being implemented through NGOs. NGO activities are governed by guidelines and policy criteria. NGOs receive grants of up to 50% of project costs when operating within main partner countries, up to 25% when operating in other developing countries and up to 75% for projects in Southeast and Eastern Europe as well as Central Asia. As the Austrian Development Agency focuses increasingly on its priority and co-operation countries and the introduction of country and sector programmes, NGOs have had to readjust their regional and sectoral priorities. In principle, NGOs have welcomed this move towards a stronger focus on development activities and greater political convergence and complementary working relationships have already been achieved in a number of countries.

In addition to efforts to achieve greater geographical coherence in NGO activities, ensuring that NGO activities are consistent with government policy and priorities remains a challenge. This may be facilitated by multi-annual funding schemes and the joint development of policies but is more difficult when a large number of NGOs are in receipt of government funding for small-scale projects. A greater emphasis on project monitoring and evaluation can have a positive impact but generates significant management challenges for development agencies as well.

The extent to which government priorities may and should guide the activities of NGOs may depend on the amount of funding received from government as a proportion of an organisation's total income. In some DAC member countries, almost all funds are received from government and NGOs may consequently be perceived as lacking autonomy whereas in some other countries organisations may receive at least as much funding for development activities independent of government and may even voluntarily limit the share of government funding they receive so as to maintain their independence.

Some DAC member countries have taken active steps to encourage NGOs to be more strategic, to have a longer-term vision, to have clearer priorities, more defined areas of expertise and a greater focus on evaluation. As part of this, some development agencies have funded capacity development initiatives for NGOs to support the development of skills and policies in these areas. This is particularly important for smaller NGOs who risk being crowded out by larger and more formalised organisations.

One aspect of this capacity development process may be support through umbrella organisations. NGO umbrella organisations can facilitate dialogue with government and the development of joint strategies, create a forum for information sharing and may be better able to represent the concerns and views of their constituents than the disparate voices of a large number of NGOs operating individually. Umbrella organisations may find they have a greater voice in the policy development process as they facilitate communications with government. In some DAC member countries, representatives of NGOs or from NGO umbrella organisations may also sit on development advisory committees and have a formal role in reviewing and providing input into policy formulation.

ISBN 92-64-00761-X
Managing Aid: Practices of DAC Member Countries

Chapter 10

Multilateral Assistance and Contributions to Global Funds

Contributions to multilateral institutions are an important channel for DAC member countries' ODA and official aid. In the view of many countries, multilateral organisations offer the benefits of being able to mobilise significant volumes of resources and to co-ordinate donor responses to global development problems. However, in many DAC member countries greater attention could be given to the management and co-ordination of multilateral assistance with bilateral assistance. Recently, some member countries have been more pro-active with regard to multilateral assistance including the assessment of multilateral agencies' performance at the field level. Global funds, which typically address specific issues such as health or the environment, are a comparatively new and alternative means for DAC member countries to address development challenges at a regional or global level. While Global funds have a number of strengths, concerns remain about the accountability of such funds and the extent to which they adopt a partnership approach.

Multilateral assistance

For DAC purposes, aid contributions qualify for recording as multilateral assistance only if:

- They are made to an international institution whose members are governments and who conduct all or a significant part of their activities in favour of developing (or transition) countries.
- Those contributions are pooled with other amounts received so that they lose their identity and become an integral part of the institutions financial assets.
- The pooled contributions are disbursed at the institution's discretion.

Any ODA or official aid which does not fulfil these criteria is classified as bilateral assistance. This includes multi-bilateral (multi-bi) assistance, *i.e.* voluntary external assistance from donors for a multilateral agency, supplementary to core membership contributions, which is earmarked for specific purposes.

Multilateral aid is channelled through a large number of institutions. The principal categories are:

- **Multilateral development banks:** the World Bank Group, including its International Development Association (IDA), and the four regional development banks and their soft-loan windows (the African Development Bank [AfDB], the Asian Development Bank, the European Bank for Reconstruction and Development [EBRD] and the Inter-American Development Bank [IDB]).
- **United Nations agencies** including the United Nations Development Programme (UNDP), the United Nations Children's Fund (UNICEF), WFP and UNHCR.
- **European Community** (for European Union Member States). This mainly includes the European Development Fund (EDF) as well as development activities financed from the European Commission's own resources. In DAC statistics, these are notionally reallocated back to each member state on a *pro rata* basis.

The management of multilateral assistance and strategic relationships with multilateral agencies varies somewhat across DAC member countries. In relation to multilateral development banks, especially the World Bank, the ministry of finance in many countries manages core contributions and leads on policy dialogue whereas the ministry of foreign affairs, or the development agency where one exists, is responsible for relations with most other multilateral agencies active in development. This is typically done by a specific department or section divided into different teams for United Nations agencies, the European Union (for European Union Member States) and international financial institutions, due to their important role in promoting development even if main responsibility rests with the ministry of finance.

In the case of the more specialised United Nations agencies, relationships may span a number of ministries. The management of core contributions and relationships with the governing authorities of the World Health Organization, for example, are usually led by the ministry of health but may be backed up by both development and technical specialists within the development agency or the ministry of foreign affairs.

The management of development and broader policy coherence issues within the European Community is a complex area that European Union Member States need to structure themselves carefully to address. Decision-making procedures are influenced by member states, the European Parliament and the European Commission itself, all of which often have different and sometimes conflicting agendas. The implementation of development co-operation activities is largely the work of the Commission. The key actors are the Directorate-General (DG) External Relations, DG Development, ECHO and Europe Aid, the office created in 2001 to implement the Commission's external aid instruments (see also Box 10.1). Implementation of external assistance programmes in partner countries is organised through European Community delegations in the field.

Box 10.1. **Foreign assistance programmes managed by the European Community**

The European Community is a unique donor in that it plays a dual role in development, as a substantial donor providing direct support to partner countries and as a co-ordinating framework for European Union Member States' foreign assistance programmes. The European Commission is the world's largest multilateral grant provider, while the European Union is the world's largest single market and the main trading partner of most developing countries.

The European Commission is an executive body, accountable to the European Parliament and members states meeting in Council. The General Affairs and External Relations Council, one of nine configurations of the Council, is responsible for the European Union's external relations, including external economic relations, development co-operation assistance and humanitarian aid. The Council is charged with co-ordinating member states' efforts in these areas and with ensuring coherence between the different aspects of the Union's external relations. Currently, the chairperson is the Foreign Minister of the member state holding the six-month rotating presidency of the European Union who works with the Secretary-General of the Council.

The European Commission and the European Union Council adopted an important joint Declaration on development policy in November 2000. This declaration outlined the principal aim of the European Community's development policy as poverty reduction. It stated that development activities would concentrate on six areas: *i)* trade and development; *ii)* regional integration and co-operation; *iii)* support for macroeconomic policies and the promotion of equitable access to social services; *iv)* transport; *v)* food security and sustainable rural development; and *vi)* institutional capacity development. Attention would also be given to human rights, the environment, gender equality and good governance. The least-developed countries and other low-income countries would be given priority.

The European Commission finances development activities through European Union budget lines for external relations and through the EDF. External relations funds cover more activities than are eligible for reporting as ODA and come from member states' contributions to the regular budget and other own resources such as customs duties. The EDF is a multi-annual programme supporting developing countries in the African, Caribbean and Pacific (ACP) region, South Africa, activities in member states' overseas territories and some thematic funds such as food aid. It is funded by voluntary contributions from member states and managed by DG Development, EuropeAid and, in the case of emergency assistance, ECHO. Both external relations and EDF funds are divided into a number of programming instruments, including significant regional/geographic programmes.

On average, DAC member countries provide nearly 30% of their gross ODA as multilateral assistance. To date, there has been only limited formal analysis of the main factors influencing the level of DAC member countries' contributions to multilateral agencies. However one available study of funding to multilateral organisations between 1970 and 2000 provides a number of insights. The financial burden of funding is carried by smaller donors. The financing of multilateral agencies is a largely residual item in overall aid budgets. With the exception of the European Commission, multilateral agencies are a channel for assisting developing countries. In European Union Member States, European Commission contributions do not crowd out contributions to other multilateral agencies. Finally, neither the phase of a country's economic cycle nor its rate of economic growth affects the burden sharing responsibility of donors.[1]

Two recent trends can be highlighted in DAC member countries' approach to multilateral assistance. First, some DAC member countries are concentrating their funding on a more limited number of multilateral agencies, guided by their priorities and policy approaches (see below).

An example: Ireland

Ireland has adopted a more selective and targeted approach to the United Nations agencies it funds and increased contributions to agencies that reinforce its policy objectives, in particular poverty reduction. In parallel, Ireland has reduced the number of United Nations agencies it funds from around 35 to 20. This has been done by withdrawing from institutions to which Ireland was making only symbolic contributions or which had a poor fit with Ireland's overall policy objectives. Ireland has also developed a set of criteria to identify possible multilateral partners which include the organisation's poverty reduction focus; its relevance to achieving the Millennium Development Goals; its management strength; its commitment to reform; its commitment to co-ordinate with other multilateral and bilateral partners, especially as part of pooled-funding arrangements in partner countries; and its transparency of reporting arrangements. This has resulted in Ireland engaging more substantially and strategically with five agencies: UNDP, UNHCR, UNICEF, WFP and the United Nations Population Fund (UNFPA). In addition, Ireland has stepped up its capacity to monitor its performance through membership of agencies' governing boards and annual bilateral consultations.

A second trend is that some DAC member countries are developing strategic policy documents or assessment frameworks which set out the strengths and weakness of major multilateral agencies, assess the impact of current engagements, assess the effectiveness of the agency and evaluate its fit with government policy and priorities (see below). In some cases, emphasis is also being placed on the country-level performance of multilateral organisations, with DAC member countries' field-based staff monitoring and evaluating performance in partner countries (see below). This should form part of wider efforts to create greater linkages and lesson learning between multilateral and bilateral assistance. Strategic policy documents produced may form the basis for decisions about the ongoing relationship, funding levels and set out the whole-of-government strategy for managing the future partnership.

An example: Australia

The International Fund for Agricultural Development (IFAD) was set up in 1977 to provide loans and grants to alleviate rural poverty. Australia was a founding member and has committed a total of USD 50 million to IFAD. However, Australia has now decided to withdraw from IFAD for a number of reasons: *i)* its limited relevance to the Australian aid programme's priority countries in South-East Asia and the Pacific due to IFAD being largely focussed on Africa; *ii)* its lack of comparative advantage and focus – other organisations are more strongly involved in rural development in the region; and *iii)* its failure to respond to concerns that Australia has raised with IFAD senior management. Since IFAD is a treaty-based organisation, Australia must undertake a formal process for treaty withdrawal which includes tabling the reasons for withdrawal in parliament and holding public hearings.

An example: Canada, Denmark, Germany, the Netherlands, Norway, Sweden, Switzerland and the United Kingdom

Eight donor countries established the Multilateral Organisations Performance Assessment Network (MOPAN) in 2002 to carry out regular performance assessments of multilateral organisations at the country level. The general purpose of MOPAN is to improve the flow of information on multilateral performance from country level to headquarters, to allow members to be more effective stakeholders, to increase accountability to members' parliaments and to understand better the work and priorities of the organisations concerned. A pilot exercise was conducted in 2003 that focused on the health sector and assessed the performance of WHO, UNICEF, the World Bank and the African, Asian and Inter-American Development Banks in eight partner countries: Bangladesh, Ghana, India, Malawi, Mozambique, Nicaragua, Uganda and Vietnam. The exercise found that multilateral agencies are perceived to have contributed significantly to making national health policies more poverty oriented but are not perceived to have contributed to any significant degree towards building local capacity.[2]

Some concerns have been raised recently about the increasing "bilateralisation" of multilateral assistance, *i.e.* the increasing volume of external assistance being channelled by donors through multilateral agencies as earmarked voluntary contributions. Such multi-bi assistance is a major feature of the funding profile of some of United Nations specialised agencies. For example, of WHO's global budget for 2002-03, only 38% was raised through the regular contributions assessed on member states with the remaining 62% comprising voluntary contributions.[3] Similarly, voluntary contributions from DAC member governments are the major source of UNHCR funds, with only 20% of voluntary contributions being unearmarked and 43% being tightly earmarked in 2002.[4] There are contrasting views within the DAC on multi-bi assistance. Significant volumes of multi-bi assistance, particularly when earmarked for specific sectors or countries, risk redirecting the priorities of the multilateral agency concerned and diminishing the multilateral character of the institution. On the other hand, some DAC members regard voluntary contributions as a key mechanism by which to gain influence, direct programme focus and increase the effectiveness of agencies.

Global funds

Global funds – such as the Global Environment Facility (GEF), the Global Alliance for Vaccines and Immunisation (GAVI) and the Global Fund for AIDS, Tuberculosis and Malaria (GFATM) – are emerging as an important mechanism for the financing of development activities in developing countries. Global funds are distinguishable from multilateral organisations being, according to one study,[5] "a financial instrument whose primary purpose is to attract, manage and distribute resources for global purposes" and having the following defining features:

- **Public/private partnership:** the private sector is often a financial contributor or co-financing partner and governance arrangements may include the private sector, civil society and other stakeholders.
- **Independent:** they are independent of any single institution, constituted as separate entities with independent legal personalities, as alliances with financing arms for legal purposes or as the financial mechanism of international agreements.
- **Issue-based:** the mission is often linked to single issue or policy area.

The structure and governance of three global funds – the GEF, the GAVI and the GFATM – are presented in Table 10.1.

DAC member countries are significant contributors to global funds and, in some cases, to their governance. Global funds are seen to have a number of key strengths:

- They may operate as significant vehicles for the financing of global public goods.
- They can generate additional resources from public sources where there is lack of interest in expanding bilateral programmes or providing additional financial support to established international organisations.
- They are more likely to be innovative and flexible in their operations.
- They leverage the participation of the private sector, civil society and other stakeholders.
- No single donor or agency controls the funds and there is a greater focus on meeting the needs of partner countries.

However, among the weaknesses most commonly cited are:

- The single issue focus neglects synergies across policy making and contradicts support for country led development partnerships behind national priorities and strategies, including the PRS.
- They may duplicate existing structures and increase transaction costs.
- They are less democratically accountable than multilateral organisations and governments.
- They may not attract additional funding but rather be used as a substitute channel for foreign assistance.

These strengths and weaknesses may influence significantly the funding decisions of DAC member countries particularly at a time when many countries are looking for increasingly strategic engagement with multilateral organisations in general. For example, board representation on global funds varies significantly, in some cases donors are automatically granted a seat on the executive management board whereas in other cases a seat may be shared or rotated between donors. If DAC member countries wish to engage strategically with global funds, they need to have the capacity to engage with the board and

Table 10.1. **Global funds**

The following table provides a comparison of the structure and governance of three major global funds.

	GEF	GAVI	GFATM
Mission	The GEF helps developing countries fund projects and programmes that protect the global environment. GEF supports projects related to biodiversity, climate change, international waters, land degradation, the ozone layer and persistent organic pollutants.	GAVI was formed to harness the strengths and experience of multiple partners in immunization. It provides financial resources to countries to purchase vaccines and other supplies and to support the operational costs of immunization.	The GFATM was created to increase resources to fight three of the world's most devastating diseases – AIDS, TB and malaria – and to direct those resources to areas of greatest need.
Year established	1991, restructured in 1994.	1999	2002
Main bilateral donors		The United States, Norway, the Netherlands, the United Kingdom	The United States, France, Germany, Italy, Japan.
Role of international organisations	World Bank, UNEP and UNDP are implementing agencies and key drivers of programme development.	Vaccine procurement through UNICEF, technical and operational expertise provided by WHO.	Technical support and assistance with country-level programme proposals and implementation.
Role of the private sector	No role in governance or as direct financial contributors. Some co-financing and joint projects at country level.	Key role as partners including in vaccine development and delivery. The Gates Foundation is the principal donor.	Financial contributors (around 5% of funds) with board representation.
Role of civil society	Consultation and participation in Council meetings, may be funding recipients via implementing agencies, small grants directly to grassroots NGOs.	Limited representation on board.	Voting members on board and funding recipients.
Fiduciary arrangements	World Bank is trustee.	UNIECF is trustee.	World Bank is trustee, sub-trustee at national level, disbursements made directly to government.
Use of performance-based funding	No	Yes	Yes
Programme monitoring and evaluation arrangements	Carried out mainly by implementing agencies with some external evaluation and expanding role for the Secretariat. Overseen by the governing council.	Independent performance audits conducted to verify immunisation reporting. Hands-off approach due to performance-based funding system.	Board ultimately responsible. Country Co-ordination Mechanism key at country level, emphasis in using existing systems where possible.

Note: Adapted from Heimans, J. (2002), *Multisectoral Global Funds as Instruments for Financing Spending on Global Priorities*, DESA Discussion Paper No. 24, United Nations Department of Economic and Social Affairs, available at: *www.un.org/esa/esa02dp24.pdf*.

other donors on significant issues such as governance, priorities, sustainability issues and partnership approaches. DAC members can also play a significant role by working together at the board and country levels to ensure that global funds operate within accepted international practice, particularly with regard to development partnerships and government ownership and leadership. One example of DAC members working together to monitor the country-level impact of a global fund is the *Global Fund (for AIDS, TB and Malaria) Tracking Study* being carried out in four partner countries and being funded by Denmark, Ireland, the Netherlands and the United Kingdom.

Notes

1. Addison, T., M. McGillivray and M. Odedokum (2003), *Donor Funding of Multilateral Agencies*, Discussion Paper No. 2003/17, UNU/WIDER.
2. Jerve, A.M. and H. Selbervik (2003), *MOPAN: Report from the 2003 Pilot Exercise*, Chr. Michelsen Institute, Bergen.
3. DFID (2002), *Working in Partnership with the World Health Organization*, DFID, London.
4. See *www.unhcr.ch* under Voluntary Contributions for 2002.
5. Heimans, J. (2002), *Multisectoral Global Funds as Instruments for Financing Spending on Global Priorities*, DESA Discussion Paper No. 24, United Nations Department of Economic and Social Affairs. Available at: *www.un.org/esa/esa02dp24.pdf*.

ISBN 92-64-00761-X
Managing Aid: Practices of DAC Member Countries

Chapter 11

Checks and Balances in Development Co-operation Systems

Providing foreign assistance is a unique and often poorly understood function of government and may be seen as only helping people in other countries or as having limited impact. From this perspective, aid is in a precarious and sensitive position vis-à-vis public opinion and the domestic political system. Managers of foreign assistance programmes consequently need to make sustained efforts to inform the general public about their activities and especially to demonstrate and provide evidence that it is well managed and achieving results. To the surprise of many people, foreign assistance programmes are subject to a variety of rigorous checks and balances that provide a range of verifications. But the results and findings from these are generally not well known. These checks and balances range from monitoring and evaluating activities and programmes, to systems for managing for results, to investigations conducted by national audit offices, to inputs, feedback and reviews provided by advisory bodies. Arguably, development programmes may be among the most comprehensively verified government activities in some DAC member countries. However, further steps are being taken to improve evaluation, as well as the feedback of evaluation findings, for both internal lesson-learning, external accountability and public information.

Monitoring

Monitoring implementation of development interventions is an integral part of the project/programme cycle, and should be so, regardless of the aid modality being used. The OECD/DAC defines monitoring as a "continuing function that uses systematic collection of data on specified indicators to provide management and the main stakeholders of an ongoing development intervention with indications of the extent of progress and achievement of objectives and progress in the use of allocated funds".[1] Monitoring enables progress to be reviewed and corrective actions to be proposed so that the activity's objectives can be achieved. Monitoring is the responsibility of both implementing and funding organisations but should also include the perspectives of stakeholders and beneficiaries. Logical frameworks provide a useful basis for monitoring, using the indicators and means of verification specified.

A well designed development intervention will have clear measurable objectives as well as indicators (see Annex A.5 on the management of development projects and programmes, including monitoring). Indicators measure the carrying out of specified activities, the achievement of results and the likely achievement of objectives. If not already available, it may be necessary to collect baseline information during the initial project phase in order to provide an adequate basis for subsequent monitoring of progress. A baseline study collects data that describes and analyses socio-economic and other conditions and trends during a particular period. The indicators set through a baseline study become the reference points for demonstrating change and the achievement of objectives. Monitoring should also extend to changes in the external environment and major assumptions underpinning the activity.

The field visit to Mozambique found that DAC member countries monitor the impact of their activities to different degrees. In some cases, particularly those countries with centralised management systems, there are few formal requirements to monitor activities and this is sometimes a source of frustration for staff in the field. In a few cases, logical frameworks are not prepared for any activity which means that monitoring is reduced to a rudimentary level of collecting anecdotal evidence. On the other hand, a few countries have developed sophisticated strategic management systems with results of specific activities closely monitored and aggregated, so as to gauge the impact of the country programme as a whole. Some DAC member countries choose indicators depending on the specific activity and the country's overall objectives. In others, there is a deliberate effort to use partner government systems to the maximum degree possible in monitoring exercises. Another trend noted is an increasing use of computer-based systems, where appropriate communications systems are available, for scoring and monitoring all activities funded by a development agency throughout the world.

Evaluation

The OECD/DAC defines an evaluation as "an assessment, as systematic and objective as possible, of an ongoing or completed project, programme or policy, its design, implementation and results. The aim is to determine the relevance and fulfilment of objectives, developmental efficiency, effectiveness, impact and sustainability. An evaluation should provide information that is credible and useful, enabling the incorporation of lessons learnt into the decision-making process of both recipients and donors."[2] The main purposes of evaluations are to provide an objective basis for assessing the performance of interventions, to improve future interventions through the feedback of lessons learnt and to provide accountability. For evaluations to fulfil these objectives, they must be used as learning tools within the organisation and, where necessary, be used to change organisational behaviour. Several DAC member countries, including Australia[3] and the United States,[4] have recognised both the need and the value of more systematic identification and sharing of lessons learnt and have established Internet-based systems to manage their knowledge base.

The main issues to be addressed during evaluations of development activities are:

- The **relevance** of the intervention within the context of its environment.
- The intended and unintended **impact** of the intervention and any contribution to achievement of the overall goal.
- The **effectiveness** of the intervention in achieving its purpose and the extent to which achievement of the purpose can be attributed to the intervention.
- The **efficiency** of the intervention in terms of the inputs used for the outputs achieved.
- The **sustainability** of the benefits after external assistance is ended.

As part of its on-going efforts to improve aid effectiveness, the DAC adopted in 1991 a set of *Principles for Evaluation of Development Assistance* which were reviewed in 1998 and are still used as the basis for the DAC Peer Review process (see Box 11.1). In recent years, peer reviews have highlighted a number of evaluation issues where progress still needs to be made including:

- A lack of impartiality and independence of evaluation systems from operational management.
- Weakness in effective monitoring and self-evaluation.
- An imbalance between internal lesson-learning and external accountability.
- Insufficient attention to effective feedback and the dissemination of results, especially in partner countries.
- Insufficient involvement of beneficiaries.

In addition, peer reviews have been able to identify some of the key challenges facing members with regard to evaluation. These include:

- The challenge of being a learning organisation, promoting an evaluation or results-based culture and creating system linkages between the field and headquarters and the various institutional actors.
- The need to link monitoring and evaluation for organisational lesson learning strategically with independent evaluation for purposes of external accountability.
- The need to go beyond project analysis and include sector, country and process evaluations.

- The need to develop appropriate methodological tools for assessing PRS and sector programme aid aimed at providing useful information for action and decision-making.
- The need to strengthen the role of communities and organisations of the poor, as well as the poor themselves, in monitoring and evaluation systems.

As the DAC Principles emphasise, independence and transparency are important if evaluation systems are to function well. DAC member countries tend to adopt a variety of approaches to promote independence and transparency which are linked, in part, to their national context (see below).

An example: Japan

Ensuring the transparency and credibility of ODA performance is an important issue for Japan. Each ODA institution has its own evaluation committee composed of external specialists through which individual evaluation quality and methodology can be examined. All evaluation reports are made public and most are available electronically. An annual evaluation report[5] is sent separately to the Diet (Parliament) for their reference by the Ministry of Foreign Affairs, JICA and JIBC. The Diet's Board of Audit also has a special administrative section to track the use of ODA and external audits have now been extended to all aid modalities.

Evaluations can be conducted at a variety of levels and in various ways. Individual projects or activities may be evaluated during implementation or upon completion. However, there are also clear tendencies for donors to conduct evaluations at a more aggregate level covering similar activities in a number of partner countries or a range of activities in the same partner country. Joint evaluations are also occurring increasingly regularly and are the logical way to evaluate the impact of donors' collective contribution to pooled funding mechanisms such as general budget support. The DAC Network on

Box 11.1. **DAC Principles for evaluation of development assistance**

The DAC Principles incorporate the following essential elements:

- Aid agencies should have an evaluation policy with clearly established guidelines and methods and with clear definition of its roles and responsibilities and its place in institutional aid structure.
- The evaluation process should be impartial and independent from the process concerned with policy-making, and the delivery and management of development assistance.
- The evaluation must be as open as possible with results made widely available.
- For evaluations to be made useful, they must be put into practice. Feedback to both policy-makers and operational staff is essential.
- Partnership with recipients and donor co-operation in aid evaluation are both essential; they are an important aspect of recipient institution building and of aid co-ordination and may reduce administrative burdens on recipients.
- Aid evaluation and its requirements must be an integral part of aid planning from the start. Clear identification of the objectives which an aid activity is to achieve is an essential prerequisite for ongoing effectiveness in evaluation.

Development Evaluation has produced guidance on how to plan and conduct joint evaluation of development programmes.[6]

This move towards aggregate and joint evaluations reflects a desire to evaluate the overall impact of development programmes on the progress of the partner country or a sector towards the achievement of the Millennium Development Goals; an increasingly important area of focus for DAC member countries. This stems in part from the increasing application of partnership approaches and increasing alignment with national poverty reduction strategies which generates the difficulty of evaluating the contribution of one donor in isolation from other bilateral and multilateral agencies. In order to evaluate the aggregate impact of aid programmes, a more integrated and collaborative evaluation process may be needed which builds on the joint evaluations already taking place. This process should be led, in principle, by partner countries with greater support to build their capacity to monitor and evaluate results. This type of evaluation is necessary in order to provide reliable feedback on the effectiveness of overall efforts to support progress towards the Millennium Development Goals to parliaments, the general public and decision makers.

An important aspect of evaluation is the development of feedback mechanisms and DAC member countries have acknowledged the need to improve and develop their evaluation feedback practices.[7] There are a large number of potential audiences for evaluation feedback, a variety of reasons for targeting them, and different approaches needed for each. A choice may need to be made on the most important audiences for each agency and the methods that will be used to reach them. Work by DANIDA[8] shows how feedback approaches can be tailored to selected audiences (see Table 11.1).

Table 11.1. **DANIDA's approach to matching feedback vehicles to specific audiences**

	AUDIENCE GROUPS		
Primary purpose	*Accountability*	*Learning*	*Partners*
FEEDBACK VEHICLES	Parliament opinion makers Leaders General public	Academics, students, researchers External resource base (consultants, etc.) NGOs	Developing country partners Other development agencies
Evaluation reports		•	•
4 page summary	•	•	•
25 page popular version	•		
Press events	•		
Video/film	•		•
Annual report to board	•		
DANIDA's annual report	•		
Danid@visen newsletter	•		
Public meetings and professional associations		•	
Lectures at universities and high schools		•	
World Wide Web	•	•	•
Seminars/ workshops			•
Participation in evaluations			•

Source: DANIDA (2000), *External Feedback – DANIDA's Dissemination Vehicles*, paper presented at the DAC Tokyo Workshop on Evaluation Feedback for Effective Learning and Accountability, September 2000.

Managing for development results

As part of the donor community's broader efforts to improve the effectiveness of aid, several DAC member countries are focusing increasingly on the measurement of development results and the impact of their activities and establishing the extent to which these results can be attributed to specific development activities. A variety of terms including Results-Based Management and Performance Management are also used to describe this process.

The DAC Development Partnership Forum in 2002 brought together donors and partners to discuss managing for development results and aid effectiveness.[9] Discussions highlighted the need for a greater focus on the assessment of results of aid programmes and the implementation of results-oriented systems.

The Second International Roundtable on Managing for Development Results in Marrakech in February 2004, attended by DAC members and multilateral agencies, defined results as "sustainable improvements in country outcomes" and Managing for Development Results as a "management strategy focusing on performance and the achievement of outputs, outcomes and impact".[10] The five core principles of Managing for Development Results adopted at the Roundtable are:[11]

- At all phases – from strategic planning through implementation to completion and beyond – focus the dialogue on results for partner countries, development agencies and other stakeholders.
- Align actual programming, monitoring and evaluation activities with the agreed expected results.
- Keep the results reporting system as simple, cost-effective and user-friendly as possible.
- Manage for, not by, results.
- Use results information for management learning and decision making as well as for reporting and accountability.

DAC member countries, including the United Kingdom and the United States, are increasingly pursuing the application of Managing for Development Results within their development programmes (see below).

An example: the United States

The USAID approach to Performance Management is based on the setting of strategic objectives (SOs) which are the highest level result that a USAID operating unit and its partners can materially affect, given the time and resources available. Each operating unit has a performance management plan which lays out specific annual and long-term performance targets. In Mozambique, the USAID results framework has four strategic objectives, each of which has a number of intermediary results, sub-intermediary results and associated indicators. For example, the strategic objective of "increased rural household incomes in focus areas" has an intermediary result of "increased access to markets" and four sub-intermediary results: *i)* "improved enabling environment for market activities"; *ii)* "roads rehabilitated and maintained"; *iii)* "expanded capacity to market and transport"; and *iv)* "market information and commodity trading system operational".

An example: the United Kingdom

The central architecture of the Results-Based Management approach across the British civil service is the Public Service Agreement (PSA) and its associated Service Delivery Agreement (SDA). As for other departments, the PSA sets out time-bound targets that DFID aims to deliver on with resources provided over the period 2003-2006. The targets set are interim *outcomes* directly linked to the Millennium Development Goals. It uses proxy indicators (for example, child mortality and maternal health) on the assumption that progress against the proxy indicators provides a reasonable sense of progress at the country level where the outcomes are delivered. The SDA underpins the PSA and sets out what DFID will do to contribute to PSA outcomes during the same time frame. SDA targets are a mixture of intermediate *outputs*, activities and processes that are more within DFID's control to deliver on than the PSA outcome targets. Directors, who head DFID divisions, have triennial Delivery Plans which provide the performance ladder describing how achievement of SDA targets will contribute to PSA outcomes. These in turn are supported by annual plans for each department and country office and work plans and objectives for teams which cascade down to performance plans for individual staff members (see below).

Figure 11.1. **From MDGs to you: DFID strategy and organisation**

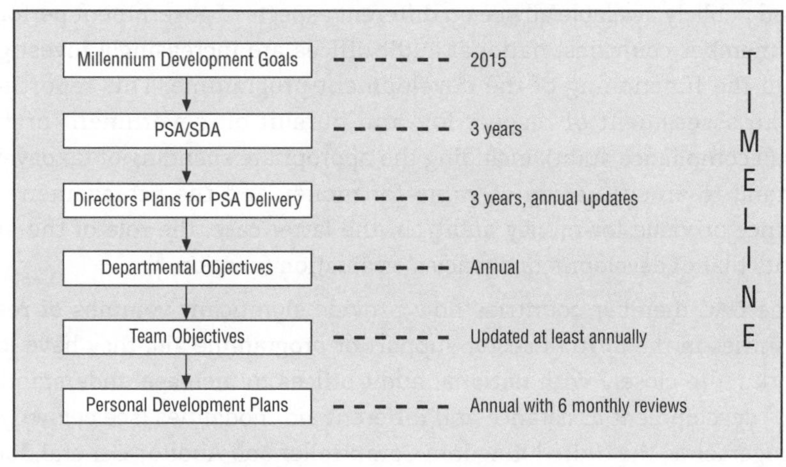

Some of the challenges created by the introduction and use of Managing for Development Results have been identified by DAC member countries as:

- **Organisational challenges:** ensuring commitment within the organisation; developing a change of organisational culture; lack of capacity including the right skills and competencies; the need for additional resources to support capacity development; the difficulty of developing consistent and integrated objectives shared by all responsible agencies within a development co-operation programme; the ability to develop simple, flexible and adaptable systems; and the need for clearer guidance on the application of Management for Development Results for multi-donor initiatives such as sector programmes.

- **Measurement difficulties:** the setting of measurable indicators; the collection of too much information and associated management difficulties; and the difficulty of measuring results.
- **Attribution difficulties:** the difficulty of defining an agency's contribution; sharing responsibility for the achievement of intermediate outcomes with other donors; and identifying attributable impacts.
- **Partner country challenges:** lack of capacity in partner systems to collect performance information; PRS or other national targets that are over-ambitious; and the need to harmonise information requirements in order to reduce demands on partner country systems.

The DAC, through its Working Party on Aid Effectiveness and Donor Practices' Joint Venture on Managing for Development Results, is helping donors to address these challenges by providing a platform for sharing emerging practices and joint learning. It is placing Managing for Development Results on the broader agenda of DAC members and partners and developing and promoting shared values, methodological approaches and co-operation procedures, in line with general DAC policy and guidance.

Involvement of national audit offices

The auditors attached to parliaments in DAC member countries – sometimes known as the National Audit Office or the Auditor General – are independent agencies that provide objective and publicly available advice on different aspects of government performance. In many DAC member countries, national audit offices are increasingly investigating and reporting on the functioning of the development programme. This reporting may be limited to an assessment of respect for, and pursuit of, government practices and procedures (a compliance audit), including the appropriate spending of taxpayers' money, or may extend to an evaluation of value-for-money and the achievement of results (a performance or value-for-money audit). In the latter case, the role of the audit office complements that of development agencies' evaluation function.

As some DAC member countries now provide significant volumes of resources to partner countries in the form of sector support or programme aid, they have identified a need to work more closely with national audit offices to increase understanding of the objectives of development assistance and different aid modalities (see below). As a result of such engagements, the United Kingdom Comptroller and Auditor-General, for example, has emphasised the importance of value-for-money and development impact but acknowledged that there are challenges to effective performance management and measurement in the field of development. The time scale for discernable results to show through are often longer than those set for public expenditure monitoring and reporting. In addition, there are difficulties in measuring and attributing impact and in obtaining reliable data.[12]

An example: Canada

CIDA regularly performs audits of its programmes to help ensure effective and efficient use of its resources. For a better integration of the audit function in the overall performance assessment process, internal audit has been re-oriented to focus on best practices rather than compliance. In addition, periodic independent reviews are conducted by the Office of the Auditor General (OAG) to provide

MANAGING AID: PRACTICES OF DAC MEMBER COUNTRIES – ISBN 92-64-00761-X – © OECD 2005

objective information and advice to parliament. A very collaborative and constructive relationship has developed over the years between CIDA and the OAG. The OAG has, for example, been encouraging CIDA to provide to the public a more meaningful and balanced picture of its performance. More recently, the OAG has closely followed CIDA's discussions on aid effectiveness and has indicated its support for the agency's shift towards programme-based approaches, provided that development results can be measured and proper financial assessment and reporting mechanisms established.

The field visit to Mozambique noted greater interest by auditors-general or national audit offices in DAC member countries in the activities donors are funding. However, the missions of national auditors to Mozambique have tended to be fairly unco-ordinated and more can be done to promote greater harmonisation in these activities, including standards and norms used, as is occurring with evaluations. A group of seven DAC member countries – Denmark, Finland, Ireland, the Netherlands, Norway, Sweden and the United Kingdom – known as the Nordic + group, are working to address such issues by promoting greater harmonisation of standards regarding financial, procedural and legal requirements.[13] These could include agreement on legal frameworks for pooling funds and on mutually acceptable audit standards and reporting requirements. Ultimately, the acceptance and use by National Audit Offices of audits carried out at country level by the audit offices of other DAC member countries could significantly reduce the administrative burden on partner countries. Although progress in this direction has been slow, the discussion of the possibility demonstrates the degree to which many donors are exploring new ways to work together in partnership.

Advisory bodies

Approximately half the DAC member countries have some form of committee that advises either the responsible minister or the main development agency. The structure, function, membership and role of these committees take different forms but they usually differ from consultative bodies in that there is an explicit advisory role and operate with a high degree of independence. A few DAC member countries have more than one advisory body.

The composition and size of advisory bodies varies significantly and may be related to the functions they carry out. Some bodies comprise technical specialists or research experts while others include broader representation of civil society including staff of development NGOs or academics. A number of advisory bodies include former ministers or government representatives, alongside members from civil society (see below). The size of such bodies can range from as few as nine people to as many as 50.

An example: Switzerland

The Swiss Consultative Commission on international development and co-operation comprises members representing the parties in parliament, civil society including trade unions, NGOs, universities and the media, as well as the private sector. Its purpose is to advise the Federal Council on development co-operation and humanitarian aid. The commission has set up at least three sub-commissions to monitor more closely institutions and activities of special interest: the Bretton Woods Institutions, the WTO and co-operation with Eastern European countries. The commission provides a unique discussion forum that facilitates dialogue between the government and civil society and plays a considerable role in ensuring that the Swiss population continue to support development co-operation and Swiss policy in this area.

Some advisory bodies carry out a range of functions while others have more circumscribed roles. These functions may include discussion of overall policy issues and more specialised tasks such as reviewing country strategies, reviewing grant proposals, commissioning or approving research and drafting planning documents. A number of bodies provide input into programme evaluation, either through the review of audit and evaluation reports or through active participation in evaluation activities. Some advisory bodies are responsible for organising development forums or dialogue between civil society and government.

The effectiveness of advisory bodies is influenced by the structure and roles set out above. Broad membership, for example, can create difficulties in achieving consensus or lead to ambiguity, while the inclusion of members of a current government may undermine the body's degree of independence. Advisory bodies also need to be adequately resourced to be effective both in terms of development agency staff time for management and consultation as well as provision being made for the time and costs of the members themselves. In some DAC member countries, the advisory bodies operate in an entirely voluntary capacity despite playing an important role in the development co-operation programme.

An example: France

The High Council for International Co-operation was created in 1999 as an advisory body under the responsibility of the Prime Minister. With the aim of involving civil society in France's development policy by providing non-governmental actors with a forum, its responsibilities are to foster consultations between development co-operation actors and raise public awareness on development challenges. It has 45 members appointed for a three-year term, which include representatives of NGOs and other civil society organisations, officials from sub-national authorities involved in decentralised co-operation, as well as members of parliament. It has its own budget and a secretariat run by a team of about 10 persons. Its work is organised around a number of thematic working groups. Its major activities include the organisation of annual conferences around development topics as well as the preparation of reports and statements, sometimes in collaboration with parliamentary committees or at the request of the government. Its independence is demonstrated by the exclusion of government officials in its own work.

Notes

1. OECD (2002), *Glossary of Key Terms in Evaluation and Results Based Management*, OECD, Paris.
2. *Ibid.*
3. AusAID's Knowledge Warehouse (AKWa) at *http://akwa.ausaid.gov.au/* includes lessons learnt in delivering Australia's aid programme, examples of good practice through the activity cycle and a range of AusAID publications related to quality assurance and the evaluation of Australian aid projects and programmes.
4. To improve dissemination of lessons learnt, USAID has set up a "Knowledge for Development" site at: *http://knowledge.usaid.gov/index.html.*
5. Annual Evaluation Reports on Japan's Economic Co-operation are available at *www.infojapan.org/policy/oda/evaluation/.*
6. OECD (2000), *Effective Practices in Conducting a Joint Multi-Donor Evaluation*, OECD, Paris.
7. OECD (2001), *Evaluation Feedback for Effective Learning and Accountability*, OECD, Paris.
8. The Danish Ministry of Foreign Affairs commonly uses the name "DANIDA" to represent Denmark's development co-operation, which accounts for 90% of the programme of activities of the Ministry of Foreign Affairs' "South Group".
9. OECD (2003), "Managing for Development Results and Aid Effectiveness: A Report on the DAC Development Partnership Forum", *The DAC Journal*, Volume 4, No. 3, OECD, Paris, pp. 41-71.
10. Action Plan on Managing for Development Results. Available at *www.mfdr.org/documents/3MarrakechActionPlan05febA4.pdf.*
11. Promoting a Harmonized Approach to Managing for Development Results: Core Principles. Available at *www.mfdr.org/documents/2CorePrinciples05Feb04.pdf.*
12. Comptroller and Auditor General (2002), *Performance Management – Helping to Reduce Poverty*, Report by the Comptroller and Auditor General (HC 739, Session 2001-2002), HMSO, London.
13. Joint Action Plan for Effective Aid Delivery through Harmonisation and Alignment of Donor Practices 2003-2005 (Denmark, Finland, Ireland, the Netherlands, Norway, Sweden and the United Kingdom) available at: *www.aidharmonization.org/download/236284/NordicPlus.pdf.*

ISBN 92-64-00761-X
Managing Aid: Practices of DAC Member Countries

ANNEX A.1

Basic Profiles of DAC Member Countries' Foreign Assistance Programmes

Unless otherwise indicated, all data underlying the graphs in this publication can be found at *www.oecd.org/dac/stats*.

Australia

Objective:	To advance Australia's national interest by assisting developing countries to reduce poverty and achieve sustainable development: *Better Aid for a Better Future (*1997*)*
Legislation:	None
Overall policy statement:	Better Aid for a Better Future (1997)
Other general policy statements:	Australian Aid: Investing in Growth, Stability and Prosperity (2002) Reducing Poverty – the Central Influencing Factor of Australia's Aid Programme (2001)
Minister:	Minister for Foreign Affairs assisted by a Parliamentary Secretary
Other ministers:	The Treasurer
Principal department/development agency:	Australian Agency for International Development (AusAID) (*www.ausaid.gov.au*)
Other agencies/ministries:	The Treasury (*www.treasury.gov.au*) Australian Centre for International Agricultural Research (*www.aciar.gov.au*)
Interministerial co-ordination structures:	
Main bilateral partners:	Papua New Guinea is the largest bilateral partner. The programme focuses mainly on the Pacific and East Asia concentrating on Burma, Cambodia, China, Fiji, Indonesia, Kiribati, Laos, Mongolia, the Philippines, Samoa, the Solomon Islands, Thailand, East Timor, Tonga, Tuvalu, Vanuatu and Vietnam.
Main sectors:	Governance, health, education, agriculture and rural development, and infrastructure
Ministerial advisory bodies:	The Aid Advisory Council

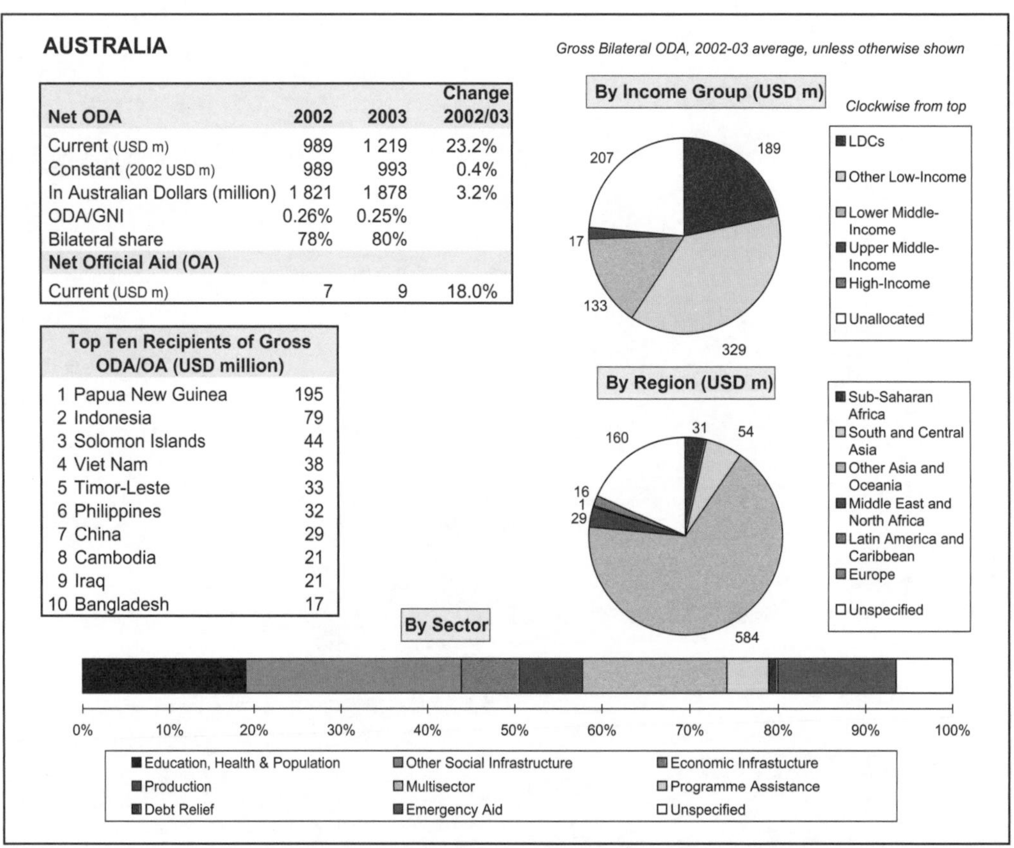

AUSTRALIA

Gross Bilateral ODA, 2002-03 average, unless otherwise shown

Net ODA	2002	2003	Change 2002/03
Current (USD m)	989	1 219	23.2%
Constant (2002 USD m)	989	993	0.4%
In Australian Dollars (million)	1 821	1 878	3.2%
ODA/GNI	0.26%	0.25%	
Bilateral share	78%	80%	
Net Official Aid (OA)			
Current (USD m)	7	9	18.0%

Top Ten Recipients of Gross ODA/OA (USD million)	
1 Papua New Guinea	195
2 Indonesia	79
3 Solomon Islands	44
4 Viet Nam	38
5 Timor-Leste	33
6 Philippines	32
7 China	29
8 Cambodia	21
9 Iraq	21
10 Bangladesh	17

Austria

Objective:	To combat poverty through economic and social development, ensure peace and human security, and preserve the environment and protect natural resources: *Federal Act on Development Co-operation* (2002).
Legislation:	Federal Act on Development Co-operation (2002, amended 2003)
Overall policy statement:	Three-Year Programme on Austrian Development Policy (adjusted annually)
Other general policy statements:	
Ministers:	Federal Minister for Foreign Affairs
Other ministers:	
Principal department/development agency:	Ministry for Foreign Affairs (Department for Development Cooperation and Cooperation with Eastern Europe) (*www.eza.gv.at*)
Other agencies/ministries:	The Austrian Development Agency (ADA) (*www.ada.gv.at*) Federal Ministry of Finance Federal Ministry for Education, Science and Culture Federal Ministry of the Interior Provinces Ministry for Agriculture, Forestry, Environment and Water Management
Interministerial co-ordination structures:	ADA Board of Directors Private Sector Development Platform
Main bilateral partners:	In the South, Austria has 7 priority countries, 13 co-operation countries and 4 special programmes. In Eastern Europe, there are 8 priority countries (2 of them being phased out, 1 planned) and in another 11 countries small local activities are carried out.
Main sectors:	Education, energy, rural development, investment and employment, support for micro, small and medium sized enterprises, transport and mobility, water supply and sanitation, democratisation, rule of law, human rights, conflict prevention and good governance
Ministerial advisory bodies:	The Advisory Board on Development Policy

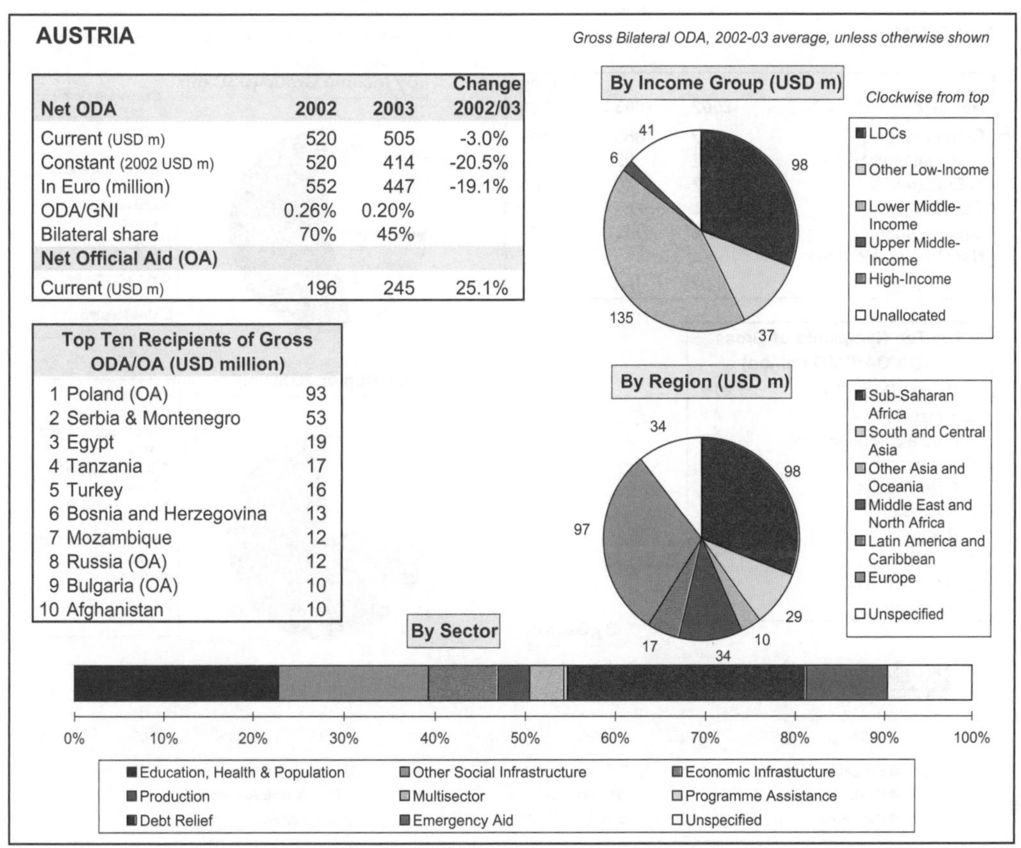

Net ODA	2002	2003	Change 2002/03
Current (USD m)	520	505	-3.0%
Constant (2002 USD m)	520	414	-20.5%
In Euro (million)	552	447	-19.1%
ODA/GNI	0.26%	0.20%	
Bilateral share	70%	45%	
Net Official Aid (OA)			
Current (USD m)	196	245	25.1%

Top Ten Recipients of Gross ODA/OA (USD million)	
1 Poland (OA)	93
2 Serbia & Montenegro	53
3 Egypt	19
4 Tanzania	17
5 Turkey	16
6 Bosnia and Herzegovina	13
7 Mozambique	12
8 Russia (OA)	12
9 Bulgaria (OA)	10
10 Afghanistan	10

Belgium

Objective:	Sustainable development to be achieved by combating poverty, on the basis of the concept of partnership and in accordance with the criteria for determining relevance to development: *Law on Belgian Development Co-operation* (1999).
Legislation:	Law on Belgian Development Co-operation (1999).
Overall policy statement:	Policy Plan for Belgian International Co-operation.
Other general policy statements:	
Ministers:	Minister for Development Co-operation.
Other ministers:	Minister for Foreign Affairs.
Principal department/development agency:	Directorate General for Development Co-operation (DGDC) of the Federal Department of Foreign Affairs, Foreign Trade and Development Cooperation (*www.dgdc.be*).
Other agencies/ministries:	Belgian Technical Co-operation (BTC) (*www.btcctb.org*). Federal Ministry of Finance Ministry of Foreign Affairs National Ducriore office Flemish government Walloon government
Interministerial co-ordination structures:	
Main bilateral partners:	Belgium has 18 main programme countries. In Africa these are: Algeria, Benin, Burundi, Congo, Mali, Morocco, Mozambique, Niger, Rwanda, Senegal, South Africa, Tanzania and Uganda; in Latin America these are Bolivia, Ecuador, and Peru, and in Asia, Vietnam plus the Palestinian Administered Areas.
Main sectors:	Health, education, agriculture and food security, basic infrastructure, conflict prevention and societal consolidation.
Ministerial advisory bodies:	

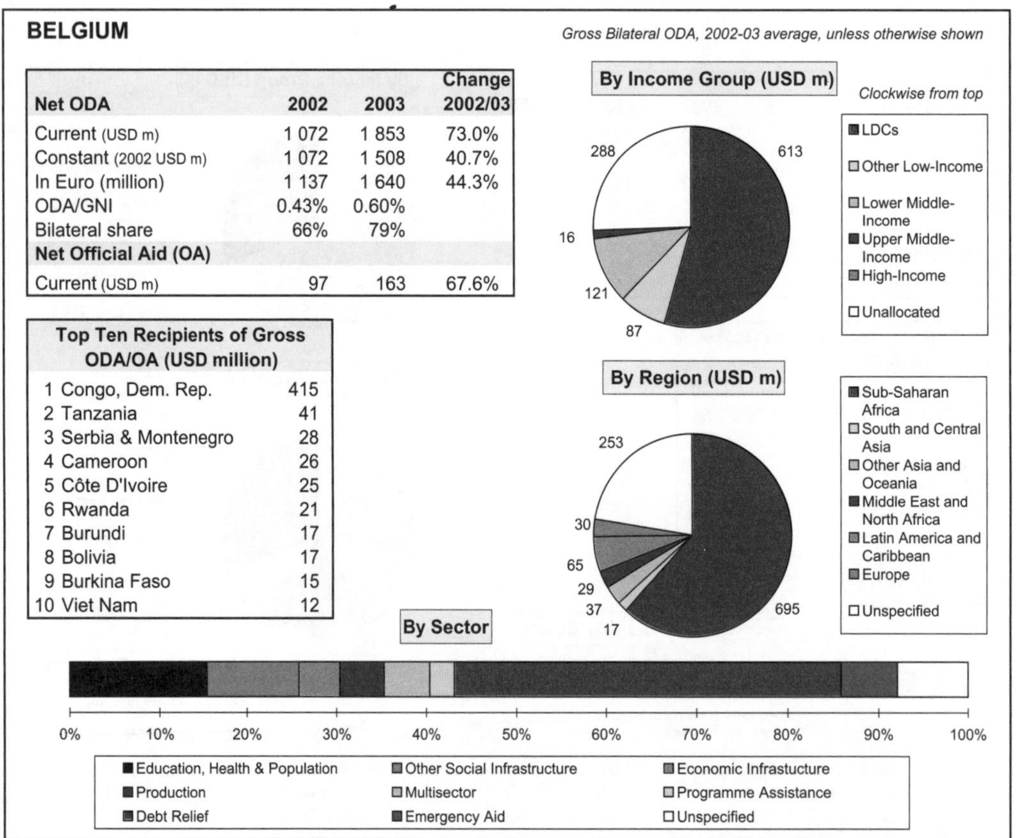

Net ODA	2002	2003	Change 2002/03
Current (USD m)	1 072	1 853	73.0%
Constant (2002 USD m)	1 072	1 508	40.7%
In Euro (million)	1 137	1 640	44.3%
ODA/GNI	0.43%	0.60%	
Bilateral share	66%	79%	
Net Official Aid (OA)			
Current (USD m)	97	163	67.6%

Top Ten Recipients of Gross ODA/OA (USD million)	
1 Congo, Dem. Rep.	415
2 Tanzania	41
3 Serbia & Montenegro	28
4 Cameroon	26
5 Côte D'Ivoire	25
6 Rwanda	21
7 Burundi	17
8 Bolivia	17
9 Burkina Faso	15
10 Viet Nam	12

MANAGING AID: PRACTICES OF DAC MEMBER COUNTRIES – ISBN 92-64-00761-X – © OECD 2005

Canada

Objective:	To support sustainable development in developing countries, in order to reduce poverty and to contribute to a more secure, equitable and prosperous world: *Canada in the World* (1995).
Legislation:	None
Overall policy statement:	Canada in the World (1995).
Other general policy statements:	Canada Making a Difference in the World: A Policy Statement on Aid Effectiveness (2002).
Minister:	Minister for International Cooperation.
Other ministers:	Minister of Foreign Affairs. Minister of Finance.
Principal department/development agency:	The Canadian International Development Agency (CIDA) (*www.acdi-cida.gc.ca*).
Other agencies/ministries:	Department of Foreign Affairs (*www.fac-aec.gc.ca*). Department of International Trade (*www.dfait-maeci.gc.ca*). Department of Finance (*www.fin.gc.ca*). International Development Research Centre (*www.idrc.ca*). Rights and Democracy. Health Canada. Public Works and Government Services. Environment Canada. Canadian Heritage and the Privy Council Office.
Interministerial co-ordination structures:	
Main bilateral partners:	Canadian development assistance supports bilateral activities in approximately 100 countries but has selected a limited number of countries for an enhanced partnership.
Main sectors:	CIDA priority areas are basic social needs including basic education, health, nutrition, HIV/AIDS, and child protection, and human rights, democracy and governance.
Ministerial advisory bodies:	

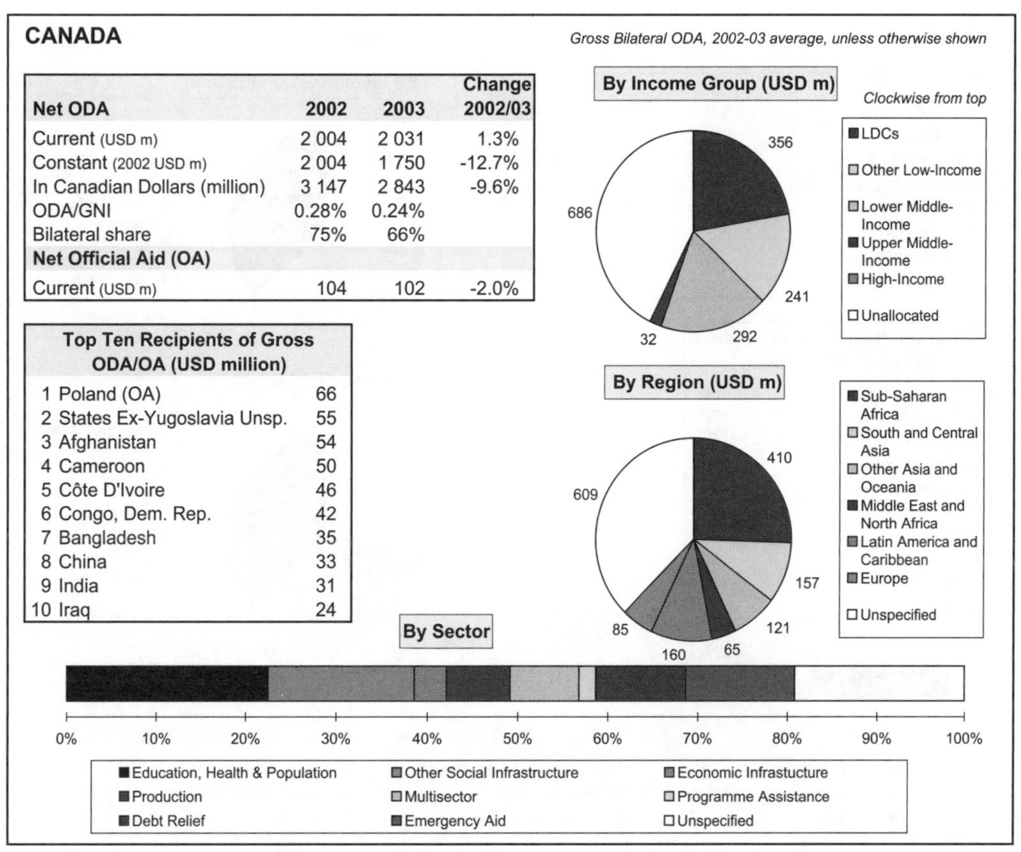

CANADA

Gross Bilateral ODA, 2002-03 average, unless otherwise shown

Net ODA	2002	2003	Change 2002/03
Current (USD m)	2 004	2 031	1.3%
Constant (2002 USD m)	2 004	1 750	-12.7%
In Canadian Dollars (million)	3 147	2 843	-9.6%
ODA/GNI	0.28%	0.24%	
Bilateral share	75%	66%	
Net Official Aid (OA)			
Current (USD m)	104	102	-2.0%

Top Ten Recipients of Gross ODA/OA (USD million)	
1 Poland (OA)	66
2 States Ex-Yugoslavia Unsp.	55
3 Afghanistan	54
4 Cameroon	50
5 Côte D'Ivoire	46
6 Congo, Dem. Rep.	42
7 Bangladesh	35
8 China	33
9 India	31
10 Iraq	24

Denmark

Objective:	Through co-operation with governments and public authorities in [developing] countries, to support their endeavours aimed at providing economic growth, thereby making contributions to ensuring social progress and political independence in accordance with the aims and principles of the UN Charter, and to promote mutual understanding and solidarity through cultural co-operation: *Act on International Development Co-operation* (1971).
Legislation:	Act on International Development Co-operation (1971, amended 1998 and June 2002).
Overall policy statement:	Partnership 2000
Other general policy statements:	A World of Difference: the Government's Vision for New Priorities in Danish Development Assistance 2004-2008.
Minister:	Minister for Foreign Affairs
Other ministers:	
Principal department/development agency:	The South Group within the Ministry of Foreign Affairs (*www.um.dk*).
Other agencies/ministries:	
Interministerial co-ordination structures:	
Main bilateral partners/programme countries:	There are 15 programme countries. In Africa these are: Benin, Burkina Faso, Egypt, Ghana, Kenya, Mozambique, Tanzania, Uganda, and Zambia; in Asia: Bangladesh, Bhutan, Nepal and Vietnam and in Latin America: Nicaragua and Bolivia.
Main sectors:	The social sectors – health, education, water and sanitation, economic infrastructure – together with transport, energy and the productive sectors – agriculture and the private sector. The principle is to be involved in a maximum of three to four sectors per programme country.
Ministerial advisory bodies:	The Board of International Development Co-operation. The Council of International Development Co-operation.

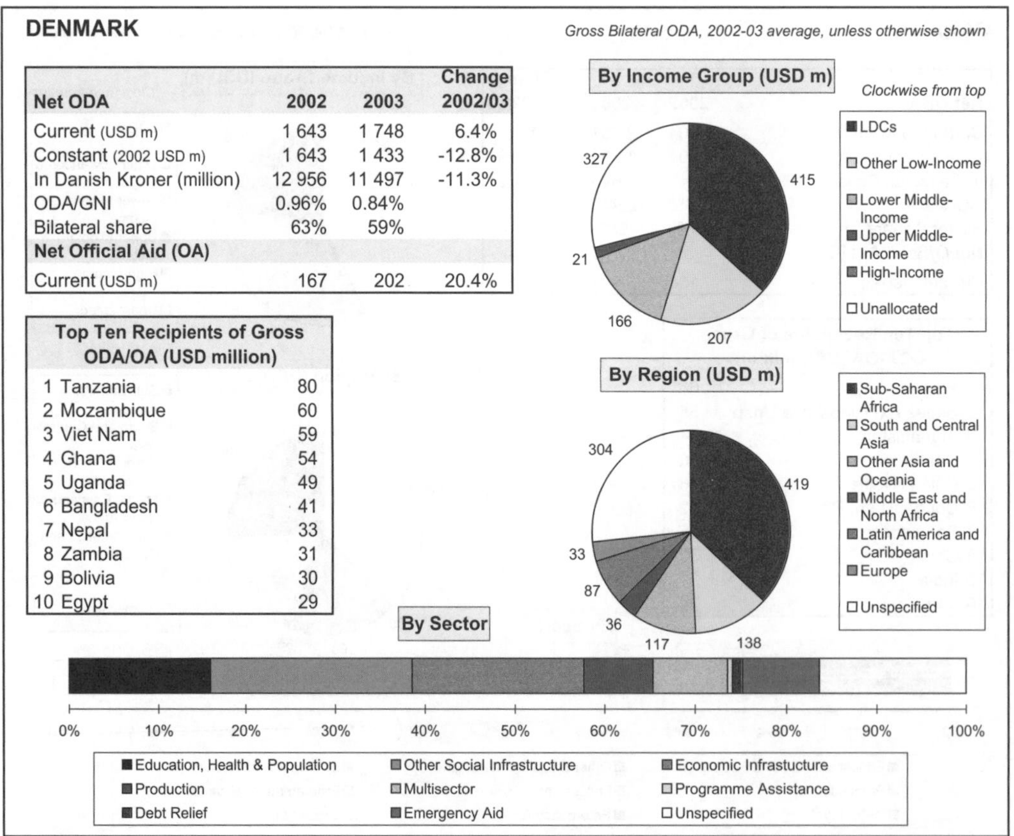

Net ODA	2002	2003	Change 2002/03
Current (USD m)	1 643	1 748	6.4%
Constant (2002 USD m)	1 643	1 433	-12.8%
In Danish Kroner (million)	12 956	11 497	-11.3%
ODA/GNI	0.96%	0.84%	
Bilateral share	63%	59%	
Net Official Aid (OA)			
Current (USD m)	167	202	20.4%

Top Ten Recipients of Gross ODA/OA (USD million)	
1 Tanzania	80
2 Mozambique	60
3 Viet Nam	59
4 Ghana	54
5 Uganda	49
6 Bangladesh	41
7 Nepal	33
8 Zambia	31
9 Bolivia	30
10 Egypt	29

Finland

Objective:	To contribute to the eradication of extreme poverty: *White Paper on Development Policy* (2004).
Legislation:	None
Overall policy statement	Development Policy, Government Resolution (2004).
Other general policy statements:	Government Decisions-in-Principle (2001).
Minister:	Minister for Foreign Trade and Development Co-operation.
Other ministers:	Minister for Foreign Affairs.
Principal department/development agency:	Ministry for Foreign Affairs (*http://formin.finland.fi/english*).
Other agencies/ministries:	Finnfund (*www.finnfund.fi*). The Service Centre for Development Cooperation (KEPA) (*www.kepa.fi*).
Interministerial co-ordination structures:	
Main bilateral partners/programme countries:	There are 8 long-term partner countries. In Africa: Ethiopia, Kenya, Mozambique, Tanzania and Zambia. In Asia: Nepal and Vietnam, and in Latin America: Nicaragua.
Main sectors:	Finland supports partner countries' efforts to achieve the MDGs. The sectors for Finnish support are selected on a case-by-case analysis of the Finnish added value.
Ministerial advisory bodies:	The Development Policy Committee.

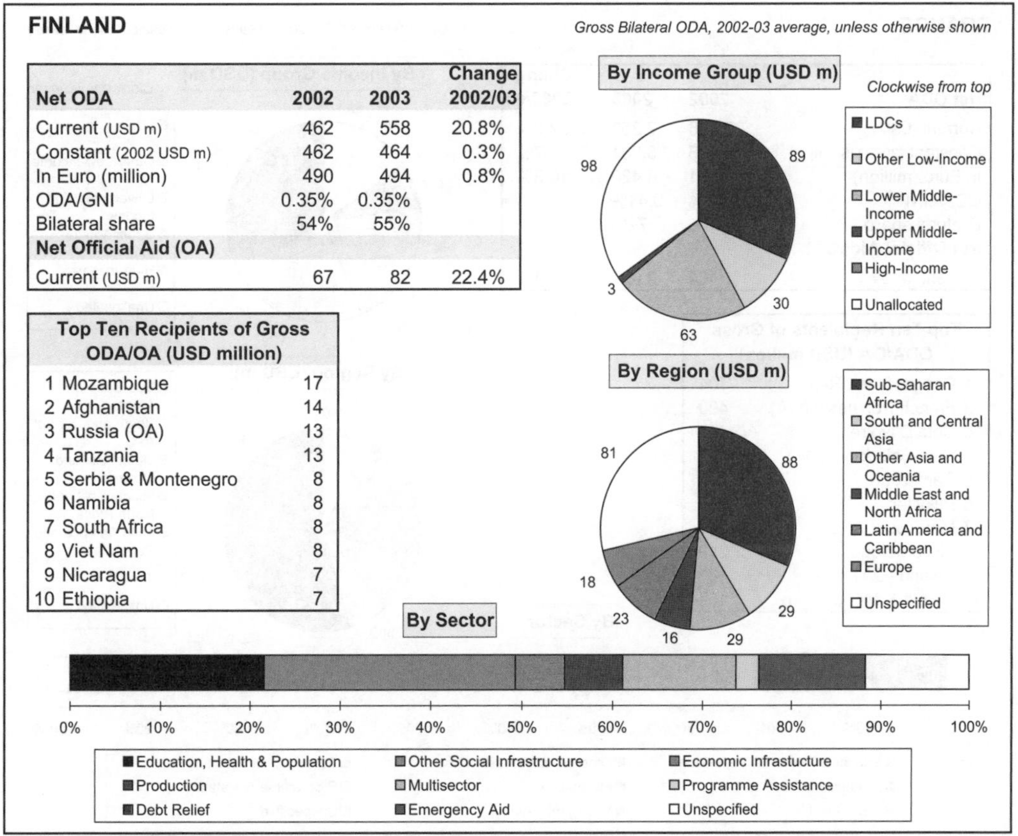

FINLAND

Net ODA	2002	2003	Change 2002/03
Current (USD m)	462	558	20.8%
Constant (2002 USD m)	462	464	0.3%
In Euro (million)	490	494	0.8%
ODA/GNI	0.35%	0.35%	
Bilateral share	54%	55%	
Net Official Aid (OA)			
Current (USD m)	67	82	22.4%

Top Ten Recipients of Gross ODA/OA (USD million)	
1 Mozambique	17
2 Afghanistan	14
3 Russia (OA)	13
4 Tanzania	13
5 Serbia & Montenegro	8
6 Namibia	8
7 South Africa	8
8 Viet Nam	8
9 Nicaragua	7
10 Ethiopia	7

France

Objective:	The objectives of France's development co-operation programmes are to support the achievement of sustainable development in partner countries, encouraging also poverty reduction, and to give particular emphasis to African countries, notably the least developed counties on that continent, and via its partnership with NEPAD.
Legislation:	None
Overall policy statement:	
Other general policy statements:	
Ministers:	Minister of Foreign Affairs assisted by the Associate Minister for Co-operation and Francophonie. Minister of the Economy, Finance and Industry.
Other ministers:	
Principal department/development agency:	Directorate-General for International Co-operation and Development (DGCID) within the MFA (*www.france.diplomatie.fr*).
Other agencies/ministries:	Ministry of the Economy, Finance and Industry (*www.mineti.gouv.fr/minefi/europe/index.htm*) French Development Agency (AFD) (*www.afd.fr*). Ministry of Education. Ministry of Agriculture. Ministry of the Interior. Ministry of the Environment. Ministry of Culture. Ministry of Social Affairs. Ministry of Infrastructure.
Interministerial co-ordination structures:	Interministerial Committee for International Co-operation and Development (CICID).
Main bilateral partners/programme countries:	The Priority Zone for Partnerships (ZSP) includes 54 countries.
Main sectors:	Water and sanitation, education, health and HIV/AIDS, agriculture and rural development, and infrastructure.
Ministerial advisory bodies:	The High Council for International Co-operation (HCCI).

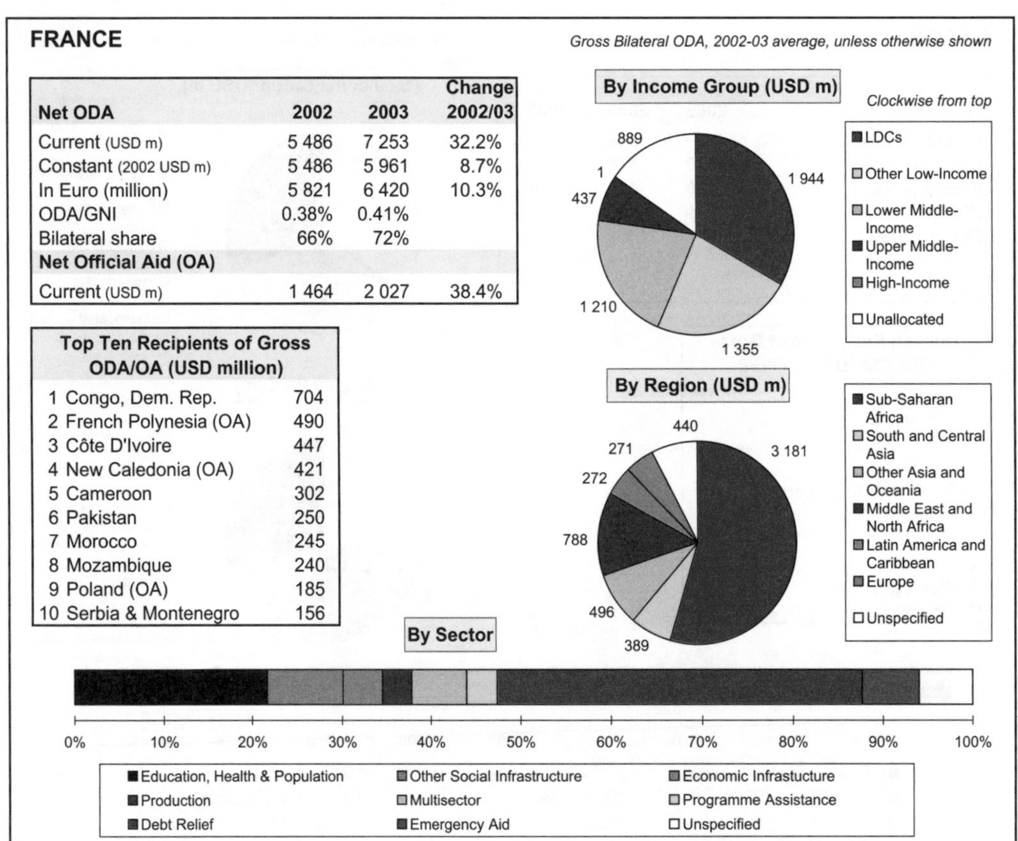

Net ODA	2002	2003	Change 2002/03
Current (USD m)	5 486	7 253	32.2%
Constant (2002 USD m)	5 486	5 961	8.7%
In Euro (million)	5 821	6 420	10.3%
ODA/GNI	0.38%	0.41%	
Bilateral share	66%	72%	
Net Official Aid (OA)			
Current (USD m)	1 464	2 027	38.4%

Top Ten Recipients of Gross ODA/OA (USD million)	
1 Congo, Dem. Rep.	704
2 French Polynesia (OA)	490
3 Côte D'Ivoire	447
4 New Caledonia (OA)	421
5 Cameroon	302
6 Pakistan	250
7 Morocco	245
8 Mozambique	240
9 Poland (OA)	185
10 Serbia & Montenegro	156

Germany

Objective:	Reducing global poverty, safeguarding peace and making globalization equitable and sustainable German Development Co-operation is contributing to common international effort towards fulfilment of MDGs: *Programme of Action 2015 for Poverty Reduction* (2001).
Legislation:	None
Overall policy statement:	Programme of Action 2015 for Poverty Reduction – The German Government's contribution towards halving extreme poverty worldwide (2001).
Other general policy statements:	The German Government's 11th Development Policy Report (2001): Government's Coalition Statement (2002).
Minister:	Minister for Economic Co-operation and Development.
Other ministers:	The Foreign Minister. Minister of Finance.
Principal department/development agency:	The Federal Ministry for Economic Co-operation and Development (BMZ) (*www.bmz.de*).
Other agencies/ministries:	Agency for Technical Co-operation (GTZ) (*www.gtz.de*). Bank for Development (KfW) (*www.kfw.de*). Federal Foreign Office (*www.auswaertiges-amt.de/www/en/index_html*). German Investment and Development Corporation (DEG) (*www.deginvest.de*). German Development Service (DED) (*www.ded.de*). InWEnt – Capacity Building International (*www.inwent.org*).
Interministerial co-ordination structures:	BMZ co-ordinates German Development Co-operation with other ministries.
Main bilateral partners:	BMZ focuses on 40 priority countries and 35 partner countries.
Main sectors:	Sector oriented objectives are in the following areas: HIV/AIDS, basic education, rain forests, renewable energies, energy efficiency, water supply and sanitation, peacebuilding and conflict prevention. Other priority areas agreed with partners include: economic reform, democracy, civil society, public advice, water and sanitation, environmental protection, health, family planning and HIV/AIDS.
Ministerial advisory bodies:	Advisory Council to the Ministry.

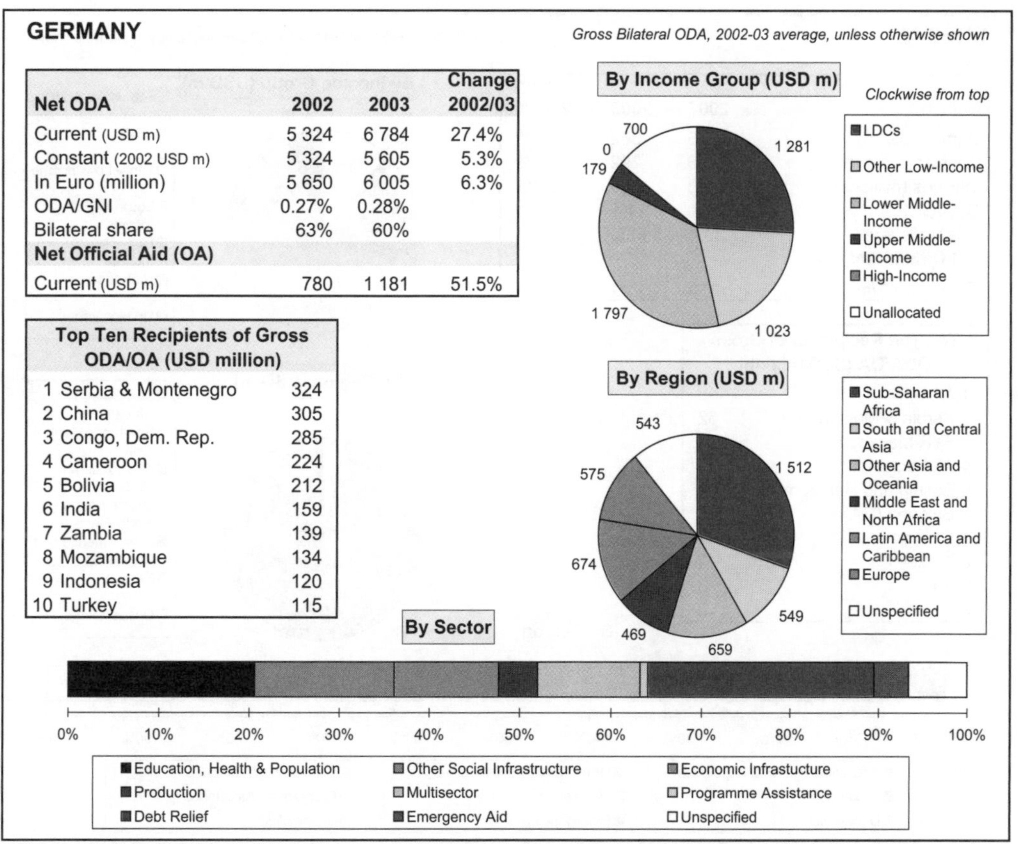

Greece

Objective:	To contribute to economic and social development, poverty reduction, strengthening of democracy and state of law, respect of human rights and fundamental freedoms gender equality and protection of the environment: *Second Medium-Term Five-Year Development Co-operation Programme 2002-2006.*
Legislation:	Law 2731/1999 (Official Gazette 138/A/5-7-1999) and Presidential Decree 224/2000 (Official Gazette 193/A/6-9-2000).
Overall policy statement:	Second Medium-Term Five-year Development Co-operation Programme (2002-2006).
Other general policy statements:	
Ministers:	Deputy Minister of Foreign Affairs responsible for International Economic Relations and Development Co-operation.
Other ministers:	Minister of National Economy.
Principal department/development agency:	Hellenic International Development Co-operation Department (YDAS or HELLENIC AID) within the Ministry of Foreign Affairs (*www.mfa.gr*).
Other agencies/ministries:	Ministry of National Economy. Ministry of National Defence. Ministry of Agriculture. Ministry of the Environment. Ministry of the Interior Public Administration and Decentralisation. Ministry of the Environment, Land Planning, and Public Works. Ministry of National Education and Religions. Ministry of Health and Welfare. Ministry of Merchant Marine. Hellenic Foreign Trade Board. Hellenic Organisation for Small and Medium Industries and Handicraft. National Tourist Organisation of Greece. Manpower Employment Organisation.
Interministerial co-ordination structures:	Committee for the Organisation and Co-ordination of International Economic Relations (EOSDOS).
Main bilateral partners:	There are 18 partner countries. In the Balkans these are: Albania, Bosnia and Herzegovina, Bulgaria, Federal Republic of Yugoslavia, Former Yugoslav Republic of Macedonia, and Rumania. In the Black Sea area these are: Armenia and Georgia. In the Middle East these are: Afghanistan, Iraq, Jordan, Lebanon, the Palestinian Administered Areas, Syria and Turkey. In sub-Saharan Africa these are: Ethiopia, Eritrea, and Ivory Coast.
Main sectors:	Basic and secondary education infrastructure and vocational training, basic health infrastructure, water supply and sanitation, environment and agriculture, and support for democratisation and human rights activities, institution building, micro-credit and income generation.
Ministerial advisory bodies:	

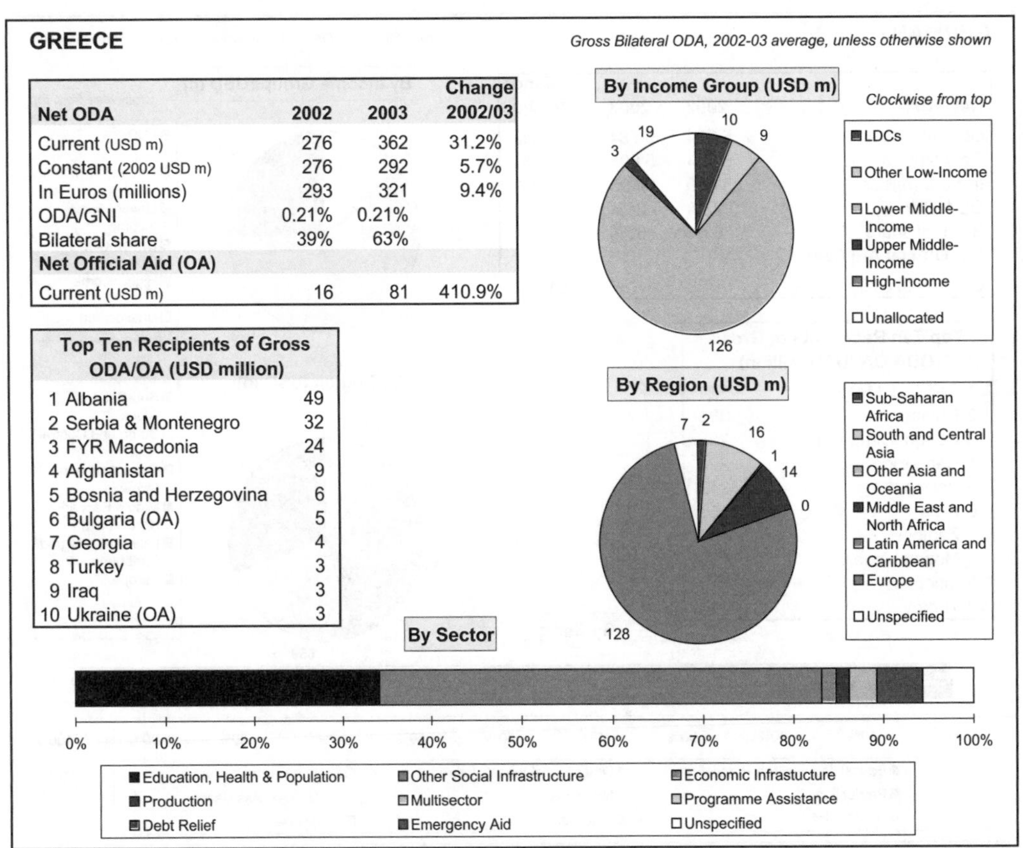

Net ODA	2002	2003	Change 2002/03
Current (USD m)	276	362	31.2%
Constant (2002 USD m)	276	292	5.7%
In Euros (millions)	293	321	9.4%
ODA/GNI	0.21%	0.21%	
Bilateral share	39%	63%	
Net Official Aid (OA)			
Current (USD m)	16	81	410.9%

Top Ten Recipients of Gross ODA/OA (USD million)	
1 Albania	49
2 Serbia & Montenegro	32
3 FYR Macedonia	24
4 Afghanistan	9
5 Bosnia and Herzegovina	6
6 Bulgaria (OA)	5
7 Georgia	4
8 Turkey	3
9 Iraq	3
10 Ukraine (OA)	3

Ireland

Objective:	Reducing poverty and promoting sustainable development in some of the poorest countries of the world: *White Paper on Foreign Policy* (1996).
Legislation:	Non
Overall policy statement:	White Paper on Foreign Policy (1996).
Other general policy statements:	Report of the Ireland Aid Review Committee (2002).
Ministers:	Minister of State with special responsibility for Development Co-operation and Human Rights.
Other ministers:	Minister of Foreign Affairs. Minister of Finance.
Principal department/development agency:	The Development Co-operation Directorate within the Department of Foreign Affairs manages Development Co-operation Ireland (DCI) (*www.dci.gov.ie*).
Other agencies/ministries:	Department of Finance.
Interministerial co-ordination structures:	
Main bilateral partners/programme countries:	The seven programme countries are: Ethiopia, Lesotho, Mozambique, Tanzania, Uganda, Zambia and East Timor. DCI also has a significant engagement with Afghanistan, the Palestinian Administered Areas and South Africa.
Main sectors:	Education, health, water and sanitation, and governance.
Ministerial advisory bodies:	Advisory Board for DCI.

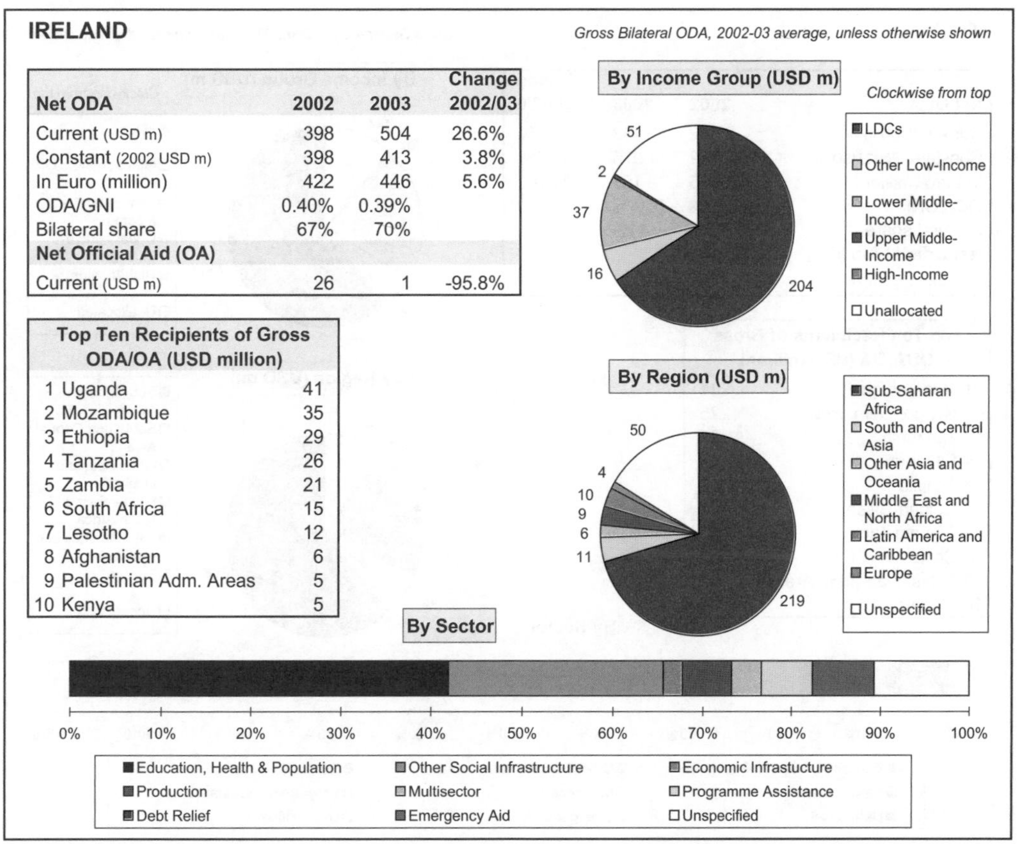

IRELAND

Gross Bilateral ODA, 2002-03 average, unless otherwise shown

Net ODA	2002	2003	Change 2002/03
Current (USD m)	398	504	26.6%
Constant (2002 USD m)	398	413	3.8%
In Euro (million)	422	446	5.6%
ODA/GNI	0.40%	0.39%	
Bilateral share	67%	70%	
Net Official Aid (OA)			
Current (USD m)	26	1	-95.8%

Top Ten Recipients of Gross ODA/OA (USD million)	
1 Uganda	41
2 Mozambique	35
3 Ethiopia	29
4 Tanzania	26
5 Zambia	21
6 South Africa	15
7 Lesotho	12
8 Afghanistan	6
9 Palestinian Adm. Areas	5
10 Kenya	5

Italy

Objective:	Development Co-operation is an integral part of Italian foreign policy and pursues the ideals of solidarity among peoples, seeking the fulfilment of fundamental human rights, in accordance with the principles sanctioned by the UN and European Commission African, Caribbean and Pacific States (EC-ACP) conventions. *(Law No. 49/87 Annex 1)*
Legislation:	Law No. 49/87 (1987)
Overall policy statement:	
Other general policy statements:	Interministerial Committee for Economic Planning (CIPE) Guidelines (1995).
Minister:	Minister of Foreign Affairs supported by four under-secretaries of state.
Other ministers:	Minister of Economy and Finance.
Principal department/development agency:	Directorate General for Development Co-operation (DGCS) in the Ministry of Foreign Affairs (*www.esteri.it*).
Other agencies/ministries:	Ministry of Economy and Finance. Ministry of Productive Activities. Ministry of the Environment. Ministry of the Interior. Ministry of Education, Universities and Research. Ministry of Justice. Presidency of the Council of Ministers. Ministry of Agriculture. Regions and Municipalities.
Interministerial co-ordination structures:	Interministerial Committee on Economic Policy (CIPE).
Main bilateral partners:	There are 16 concentration countries. In North Africa these are: Algeria, Egypt, Morocco, and Tunisia, in sub-Saharan Africa these are: Angola, Eritrea, Ethiopia, Mozambique, South Africa and Uganda. In Asia these are: China and India and in the Middle East these are: Jordan, Lebanon, the Palestinian Administered Areas and Syria..
Main sectors:	Health, education, rural development and food security, humanitarian assistance, and private sector (in particular SMEs) development.
Ministerial advisory bodies:	

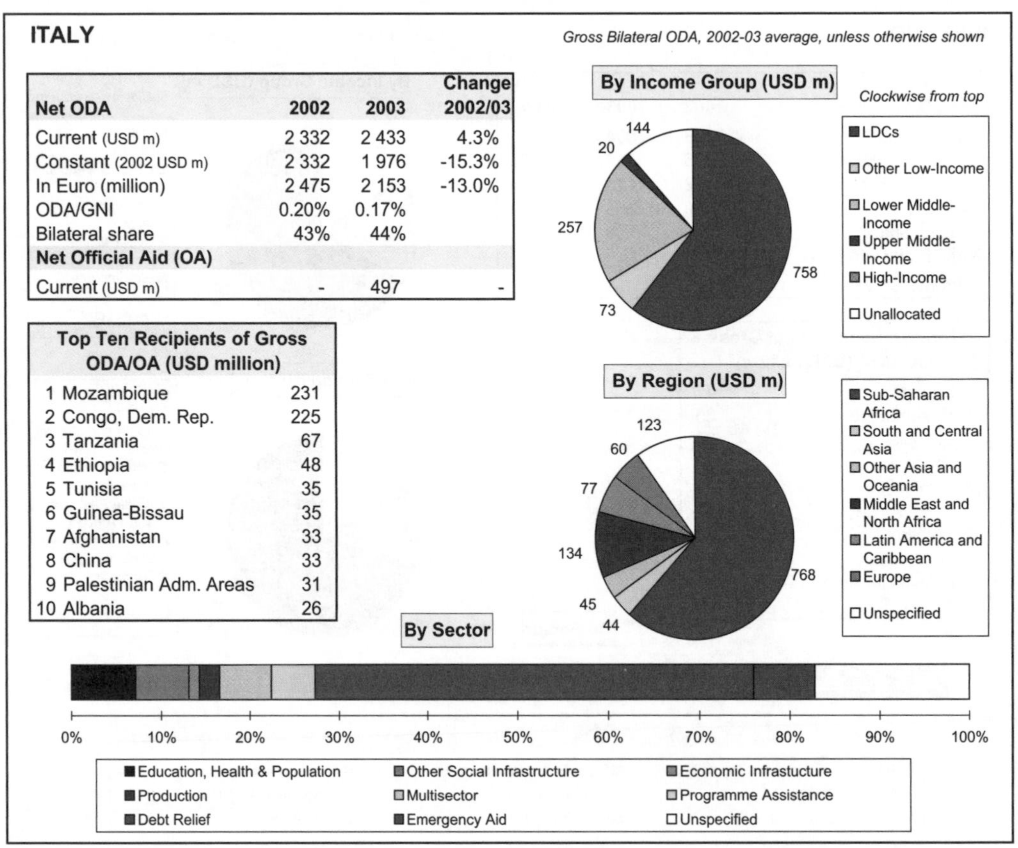

ITALY

Gross Bilateral ODA, 2002-03 average, unless otherwise shown

Net ODA	2002	2003	Change 2002/03
Current (USD m)	2 332	2 433	4.3%
Constant (2002 USD m)	2 332	1 976	-15.3%
In Euro (million)	2 475	2 153	-13.0%
ODA/GNI	0.20%	0.17%	
Bilateral share	43%	44%	
Net Official Aid (OA)			
Current (USD m)	-	497	-

Top Ten Recipients of Gross ODA/OA (USD million)	
1 Mozambique	231
2 Congo, Dem. Rep.	225
3 Tanzania	67
4 Ethiopia	48
5 Tunisia	35
6 Guinea-Bissau	35
7 Afghanistan	33
8 China	33
9 Palestinian Adm. Areas	31
10 Albania	26

Japan

Objective:	To contribute to the peace and development of the international community, and thereby help ensure Japan's own security and prosperity: *ODA Charter* (2003).
Legislation:	Official Development Assistance Charter (2003).
Overall policy statement:	Official Development Assistance Charter (1992, updated 2003).
Other general policy statements:	White Paper on Official Development Assistance (2003).
Minister:	Minister of Foreign Affairs.
Other ministers:	Minister of Finance.
Principal department/development agency:	Economic Co-operation Bureau in the Ministry of Foreign Affairs (*www.mofa.go.jp/policy/oda*).
Other agencies/ministries:	Japanese International Co-operation Agency (JICA) (*www.jica.go.jp*). Japan Bank for International Co-operation (JBIC) (*www.jbic.go.jp*). Ministry of Finance (*www.mof.go.jp*). Ministry of Economy Trade and Industry (*www.meti.go.jp*). Ministry of Education, Culture, Sports Science and Technology. Ministry of Agriculture, Forestry and Fisheries. Ministry of Health, Labour and Welfare. Ministry of Land, Infrastructure and Transport. Ministry of Internal Affairs and Communications. Ministry of Justice. Ministry of the Environment. Cabinet Office. Financial Agency. Police Agency.
Interministerial co-ordination structures:	Council of Overseas Economic Co-operation-related Ministers. Inter-Ministerial Meeting on ODA.
Main bilateral partners/programme countries:	Operational in over 140 countries with the largest programmes concentrated in Asia.
Main sectors:	Sector priorities as laid down by the ODA Charter. Poverty Reduction (education, health, water and sanitation, agriculture). Sustainable growth (infrastructure, trade and investment). Global issues (environment, infectious diseases, population, food, energy, natural disasters, drugs, organised crime). Peacebuilding (conflict prevention, emergency assistance.
Ministerial advisory bodies:	Board on Comprehensive ODA Strategy.

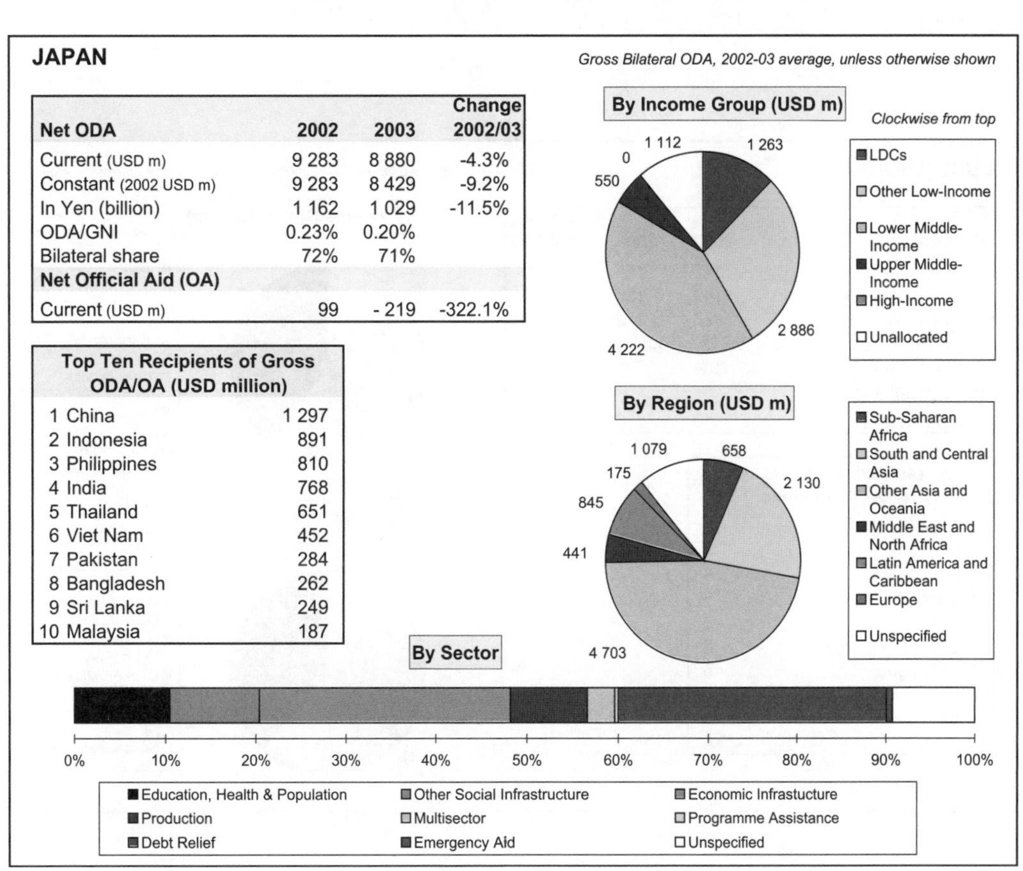

JAPAN

Net ODA	2002	2003	Change 2002/03
Current (USD m)	9 283	8 880	-4.3%
Constant (2002 USD m)	9 283	8 429	-9.2%
In Yen (billion)	1 162	1 029	-11.5%
ODA/GNI	0.23%	0.20%	
Bilateral share	72%	71%	
Net Official Aid (OA)			
Current (USD m)	99	- 219	-322.1%

Top Ten Recipients of Gross ODA/OA (USD million)	
1 China	1 297
2 Indonesia	891
3 Philippines	810
4 India	768
5 Thailand	651
6 Viet Nam	452
7 Pakistan	284
8 Bangladesh	262
9 Sri Lanka	249
10 Malaysia	187

Luxembourg

Objective:	Sustainable development and the fight against poverty: *A Policy of Solidarity With Those Most in Need (1999).*
Legislation:	Development Co-operation Act (1996).
Overall policy statement:	A Policy of Solidarity With Those Most in Need *(1999).*
Other general policy statements:	Statement on Development Co-operation and Humanitarian Action *(2003).*
Ministers:	Minister of Co-operation and Humanitarian Action.
Other ministers:	Minister of Foreign Affairs and Foreign Trade. Minister of Finance.
Principal department/development agency:	Department for Development Co-operation within the Ministry of Foreign Affairs (*www.mae.lu*) Lux-Development (*www.lux-development.lu*).
Other agencies/ministries:	Ministry of Finance.
Interministerial co-ordination structures:	Interministerial Development Co-operation Committee.
Main bilateral partners/programme countries:	There are ten "target" countries. In Africa, these are: Burkina Faso, Cape Verde, Mali, Namibia, Niger and Senegal. In Asia: Laos and Vietnam. In Latin America, El Salvador and Nicaragua. In addition, there are 20 "project" countries including in Africa: Burundi, Guinea, Morocco, Mauritius, Rwanda, Sao Tome and Principe, South Africa and Tunisia. In Asia: China, East Timor India, and Mongolia. In Latin America: Brazil, Chile, Ecuador and Peru, and in Europe: Albania, Bosnia and Herzegovina, Croatia and the Federal Republic of Yugoslavia.
Main sectors:	Health, water and sanitation, education, other social services, and integrated rural development.
Ministerial advisory bodies:	

LUXEMBOURG

Gross Bilateral ODA, 2002-03 average, unless otherwise shown

Net ODA	2002	2003	Change 2002/03
Current (USD m)	147	194	32.1%
Constant (2002 USD m)	147	159	8.4%
In Euro (million)	156	172	10.2%
ODA/GNI	0.77%	0.81%	
Bilateral share	79%	77%	
Net Official Aid (OA)			
Current (USD m)	10	6	-38.7%

Top Ten Recipients of Gross ODA/OA (USD million)	
1 Cape Verde	9
2 Viet Nam	8
3 Burkina Faso	6
4 Laos	6
5 Mali	6
6 El Salvador	5
7 Nicaragua	5
8 Namibia	5
9 Senegal	5
10 Niger	4

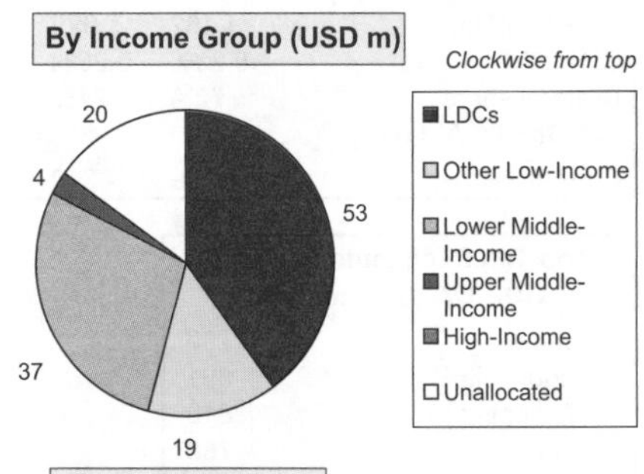

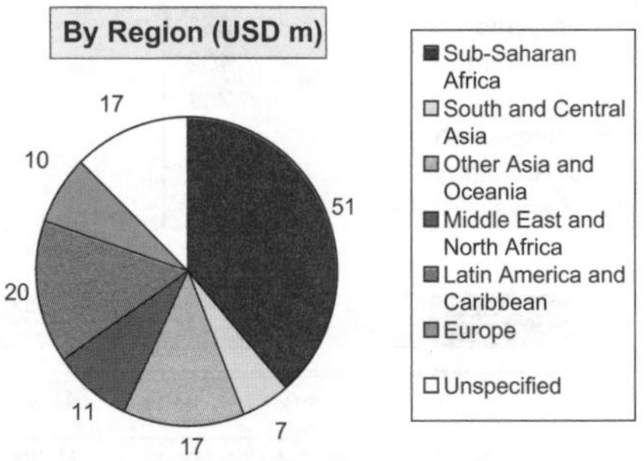

MANAGING AID: PRACTICES OF DAC MEMBER COUNTRIES – ISBN 92-64-00761-X – © OECD 2005

The Netherlands

Objective:	Sustainable poverty reduction is the main objective: *Mutual Interests, Mutual Responsibility* (2003).
Legislation:	None
Overall policy statement:	Mutual Interests, Mutual Responsibility: Dutch Development Co-operation en route to 2015 (2003).
Other general policy statements:	Aid in Progress (1995).
Ministers:	The Minister for Development Co-operation.
Other ministers:	The Minister for Foreign Affairs.
Principal department/development agency:	Directorate-General for International Co-operation (DGIS) within the Ministry of Foreign Affairs (*www.minbuza.nl*).
Other agencies/ministries:	
Interministerial co-ordination structures:	The Co-ordinating Council for International Affairs. The Co-ordination Committee for European Affairs.
Main bilateral partners/programme countries:	There are 36 long-term partner countries. In Africa these are: Benin, Burkina Faso, Cape Verde, Egypt, Eritrea, Ethiopia, Ghana, Kenya, Mali, Mozambique, Rwanda, Senegal, South Africa, Tanzania, Uganda, and Zambia; in Asia: Afghanistan, Armenia, Bangladesh, Georgia, Indonesia, Moldova, Mongolia, Pakistan, Sri Lanka and Vietnam; in Latin America: Bolivia, Colombia, Guatemala, Nicaragua, Suriname, in Europe: Albania, Bosnia-Herzegovina, Macedonia, and also the Palestinian Administered Areas and Yemen.
Main sectors:	Country programmes will operate in two to three sectors only. Overall, basic education, reproductive health, and local rural development are the main sectors supported.
Ministerial advisory bodies:	

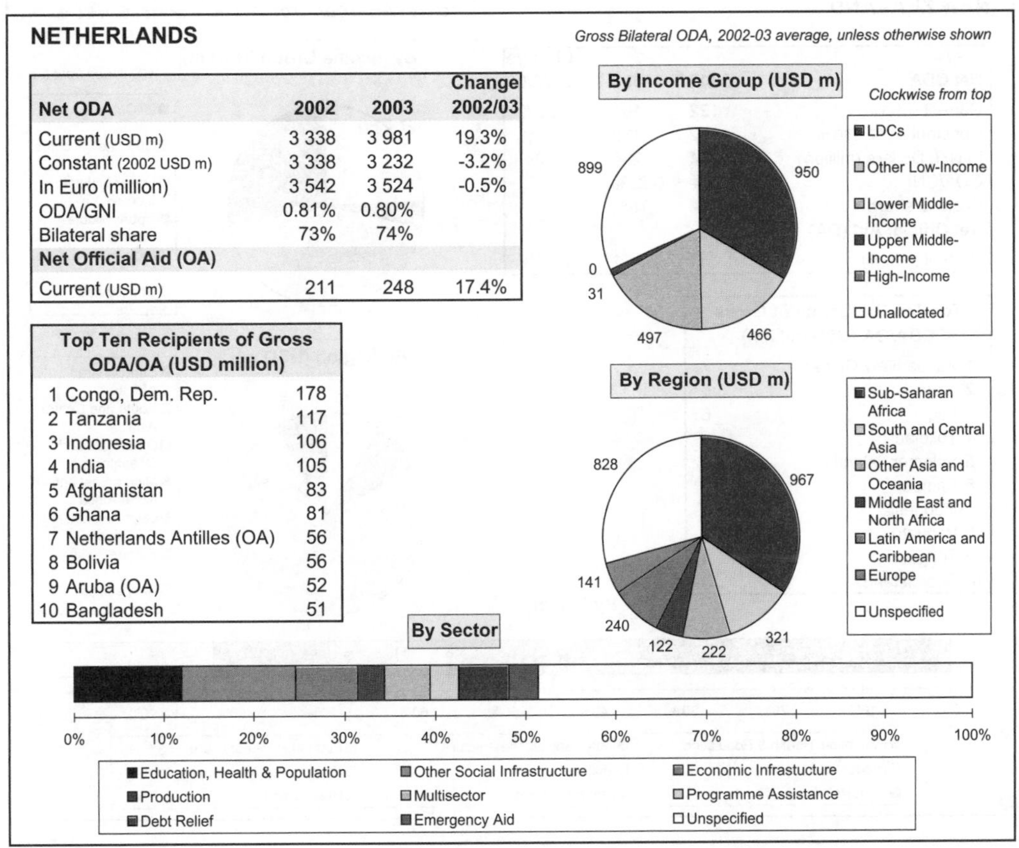

New Zealand

Objective:	The elimination of poverty in developing countries through working with partners to achieve sustainable and equitable development for those most in need: *Policy Statement* (2002).
Legislation:	None
Overall policy statement:	Policy Statement: Towards a Safe and Just World Free of Poverty (2002).
Other general policy statements:	
Ministers:	Associate Minister of Foreign Affairs and Trade (Official Development Assistance).
Other ministers:	Minister of Foreign Affairs and Trade.
Principal department/development agency:	New Zealand Agency for International Development (NZAID), a semi autonomous body within the Ministry of Foreign Affairs and Trade (*www.nzaid.govt.nz*).
Other agencies/ministries:	
Interministerial Co-ordination structures:	
Main bilateral partners:	New Zealand has 20 core partner countries eleven in the Pacific – the Cook Islands, Fiji, Kiribati, Niue, Papua New guinea, Samoa, the Solomon Islands, Tokelau, Tonga, Tuvalu and Vanuatu; seven countries in Asia – Cambodia, China, East Timor, Indonesia, Laos, the Philippines, and Vietnam; and one country in Africa – South Africa.
Main sectors:	Social development with a strong emphasis education, health, sustainable livelihoods, gender, governance and human rights.
Ministerial advisory bodies:	The International Development Advisory Committee (IDAC).

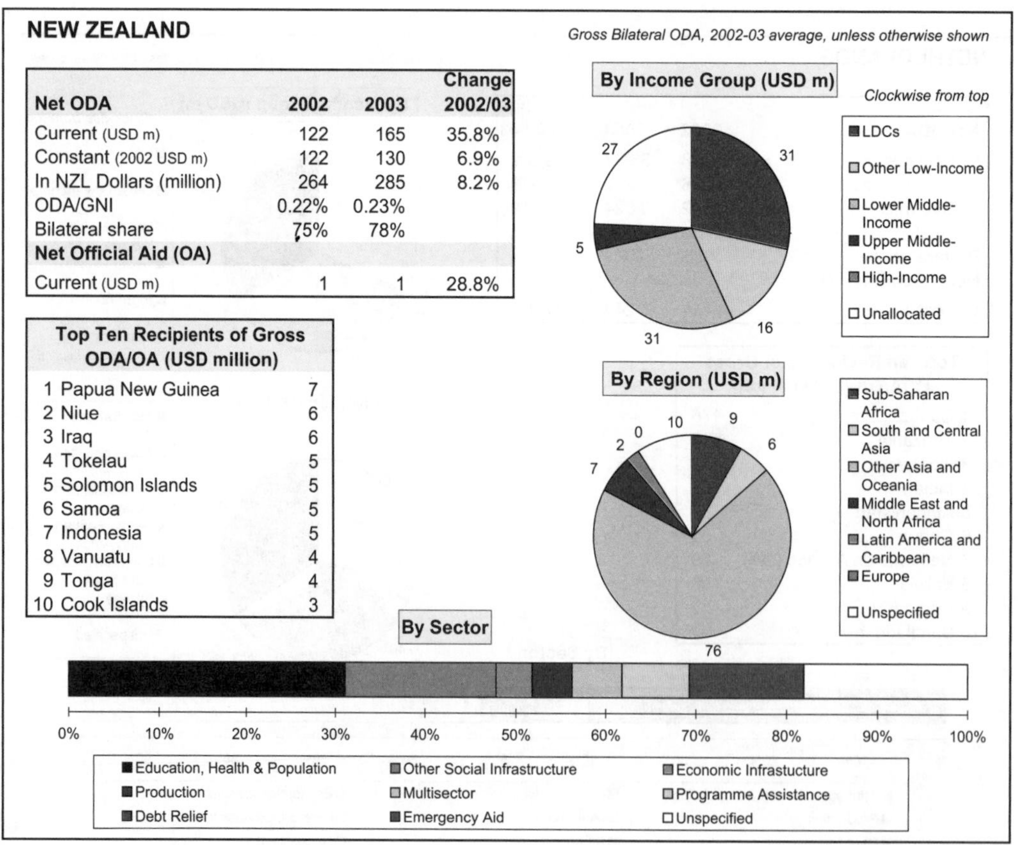

NEW ZEALAND

Net ODA	2002	2003	Change 2002/03
Current (USD m)	122	165	35.8%
Constant (2002 USD m)	122	130	6.9%
In NZL Dollars (million)	264	285	8.2%
ODA/GNI	0.22%	0.23%	
Bilateral share	75%	78%	
Net Official Aid (OA)			
Current (USD m)	1	1	28.8%

Top Ten Recipients of Gross ODA/OA (USD million)	
1 Papua New Guinea	7
2 Niue	6
3 Iraq	6
4 Tokelau	5
5 Solomon Islands	5
6 Samoa	5
7 Indonesia	5
8 Vanuatu	4
9 Tonga	4
10 Cook Islands	3

MANAGING AID: PRACTICES OF DAC MEMBER COUNTRIES – ISBN 92-64-00761-X – © OECD 2005

Norway

Objective:	The main objective is to contribute to the fight against poverty, by supporting partner countries poverty reduction strategies and other national strategies and thereby contribute to the achievement of the MDGs *(St.prp.nr. 1 2003-2004, Development aid budget, approved by the Norwegian Parliament).*
Legislation:	
Overall policy statement:	Policy Report No. 35 Fighting Poverty Together: A Comprehensive Development Policy (2003-2004) to the Storting.
Other general policy statements:	Fighting Poverty: The Norwegian Government's Action Plan for Combating Poverty in the South towards 2015 (2002).
Ministers:	Minister for International Development assisted by a State Secretary.
Other ministers:	Minister of Foreign Affairs assisted by a State Secretary.
Principal department/development agency:	Ministry of Foreign Affairs (*http://odin.dep.no/ud/engelsk/*).
Other agencies/ministries:	Norwegian Agency for Development Co-operation (NORAD) (*www.norad.no*). Fredskorpset (Norwegian volunteer service) (*www.fredskorpest.no*).
Interministerial co-ordination structures:	
Main bilateral partners/programme countries:	There are seven main partner countries: Bangladesh, Malawi, Mozambique, Nepal, Tanzania, Uganda and Zambia. There are 18 partner countries: In Africa these are: Angola, Eritrea, Ethiopia, Kenya, Madagascar, Mali, Nigeria and South-Africa. In Asia: Afghanistan, China, East Timor, Indonesia, Pakistan, Sri Lanka and Vietnam. In Central America: Guatemala and Nicaragua. In the Middle East: the Palestinian Administered Areas.
Main sectors:	Education, HIV/AIDS, private sector and agriculture, sustainable development, good governance and anti-corruption, peacebuilding and development, and health.
Ministerial advisory bodies:	

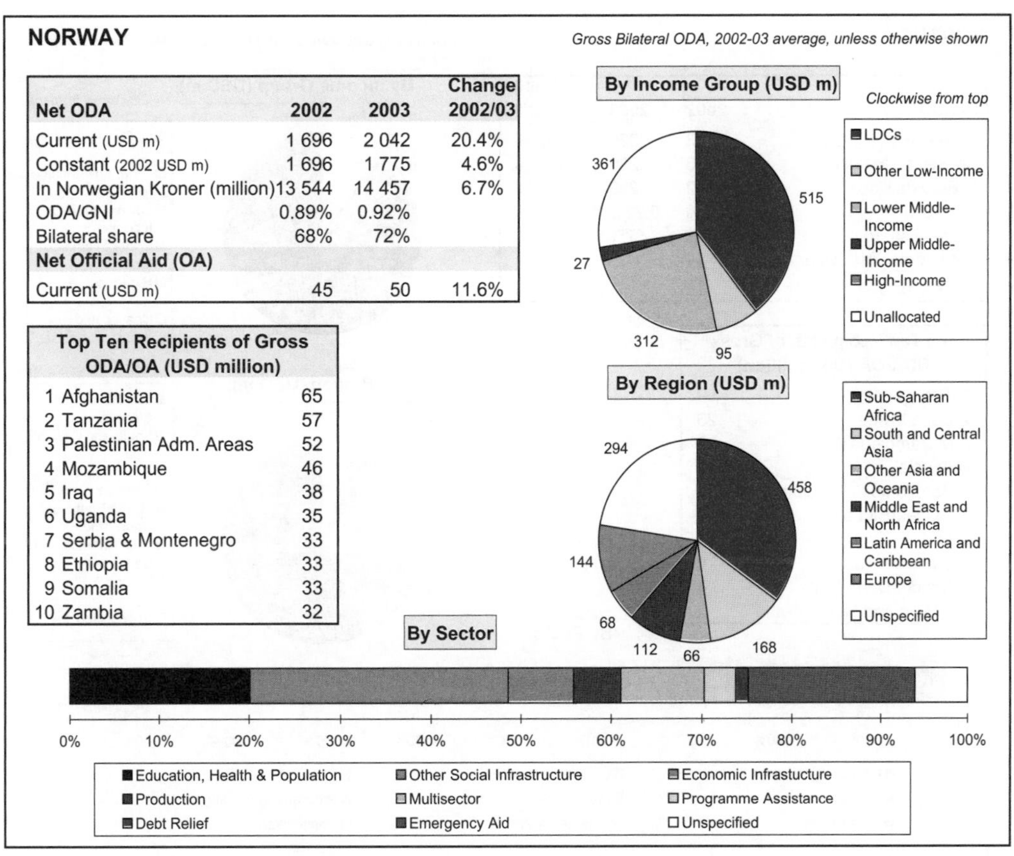

Net ODA	2002	2003	Change 2002/03
Current (USD m)	1 696	2 042	20.4%
Constant (2002 USD m)	1 696	1 775	4.6%
In Norwegian Kroner (million)	13 544	14 457	6.7%
ODA/GNI	0.89%	0.92%	
Bilateral share	68%	72%	
Net Official Aid (OA)			
Current (USD m)	45	50	11.6%

Top Ten Recipients of Gross ODA/OA (USD million)	
1 Afghanistan	65
2 Tanzania	57
3 Palestinian Adm. Areas	52
4 Mozambique	46
5 Iraq	38
6 Uganda	35
7 Serbia & Montenegro	33
8 Ethiopia	33
9 Somalia	33
10 Zambia	32

Portugal

Objective:	Reinforce democracy and the rule of law, reduce poverty, stimulate economic growth, foster regional integration and promote a European partnership for human development: *Portuguese General Policy Statement.*
Legislation:	Decree Law 5/2003 13th January
Overall policy statement:	The Portuguese Co-operation for the Incoming 21st Century – Strategy Paper (Approved by the Council of Ministers Resolution No. 43/1999 18th May).
Other general policy statements:	
Minister:	Secretary of State for Foreign Affairs and Co-operation in the Ministry of Foreign Affairs.
Other ministers:	Secretary of State for European Affairs. Secretary of State for the Portuguese Communities Minister of Finance.
Principal department/development agency:	Institute for Portuguese Development Support (IPAD) (*www.ipad.mne.pt*).
Other agencies/ministries:	Ministry of Finance. Seventeen ministries and agencies and over 300 municipalities from 22 districts.
Interministerial co-ordination structures:	
Main bilateral partners:	Seven main partner countries: Angola, Cape Verde, East Timor, Guinea Bissau, Mozambique, and Sao Tome and Principe.
Main sectors:	Education and training, culture and heritage, health, productive activities and infrastructure, society and its institutions, security, financial assistance, and humanitarian and emergency assistance.
Ministerial advisory bodies:	

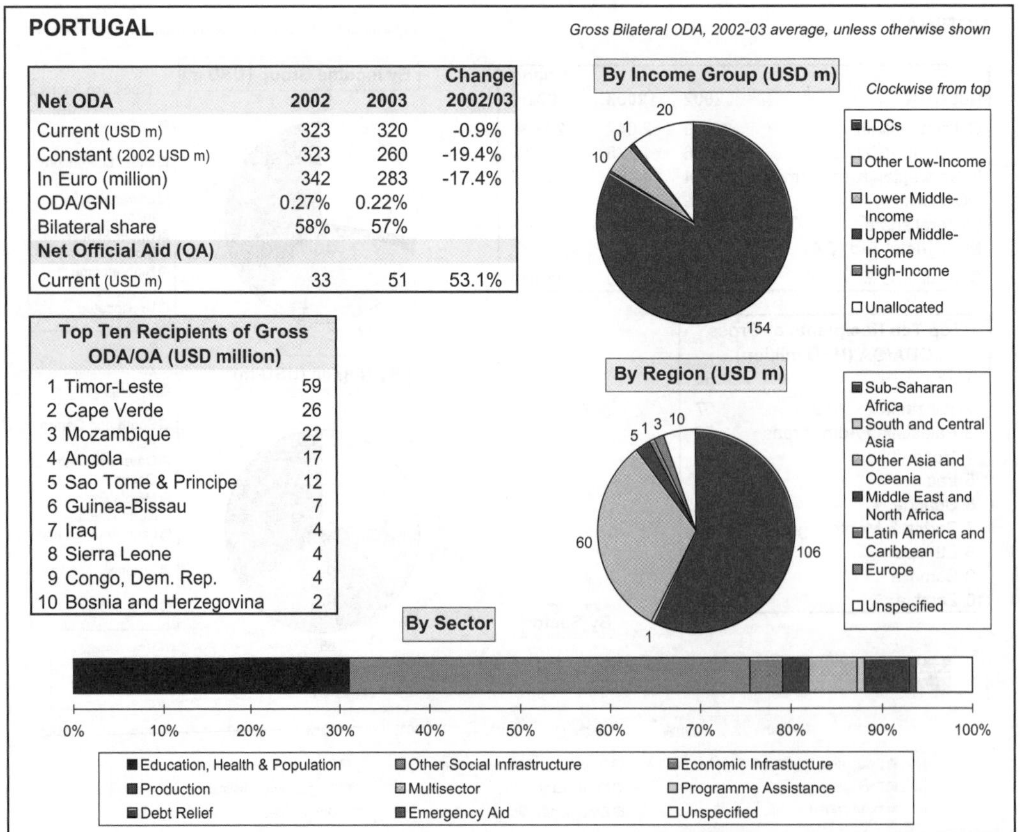

Net ODA	2002	2003	Change 2002/03
Current (USD m)	323	320	-0.9%
Constant (2002 USD m)	323	260	-19.4%
In Euro (million)	342	283	-17.4%
ODA/GNI	0.27%	0.22%	
Bilateral share	58%	57%	
Net Official Aid (OA)			
Current (USD m)	33	51	53.1%

Top Ten Recipients of Gross ODA/OA (USD million)	
1 Timor-Leste	59
2 Cape Verde	26
3 Mozambique	22
4 Angola	17
5 Sao Tome & Principe	12
6 Guinea-Bissau	7
7 Iraq	4
8 Sierra Leone	4
9 Congo, Dem. Rep.	4
10 Bosnia and Herzegovina	2

MANAGING AID: PRACTICES OF DAC MEMBER COUNTRIES – ISBN 92-64-00761-X – © OECD 2005

Spain

Objective:	The promotion of sustainable human, social and economic development in order to eliminate poverty: *Law on International Co-operation in Matters of Development* (1998).
Legislation:	Law on International Co-operation in Matters of Development (1998).
Overall policy statement:	
Other general policy statements:	Four-year Master Plan (2001-2004).
Minister:	State Secretary for International Co-operation and Latin America within the Ministry of Foreign Affairs.
Other ministers:	Minister of Economy. State Secretary for Trade and Tourism within the Ministry of Economy.
Principal department/ development agency:	State Secretariat for International Co-operation and Latin America (SECIPI) and its executing agency the Spanish Agency for International Co-operation (AECI) (*www.aeci.es*).
Other agencies/ministries:	Ministry of Economy (State Secretariat for Trade and Tourism). Ministry of Agriculture. Ministry of Fisheries and Food. Ministry of Defence. Ministry of Education and Culture. Ministry of Employment and Social Affairs. Ministry of the Environment. Ministry of Health and Consumer Affairs. Ministry of the Interior. Ministry of Justice. Ministry of Public Administration. Ministry of Public Works. Ministry of Science and Technology. Autonomous regions and municipalities.
Interministerial co-ordination structures:	The Interministerial Committee for International Co-operation. The Inter-territorial Commission for Co-operation in Matters of Development.
Main bilateral partners/ programme countries:	Spain has 29 programme countries. In Africa these are: Algeria, Angola, Cape Verde, Equatorial Guinea, Guinea Bissau, Mauritania, Morocco, Mozambique, Namibia, Sao Tome and Principe, Senegal, South Africa, and Tunisia. In Latin America these are: Bolivia, Dominican Republic, Ecuador, El Salvador, Guatemala, Honduras, Paraguay, Peru, and Nicaragua. In Asia: China, the Philippines, and Vietnam. In Europe: Albania, Bosnia Herzegovina, and the Federal Republic of Yugoslavia.
Main sectors:	Basic social services, education, human rights, democracy and civil society development, environment, culture, scientific and technological research.
Ministerial advisory bodies:	The Council for Co-operation in Matters of Development.

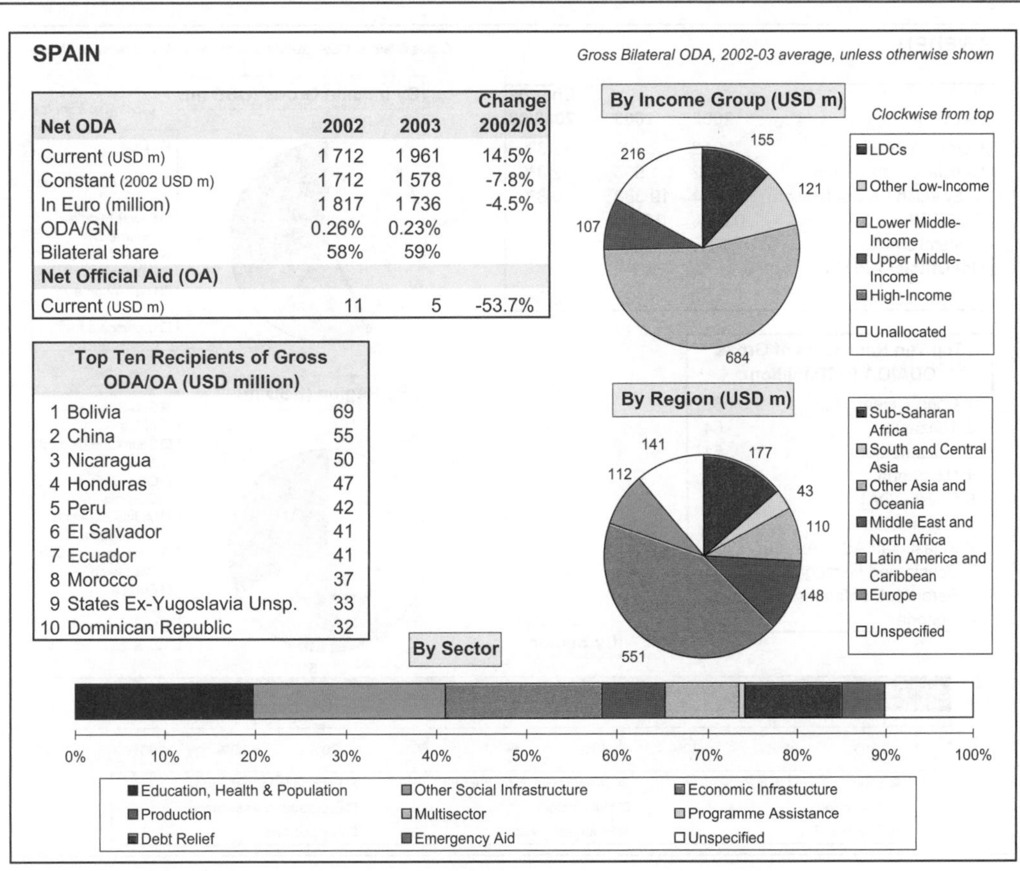

Net ODA	2002	2003	Change 2002/03
Current (USD m)	1 712	1 961	14.5%
Constant (2002 USD m)	1 712	1 578	-7.8%
In Euro (million)	1 817	1 736	-4.5%
ODA/GNI	0.26%	0.23%	
Bilateral share	58%	59%	
Net Official Aid (OA)			
Current (USD m)	11	5	-53.7%

Top Ten Recipients of Gross ODA/OA (USD million)	
1 Bolivia	69
2 China	55
3 Nicaragua	50
4 Honduras	47
5 Peru	42
6 El Salvador	41
7 Ecuador	41
8 Morocco	37
9 States Ex-Yugoslavia Unsp.	33
10 Dominican Republic	32

Sweden

Objective:	To contribute to an environment supportive of poor people's own efforts to improve their quality of life: *Act on Global Development (2003)*.
Legislation:	None
Overall policy statement:	Act on Global Development (2003).
Other general policy statements:	The Rights of the Poor: Our Common Responsibility (1997).
Minister:	Minister for International Development Co-operation assisted by a State Secretary.
Other ministers:	Minister for Foreign Affairs. Minister of Finance. Minister for International Economic Affairs and Financial Markets. Minister of Industry and Trade.
Principal department/development agency:	Global Development Department of the Ministry of Foreign Affairs (*www.ud.se*).
Other agencies/ministries:	Swedish International Development Co-operation Agency (SIDA) (*www.sida.se*). Ministry of Finance *(www.sweden.gov.se/govagencies/fiag.htm*). Ministry of Industry, Employment and Communications (*http://naring.regeringen.se/inenglish/index.htm*). Swedish Migration Board (*www.migrationsverket.se/english.html*). The Swedish Institute (*www.si.se*). The Nordic Africa Institute (*www.nai.uu.se/indexeng.html*).
Interministerial co-ordination structures:	
Main bilateral partners:	Operational in around 100 countries.
Main sectors:	Humanitarian assistance and conflict prevention, social sectors, human rights and democratic governance, infrastructure, private sector and urban development.
Ministerial advisory bodies:	Expert Group on Development Issues.

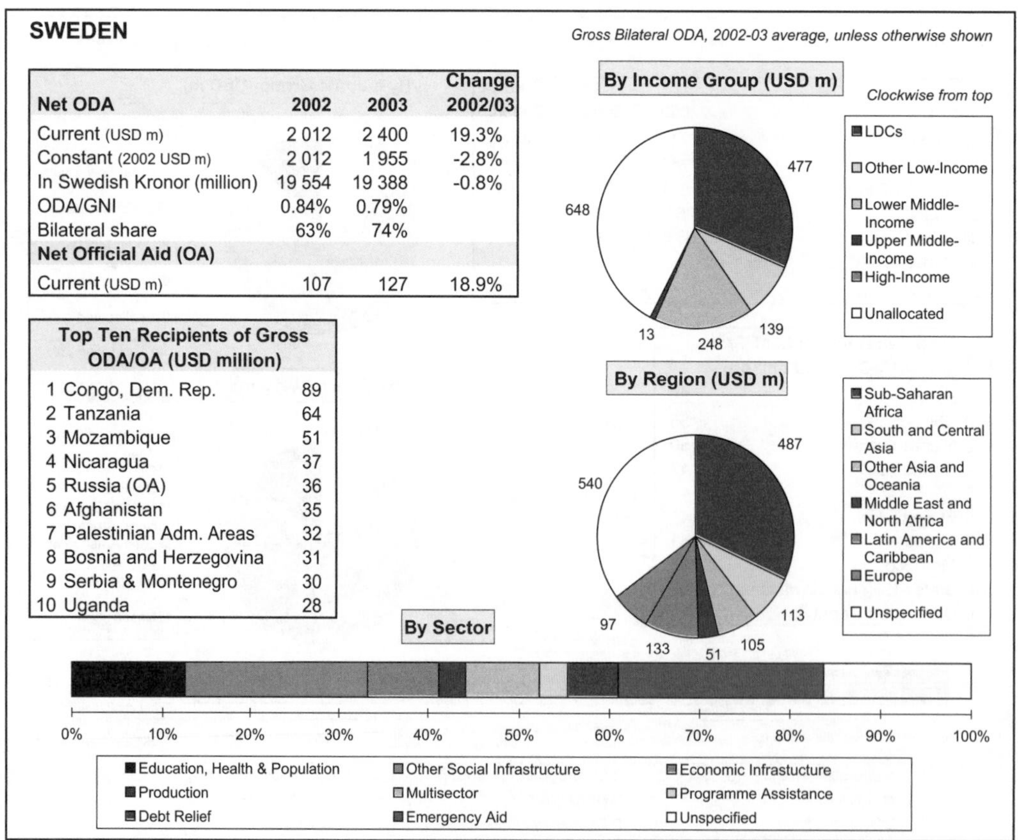

SWEDEN

Net ODA	2002	2003	Change 2002/03
Current (USD m)	2 012	2 400	19.3%
Constant (2002 USD m)	2 012	1 955	-2.8%
In Swedish Kronor (million)	19 554	19 388	-0.8%
ODA/GNI	0.84%	0.79%	
Bilateral share	63%	74%	
Net Official Aid (OA)			
Current (USD m)	107	127	18.9%

Top Ten Recipients of Gross ODA/OA (USD million)	
1 Congo, Dem. Rep.	89
2 Tanzania	64
3 Mozambique	51
4 Nicaragua	37
5 Russia (OA)	36
6 Afghanistan	35
7 Palestinian Adm. Areas	32
8 Bosnia and Herzegovina	31
9 Serbia & Montenegro	30
10 Uganda	28

MANAGING AID: PRACTICES OF DAC MEMBER COUNTRIES – ISBN 92-64-00761-X – © OECD 2005

Switzerland

Objective:	To help developing countries improve the living conditions of their populations: *Federal Law* (1976).
Legislation:	The Federal Law on International Development Co-operation and Humanitarian Aid (1976).
Overall policy statement:	SDC Strategy 2010; SECO Strategy 2006.
Other general policy statements:	Foreign Policy Report (2000). Message on the Continuation of Technical Co-operation and Financial Aid for Developing Countries 2004-2007 (2003).
Minister:	Federal Councillor of Foreign Affairs.
Other ministers:	Federal Councillor for Economic Affairs.
Principal department/development agency:	Swiss Agency for Development Co-operation (SDC) of the Federal Department of Foreign Affairs (DFA) (*www.sdc.admin.ch*).
Other agencies/ministries:	State Secretariat for Economic Affairs (SECO) (*www.seco-cooperation.ch*). Political Department IV of the Federal Department of Foreign Affairs. Cantons and municipalities.
Interministerial co-ordination structures:	
Main bilateral partners:	SDC has 17 "priority" countries: In Africa these are: Benin, Burkina Faso, Chad, Niger, Mali, Mozambique, and Tanzania. In Latin America these are: Bolivia, Ecuador, Nicaragua, Peru, and in Asia: Bangladesh, Bhutan, India, Nepal, Pakistan, Vietnam, plus six "special programme countries" including Cuba, North Korea, the Palestinian Administered Areas, South Africa, Rwanda and Madagascar. SECO has 16 "priority" countries: In Africa: Burkina Faso, Egypt, Ghana, Mozambique, and Tanzania. In Asia: Albania, Bulgaria, China, Kyrgyz Republic, Macedonia, Rumania, Tajikistan, Serbia-Montenegro, and Vietnam, and in Latin America: Peru. SECO also has 11 other "important" countries: Azerbaijan, Bolivia, Bosnia-Herzegovina, Jordan, India, Indonesia, the Maghreb, Russia, South Africa, Ukraine, and Uzbekistan.
Main sectors:	Prevention and resolution of conflicts, good governance, income generation, social justice and the sustainable use of natural resources for SDC. Macroeconomic support, investment promotion, infrastructure financing, trade and clean technology co-operation for SECO.
Ministerial advisory bodies:	Advisory Committee on International Development and Co-operation.

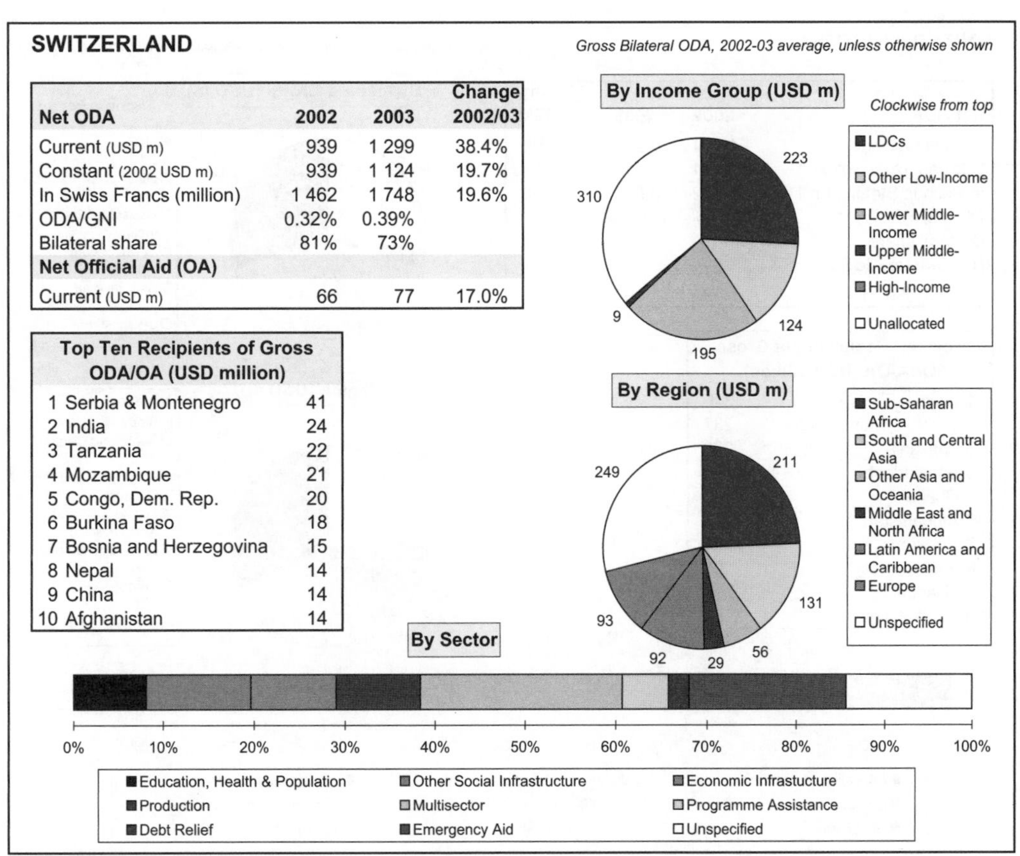

Net ODA	2002	2003	Change 2002/03
Current (USD m)	939	1 299	38.4%
Constant (2002 USD m)	939	1 124	19.7%
In Swiss Francs (million)	1 462	1 748	19.6%
ODA/GNI	0.32%	0.39%	
Bilateral share	81%	73%	
Net Official Aid (OA)			
Current (USD m)	66	77	17.0%

Top Ten Recipients of Gross ODA/OA (USD million)	
1 Serbia & Montenegro	41
2 India	24
3 Tanzania	22
4 Mozambique	21
5 Congo, Dem. Rep.	20
6 Burkina Faso	18
7 Bosnia and Herzegovina	15
8 Nepal	14
9 China	14
10 Afghanistan	14

United Kingdom

Objective:	The elimination of poverty and the encouragement of economic growth which benefits the poor: *Eliminating World Poverty* (1997).
Legislation:	International Development Act (2002).
Overall policy statement	Eliminating World Poverty: A Challenge for the 21st Century (1997); Eliminating World Poverty: Making Globalisation Work for the Poor (2000).
Other general policy statements:	
Minister:	Secretary of State for International Development assisted by a Minister of State, and a Parliamentary Under Secretary of State.
Other ministers:	Chancellor of the Exchequer.
Principal department/development agency:	Department for International Development (DFID) (*www.dfid.gov.uk*).
Other agencies/ministries:	The Foreign and Commonwealth Office (*www.fco.gov.uk*). The Home Office (*www.homeoffice.gov.uk*). The Treasury (*www.hm-treasury.gov.uk*). The British Council (*www.britishcouncil.org*).
Interministerial co-ordination structures:	
Main bilateral partners:	DFID has no formal list of priority countries but has offices or personnel in approximately 40 countries including 20 in Africa. The major DFID offices are located in the following countries, in Africa: Ghana, Kenya, Malawi, Mozambique, Nigeria, Sierra Leone, South Africa, Tanzania, Uganda, Zambia and Zimbabwe. In Asia: Afghanistan, Bangladesh, China, India, Nepal, Pakistan, and Thailand plus offices in Russia, the Ukraine and Barbados.
Main sectors:	Health, education, sustainable livelihoods, security sector reform, humanitarian assistance, private-sector development.
Ministerial advisory bodies:	

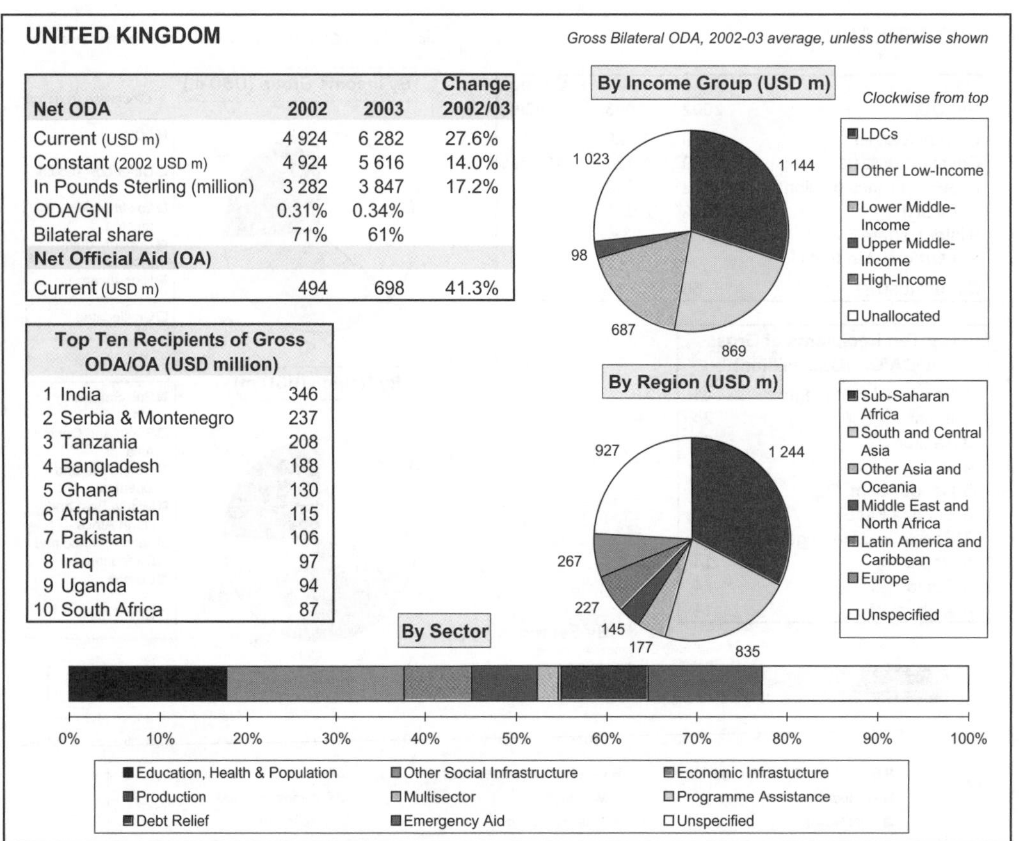

UNITED KINGDOM

Gross Bilateral ODA, 2002-03 average, unless otherwise shown

Net ODA	2002	2003	Change 2002/03
Current (USD m)	4 924	6 282	27.6%
Constant (2002 USD m)	4 924	5 616	14.0%
In Pounds Sterling (million)	3 282	3 847	17.2%
ODA/GNI	0.31%	0.34%	
Bilateral share	71%	61%	
Net Official Aid (OA)			
Current (USD m)	494	698	41.3%

Top Ten Recipients of Gross ODA/OA (USD million)	
1 India	346
2 Serbia & Montenegro	237
3 Tanzania	208
4 Bangladesh	188
5 Ghana	130
6 Afghanistan	115
7 Pakistan	106
8 Iraq	97
9 Uganda	94
10 South Africa	87

 MANAGING AID: PRACTICES OF DAC MEMBER COUNTRIES – ISBN 92-64-00761-X – © OECD 2005

United States

Objective:	
Legislation:	Foreign Assistance Act (1961 amended).
Overall policy statement:	US Department of State and US Agency for International Development, Strategic Plan: Fiscal Years 2004-2009.
Other general policy statements:	White Paper: US Foreign Aid: Meeting the Challenges of the Twenty-First Century, January 2004 National Security Strategy (2002). Foreign Aid in the National Interest: Promoting Freedom, Security and Opportunity (2002).
Minister:	USAID Administrator (who reports to the Secretary of State).
Other ministers:	Secretary of State. Secretary of the Treasury.
Principal department/development agency:	United States Agency for International Development (USAID) (*www.usaid.gov*).
Other agencies/ministries:	State Department (*www.state.gov/*). The Treasury – Office of International Affairs (*www.ustreas.gov*). The Millennium Challenge Corporation (*www.mcc.gov*). Departments of Agriculture, Defence, Health and Human Services, Interior, and others Peace Corps (www. peacecorps.gov/home.html).
Interministerial co-ordination structures:	The National Security Council is responsible for on-going, general inter-agency co-ordination. Policy Co-ordination Committees (PCC) are established to co-ordinate special policy issues on an *ad hoc* or standing basis. The Development PCC is chaired by the Department of State.
Main bilateral partners/priority countries:	USAID has offices in over 70 countries including in 22 countries in Africa, 20 countries in the Middle East and Asia, and 17 countries in Latin America.
Main sectors:	Agriculture, conflict management, democracy and governance, economic growth and trade, education, environment and population, health and nutrition.
Ministerial advisory bodies:	Advisory Committee on Voluntary Foreign Aid (ACVFA).

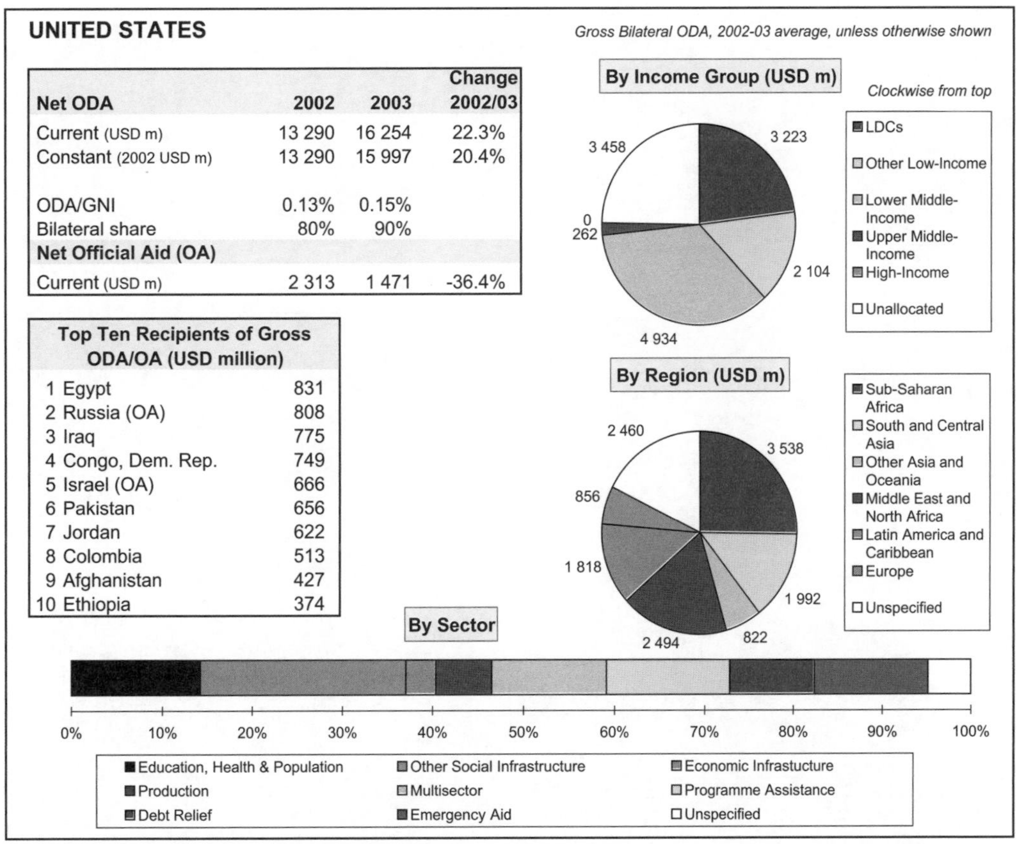
UNITED STATES

Gross Bilateral ODA, 2002-03 average, unless otherwise shown

Net ODA	2002	2003	Change 2002/03
Current (USD m)	13 290	16 254	22.3%
Constant (2002 USD m)	13 290	15 997	20.4%
ODA/GNI	0.13%	0.15%	
Bilateral share	80%	90%	
Net Official Aid (OA)			
Current (USD m)	2 313	1 471	-36.4%

Top Ten Recipients of Gross ODA/OA (USD million)	
1 Egypt	831
2 Russia (OA)	808
3 Iraq	775
4 Congo, Dem. Rep.	749
5 Israel (OA)	666
6 Pakistan	656
7 Jordan	622
8 Colombia	513
9 Afghanistan	427
10 Ethiopia	374

ISBN 92-64-00761-X
Managing Aid: Practices of DAC Member Countries

ANNEX A.2

Report on the Management of Development Co-operation Programmes in Mozambique

Introduction

As part of the preparations for a report on management structures and practices for development co-operation in member countries of the OECD's Development Assistance Committee (DAC), a mission was organised to Mozambique and South Africa from 23 February to 3 March 2004. The objective of the mission was twofold: *i)* to understand better the complexities and realities associated with managing and implementing development co-operation programmes from a field perspective; and *ii)* to collect a core set of information from most DAC member countries to enable general trends to be identified.

The findings presented in this report are drawn from the information and insights gained during meetings in either Maputo or Pretoria with representatives of 20 of the 22 DAC member countries. Eighteen DAC member countries are actively engaged and represented in Mozambique while two other DAC member countries manage activities in Mozambique from their diplomatic mission in Pretoria, in one case through a project management office in Maputo.[1] In most cases, these meetings involved the head of development co-operation stationed at the local field mission. Due to the focus of this exercise on learning more about how DAC member countries manage their development co-operation programmes, no meeting was arranged with representatives of the Government of Mozambique.

The mission was conducted by a member of the OECD Secretariat accompanied by a consultant hired for this project. The participants would like to express their appreciation for the valuable work done by the staff of the Embassy of Ireland in Maputo and the Australian High Commission in Pretoria to organise the mission.

Overview of the development context in Mozambique

Mozambique is one of the poorest countries in the world. Annual per capita income in 2002 was USD 210 (World Bank Atlas basis). Its human development index rating was 170 out of 173 (as calculated by the UNDP). It has a national HIV prevalence rate among antenatal clinic attendees of 14% but this figure masks significant regional variations and in Inhambane province the rate is 36%.[2] Little infrastructure remains after a prolonged civil war that ended in 1992 and catastrophic flooding in 2000 and 2001.

Mozambique is also one of the largest recipients of official development assistance (ODA), receiving a total of USD 1.6 billion of net ODA in 2002 (of which USD 1.1 billion took the form of debt relief).

Main findings and conclusions

Nature of the country programmes

● Priority given to Mozambique

For 17 DAC member countries, Mozambique is a designated or *de facto* "priority" country for their development co-operation or has a special place in their development co-operation system, for example by being eligible for additional funds or for special funding for high priority activities such as HIV/AIDS. For 11 DAC member countries, Mozambique was one of their five largest development co-operation partners in 2001-02.

● Size of the country programme

The size of the programme for Mozambique managed and implemented by each DAC member country's field mission varies between approximately USD 3 million and more than USD 90 million a year, with an average size of about USD 32 million annually. These figures exclude activities not managed and implemented by the field mission, notably debt relief which is a major component of some countries' ODA to Mozambique.

● Sectoral focus and cross-cutting issues

To improve efficiency and impact, a few DAC member countries have decided to concentrate on a restricted number of priority sectors. This may be contributing to most countries concentrating in the same sub-set of key sectors, possibly at the expense of some other important sectors for Mozambique's development where the partner government is trying to encourage greater involvement by donors (*e.g.* fisheries). Fourteen countries have a priority focus on the health sector (with a 15th focussed on HIV/AIDS). For 12 donors, a major focus is rural development/agriculture, 11 donors are focused on education and nine on good governance. Seven countries focussed on three of these four sectors. There may consequently be scope for a more efficient and comprehensive matching of the partner country's needs with individual donors' comparative advantages to ensure that all important sectors are adequately covered and that the number of donors in any given sector is manageable. Only one example was encountered whereby two countries had agreed to split responsibilities in their overall country programme with one concentrating on health and the other on education. Representatives of a few DAC members met declared that they were ready to pursue silent partnerships at the field level (*i.e.* providing their funding in a particular sector through another donor that is actively engaged) but that their headquarters were not yet ready to support these initiatives.

DAC member countries also work to integrate various cross-cutting themes into their activities. Both HIV/AIDS and gender are pursued by five countries. Other issues pursued are governance (by three countries), private sector development (two countries), decentralisation (two countries) and environment (one country).

● Geographic coverage

Most DAC member countries focus a part of their programme geographically; collectively they cover nine of Mozambique's ten provinces. Each country tends to focus on between one and three provinces (*e.g.* Ireland is in Niassa and Inhambane while Germany is in Inhambane, Sofala and Manica). The overall distribution is somewhat unequal, though, with several donors concentrating on Niassa and Maputo, whereas some of the poorer provinces, such as Zambézia, receive less support. To a certain extent, this results from the gradual and informal division of provinces that has taken place during the decades since independence in 1975. In provinces where a number of countries are active, a division of labour along sectoral lines may occur (*e.g.* in Sofala, Austria concentrates on rural development, Germany concentrates on education and Italy concentrates on health). Most DAC member countries find value in maintaining their provincial-level activities because it enables them to monitor the impact of actions taken by the Mozambican government and to feed lessons learnt into their policy dialogue at the national level. At this stage, only one country plans to wind down its activities at provincial level (these have been in Zambézia).

- Aid modalities

Pooled-funding mechanisms are well developed and widely supported by donors in Mozambique. As well as general budget support, sectoral funds have been set up for agriculture, education and health (where there are actually four sub-sectoral funds). A few DAC member countries are providing large shares of their assistance in the form of pooled funding. For example, one country is providing nearly two-thirds of its programme as general budget support while another is providing about 15% in general budget support and further 25% in sector support. Currently, only two countries represented in Maputo are not providing either sectoral or general budget support, but both are considering providing some pooled sectoral support in the future. With a few countries, Mozambique has been selected as a pilot to test pooled-funding modalities. This has sometimes required adopting exceptional procedures in headquarters. Few countries are able to provide the firm multi-year funding commitments that would enable Mozambique to plan medium-term macroeconomic and fiscal positions. Most countries also provide their pooled funding in their own currency, which means that Mozambique has to carry the risks associated with exchange rate variations and adjust its budgets accordingly.

The majority of DAC member countries contributing to sector funding are involved in PROAGRI, the agricultural sector fund. PROAGRI is considered to be very progressive and a few countries who are not normally involved in sectoral support have contributed to this fund. At the same time, some frustrations are building up due to perceptions that PROAGRI has mostly had an impact on improving capacity within the Ministry of Agriculture in Maputo and, so far, has had limited impact across the rest of the country. One country also found that their funding had not been appropriately administered. Another country has found similar irregularities with its funding for the education sector.

Today, 13 DAC member countries (as well as the European Union and the World Bank) provide general budget support to Mozambique. The so-called "G-15" has become one of the most active fora in Mozambique for donor co-ordination and harmonisation and for policy dialogue with the partner government, more active than the Development Partners Group (a forum for donor discussions and the sharing of policy positions). Some countries who are not able to provide budget support participate as observers in general G-15 meetings, indicating the importance of this group. Nevertheless, these countries cannot observe all meetings and do not have access to certain documents. This limits the extent to which the G-15 can legitimately become the main forum for donor-government relations. There is also a noticeable degree of variation among countries in the perception and acceptance of the risks associated with general budget support. As the experience in the agriculture and education sectors suggest (see previous paragraph), a degree of risk is involved in providing pooled funding to Mozambique, as it is in many developing counties. While a few DAC member countries are comfortable carrying this risk because they are convinced of the potentially high development impact of general budget support, others are becoming increasingly hesitant and making some of their budget support conditional on positive outcomes in terms of improvements in governance standards. It is not apparent whether countries that have joined the G-15 on a pilot basis have formed their own positions on the degree of risk they are comfortable carrying.

Among several of the countries that work principally through projects, conscious efforts are being made to increase impact by concentrating on a smaller number of more substantial activities. This will also help reduce the transaction costs for Mozambique associated with managing a very large number of development activities.[3]

- Other activities

In addition to the activities managed by the field mission, headquarters departments, other national government agencies or regional and local governments may also fund development activities in Mozambique. Many DAC member countries mentioned regional programmes for Southern Africa, multi-bilateral assistance, humanitarian assistance, debt relief, tertiary scholarships and co-financing of activities by non-governmental organisations (NGOs) as the main activities their governments were also involved in. In a few countries, the people stationed at the field mission play a modest role in co-ordinating or facilitating some of these activities by, for example, organising occasional roundtable meetings or commenting on proposed activities. For two DAC member countries, some activities in Mozambique are implemented independently of the local field mission by a different government department or a sub-national level of government, through representative offices located in a neighbouring country. For many donors, there is scope to improve the consistency and complementarity of the various strands of their development co-operation and to ensure that good development practices are applied to all ODA activities.

Field presence

- Representation in the field

Many DAC member countries declared that their development co-operation programme was the principal justification for them being represented in Mozambique. Whereas many countries' diplomatic missions were previously headed by a development person at *chargé d'affaires* level, over the last few years several countries have up-graded their representation and 15 now have a resident ambassador/high commissioner in Maputo (who may be accredited to other countries as well). For four other countries, the ambassador/high commissioner accredited to Mozambique is located in Harare or Pretoria. One country has the unusual configuration of their diplomatic mission being headed at *chargé d'affaires* level without this person reporting to a non-resident ambassador/high commissioner.

Of the 18 DAC member countries represented in Mozambique, only eight field missions are integral parts of the embassy/high commission. In each of these cases, the foreign affairs ministry has a pre-eminent role in managing or co-ordinating the development co-operation programme and the overall structure of the country's development co-operation system does not include a separate executing agency. With the remaining ten countries, the field mission is in separate premises, the executing agency for the development co-operation programme is housed separately from the embassy or the embassy is located in another country.

Now that a critical mass of countries have a resident ambassador/high commissioner in Mozambique, two levels of co-ordination and policy dialogue have emerged: heads of mission and heads of co-operation. Coherence in the messages delivered and approaches adopted by DAC member countries may be enhanced when the people occupying these two posts are from the same ministry and located in the same premises. In other circumstances, the risk of diverging positions and reduced information flow could be greater. Countries that do not have a resident ambassador/high commissioner in Mozambique may now find themselves at a disadvantage in influencing debates at the highest political levels.

- Roles and responsibilities of field missions

In all DAC member countries, projects and programmes supported in Mozambique are broadly in line with each country's general policies and approaches, with staff in both headquarters and the field playing a role in formulating and implementing activities. At the same time, there is considerable difference between countries in terms of the specific responsibilities of the field mission and the degree of delegated authority to representatives in the field. Approximately half the DAC member countries have fairly centralised systems where the field mission implements decisions made by headquarters, with little or no flexibility to change programmes or funding. At the other end of the spectrum, some field missions design and implement programmes, subject to headquarters' general approval, and make funding changes within the limits of the country framework prepared through an iterative process involving staff both at headquarters and in the field. In two countries where there are several entities involved in delivering the development co-operation programme, one entity is quite decentralised whereas others still need to consult headquarters on a regular basis. This can make internal co-ordination at the field level more difficult. In a few countries, the move towards greater decentralisation took place only recently or is in the process of being implemented. For the most part, these processes are resulting in some changes in work at the field mission, notably less routine reporting to headquarters, and are being implemented without a change in overall staffing levels at the field mission.

With regard to the amount that can be approved in the field for new activities without consulting headquarters, four countries advised that they are not able to approve any funding at all. In contrast, eight heads of mission can approve funding, usually up to a certain ceiling, within the confines of the overall country framework. These ceilings vary widely, with two countries reporting that there is no limit and another mission stating that only sums of up to USD 350 000 can be approved. However, even when large amounts can be approved by the field mission, approval for some specified activities, such as general budget support, may still need to be referred to headquarters where approval is given by the minister or the government. In at least one case, the approval ceiling was increased recently, in keeping with the move towards a transfer of authority to the field. Finally, the heads of mission of a few countries have a small fund at their discretion to be allocated for development related purposes such as cultural activities, local NGO funding and small grants schemes. The annual allocations for these funds range from approximately USD 12 000 to USD 675 000.

Staffing issues

- Staff numbers

An area where there is great interest but little reliable and comparable data available is the number of staff managing and implementing development co-operation programmes. These data are difficult to compile for a variety of reasons. The nature of individual programmes are very different with some activities possibly less staff intensive than others. The degree of support and back-up provided by headquarters varies, as does the amount of reporting to headquarters that is required and the need to consult and discuss issues with people in headquarters. Some donors contract out activities that others may perform in-house, such as regular monitoring and reporting on activities, staff training and selection or research. Some countries are free to staff their field mission as they judge best, within the budget envelope provided, including by hiring foreign nationals or local staff for professional-level positions if they prefer. Others operate within highly constrained environments with the creation of every new position needing to be approved by a range of different government entities pursuing competing objectives. Some countries can hire staff using programme funds (*i.e.* funds that could otherwise be used to fund development activities) to pay their salaries whereas others cannot. Finally, the number of hours staff work may differ, due to variations in the number of hours in the working week and differences in leave entitlements.

Despite these inherent difficulties, an attempt was made to quantify the number of professional staff[4] used by DAC member countries in the field to manage and implement their country programme for Mozambique. At one end of the scale, a few countries have a total of six or fewer professional staff while two countries have in excess of 75 (see Figure A.2.1). Although the average number of professional staff is 21, most countries have between 10 and 15 people. One country currently has 40 long-term advisors stationed

Figure A.2.1. **Programme size and staff numbers in Mozambique**

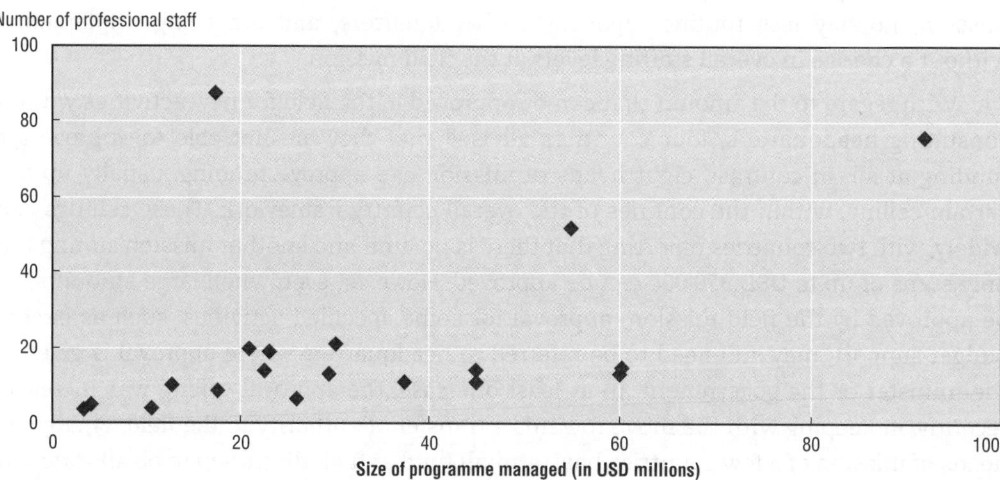

Source: Information provided by DAC member countries.

in Mozambique. Several countries reported they are phasing out their long-term advisors in the field, as part of a more general shift from project to more programmatic approaches.

A sentiment expressed by many DAC member countries was that the number of staff they have in the field is insufficient to enable them to participate in the full range of donor co-ordination mechanisms now taking place in Mozambique and to keep abreast of developments in all of their main areas of focus. A few countries recognised that a consequence of this is that staff spend too much of their time attending meetings in Maputo and may become out of touch with the situation in more isolated and poorer parts of the country. Several countries also mentioned that increased participation in pooled-funding arrangements required different staff skills, with less emphasis on process skills and greater emphasis on the capacity to engage with and influence other stakeholders and to analyse policies.

There were also clear differences in the number of staff in headquarters providing back-up for the staff located in Mozambique. In one case, four desk officers in headquarters work on the Mozambique programme alone whereas in another only two people are available for all activities in Africa. Most countries reported between one officer partially responsible to two full-time officers working on the Mozambique desk in headquarters. Many countries also indicated that sections in headquarters dealing with various thematic areas become involved in the Mozambique programme from time to time.

The information collected during this exercise enables a rough comparison to be made across DAC member countries of the size of the programme managed in the field per professional staff member. In nine countries, one professional staff member manages on average between USD 0.7 million and USD 1.5 million per year (see Figure A.2.2), irrespective of the size of the programme managed. In four countries, one professional staff member manages around USD 4 million or more a year while at the other end of the scale one

Figure A.2.2. **Programme managed in Mozambique per professional staff member**

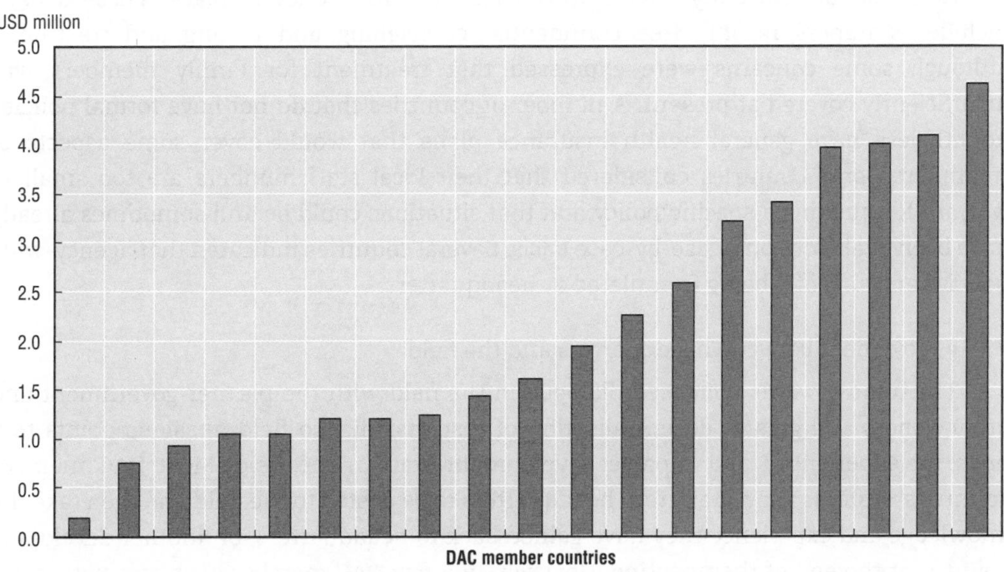

Source: Information provided by DAC member countries.

professional staff member manages USD 0.2 million. Across the DAC member countries in Mozambique, each professional staff member manages on average around USD 1.5 million a year.

- Policies for locally employed staff

Most DAC member countries acknowledge that local staff add value to their field mission because they are often the custodians of the mission's institutional memory and bring local knowledge that international staff cannot gain easily. Most countries can and do hire professional staff locally with only two stating that this was not a possibility for them. In addition, a central part of the decentralisation plans of a few countries is to rely increasingly on locally recruited staff to fulfil professional and sometimes managerial positions in the field mission. While the majority of countries indicated that no explicit policies have been put in place to foster long-term career development for locally employed staff, most of these mentioned that training is available, either in Mozambique or at headquarters. Two countries, on the other hand, do have policies in place with one offering permanent contracts complete with full training, a retirement package and the option to transfer to other field missions. A few countries maintain formal or informal policies to encourage local staff to eventually move back to broader Mozambican society while some others doubt whether this is a realistic proposition, given the substantial drop in salary that it would most likely imply. In the health sector, a growing number of counties have signed a Memorandum of Understanding with the Mozambican government stating that they will avoid recruiting local civil servants.

The increasing reliance on locally recruited staff, in both Mozambique and other main partner countries, was a factor in the decision by the development agencies of a few non-English speaking DAC member countries to adopt English as their corporate language. At the same time, representatives of some non-English speaking DAC member countries stressed the importance of actively using the national language of the partner country and of maintaining linguistic diversity so as to provide alternative conceptual bases for analysing and discussing issues.

A few donors currently have a workplace HIV/AIDS policy in place. These usually include awareness raising, free confidential counselling and testing and treatment, although some concerns were expressed that treatment for family members was insufficiently covered at present. A number of countries that do not have formal policies nonetheless have general health insurance plans that would cover some aspects of treatment. Some countries considered that their local staff numbers are too small to warrant formulating a specific policy and that situations could be and sometimes already have been dealt with on a case-by-case basis. Several countries indicated that agency-wide policies are currently being formulated at headquarters.

- Movement between headquarters and the field

The trend towards increased dialogue in the field with the partner government and other donors and greater decentralisation of responsibility to field missions points to a need for experienced and capable development staff in the field. Most DAC member countries' systems allow staff from headquarters to be posted to the field and then take the knowledge and experience they have gained back to headquarters, or another developing country, at the end of their posting. However, in a few DAC member countries with fairly centralised management approaches, no system exists for rotating staff between headquarters and the field. In these cases, the development co-operation programme may be managed in the field by diplomats stationed at the embassy or consultants recruited locally for this purpose. Neither approach would tend to build up development expertise within donors' development co-operation systems nor support greater decentralisation of responsibility to the field.

Management issues

- Country envelopes

Most DAC member countries operate with an overall budget envelope for Mozambique from which the majority of activities managed locally are funded. These envelopes may cover a number of years with funding levels for future years being indicative only. In other countries, approval is given for each specific activity with money committed over the lifetime of the activity. Through this process, a portfolio of activities can be built up that constitutes the country programme. Neither of these approaches provide the partner country with the firm multi-year funding commitments that are now considered good practice by the DAC.

- Cost of implementing the programme

The majority of DAC member countries cannot give the exact cost of administering their development co-operation programme in Mozambique and so cannot say whether the programme is being implemented more or less efficiently than last year or more or less efficiently than in other countries. Most countries can give the embassy's administrative costs as an approximation of this figure, but this includes costs for some non-development activities as well. In addition, some salaries of staff in the field, travel and training are paid from separate headquarters budgets and the salaries of some staff working on the development programme may be paid from programme funds. Four countries have identified their administrative costs, which correspond to 5.1% of programme funds managed in one case and 6.2% in another. Of these four countries, three are housed separately from their embassy/high commission and therefore also manage their administrative costs separately. While a few countries stated that their missions are relatively cheap to run, two reported that their costs have increased due to moves to separate offices.

- Communications systems

Communications systems for all DAC member countries include e-mail and fixed telephone lines to communicate with headquarters. Too narrow a bandwidth and viruses aside (which a few donors expressed concerns about), a satellite connection makes an enormous difference in the way headquarters and field offices can interact, including by enabling access to internal Intranet facilities. The majority of countries now have satellite communication facilities installed, in two cases this happened as part of the decentralisation process. Countries without satellite connections are at a clear disadvantage as local service providers are not always reliable or they need to telephone headquarters several times a day to download e-mails. Field missions housed in embassies/high commissions tend to enjoy better communication facilities, but limitations on access to secure communications systems can limit effective communication with headquarters for staff without adequate security clearances (including foreign nationals). Finally, for communicating with people throughout

Mozambique, it was indicated that mobile phones are often more practical and more reliable than fixed telephone lines.

Two countries' field missions are equipped with video-conferencing facilities and a third may have access to these facilities as part of a new satellite system that should be installed shortly. Another three countries indicated that they occasionally make use of the video-conferencing facilities at the World Bank office, the university or the main embassy building. This technology, which is mostly being used by countries with a high degree of delegated responsibility and with their headquarters located in a similar time zone, is being used for a variety of purposes including: interviewing job applicants, weekly meetings with senior managers in headquarters, participating in project appraisal committee meetings and communicating with regional offices.

Partnership

- Country strategies

Most but not all DAC member countries have prepared a country strategy for their programme in Mozambique. In two cases, these are not technically country strategies but Memoranda of Understanding signed with the partner government. Although all donors stated that their country strategy is in line with the PARPA (the Mozambican PRSP covering the period 2001 to 2005), the duration of country strategies ranges from two to six years and is mostly determined by donors' own internal processes. The country strategies of a few donors are primarily internal documents, although a short summary may be published. Some countries have a clear policy to publish their country strategy, including a version translated into the national language of the partner country.

- High-level consultations

Despite the regular contacts between donors and the partner government that have taken root in Mozambique through the rich mosaic of co-ordination mechanisms, many DAC member countries continue the practice of holding high-level bilateral consultations. In only a few cases do these consultations occur annually, the trend appears to be towards holding consultations when this is most appropriate, such as when a new country strategy is being finalised or when a minister visits Mozambique. In several cases, DAC member countries' representation at high-level consultations (as well as at Consultative Group meetings) is headed by a senior staff member from headquarters. A small group of countries advised that they no longer hold high-level consultations at all, in some cases for the reason that the G-15 budget support group meetings provide them with regular contact with the partner government.

- Monitoring, evaluation and performance assessment

DAC member countries adopt different approaches to monitoring the impact of their activities in Mozambique. In some countries, particularly those with centralised management systems, there are few formal requirements to monitor activities and this is sometimes a source of frustration for staff in the field. In a few cases, logical frameworks are not prepared for any activities which means that monitoring is reduced to a rudimentary level of collecting anecdotal evidence. On the other hand, a few countries have developed sophisticated strategic management systems with results of specific activities closely monitored and aggregated, so as to gauge the impact of the country programme as a whole. In some cases, indicators are chosen depending on the specific activity and the country's overall objectives. In others, there is a conscious effort to use partner government systems to the maximum degree possible in monitoring exercises. Another trend noted is an increasing use of computer-based systems, where appropriate communications systems are available, for scoring and monitoring all activities funded by an agency throughout the world.

Only a few DAC member countries carry out full country programme evaluations, and these tend to be donors with relatively smaller country programmes. With many countries, the annual evaluation plan is determined by headquarters although field missions can influence the choice of evaluations to be conducted. Increasingly, these are covering a range of activities in Mozambique or similar activities across a range of developing countries. With pooled-funding arrangements, particularly general budget support, attracting both an increasing number of donors and larger amounts of ODA, there is an increasing tendency in Mozambique to conduct joint evaluations. Furthermore, with some donors moving towards more of a results focus in their activities and putting more emphasis on maintaining high quality standards, the primary function of evaluations has shifted to capturing and sharing lessons learnt.

Perhaps also related to the increasing use of pooled-funding arrangements is a greater interest by auditors-general or national audit offices in DAC member countries in the activities donors are funding in Mozambique. However, the missions of national auditors to Mozambique have tended to be fairly uncoordinated and more can be done to promote greater harmonisation in these activities, including standards and norms used, as is occurring with evaluations.

Notes

1. Several non-DAC donors are also active in Mozambique including Brazil, China and Iceland.
2. UNAIDS/WHO (2003), *AIDS Epidemic Update 2003*, WHO, Geneva.
3. On average, there were 845 new development activities started in Mozambique each year between 1999 and 2001.
4. For this exercise, the following categories of personnel are not included: volunteers, administrative assistants, secretaries, drivers, security guards, cleaners and gardeners.

ISBN 92-64-00761-X
Managing Aid: Practices of DAC Member Countries

ANNEX A.3

An Introduction to DAC Statistics

Coverage

DAC statistics are designed to measure international resource flows which promote the development or welfare of developing and transition countries. Their design has been influenced:

- On a *technical* level, mainly by conventions used in balance-of-payments statistics.
- On a *policy* level, mainly by DAC members' desire to show, on a comparable basis, the full extent of their national effort in promoting development.

Types of flow

Resource flows can come either from the private sector or the official/government sector and can be either at market terms or at concessional terms. Data are collected on the following broad categories:

Official development assistance (ODA) and official aid – Flows from the official sector of the donor country which:

- Have as their main objective the promotion of the economic development and welfare of the partner country.
- Are given either as grants or as concessional loans.

Aid is referred to as official development assistance (ODA) if directed to a developing country on Part I of the *DAC List of Aid Recipients* (see below) or to a multilateral agency active in development, and official aid if directed to a transition country or to a multilateral agency primarily active in those countries.

ODA/OA includes the costs to the donor of project and programme aid, technical co-operation, forgiveness of debts not already reported as ODA, sustenance costs for refugees for their first year in a donor country, imputed student costs, food and emergency aid and associated administrative expenses.

***Other official flows* –** Consist of *i)* grants or loans from the official sector not specifically directed to development or welfare purposes (*e.g.* those given for commercial reasons) and *ii)* loans from the official sector which are for development or welfare purposes, but which are not sufficiently concessional to qualify as ODA (see also next section).

***Private flows at market terms* –** Flows for commercial reasons from the private sector of a donor country. Includes foreign direct investment, bank loans and the purchase of developing country bonds or securities by companies or individuals in donor countries.

Private grants – Funds from non-government organisations for development or welfare purposes.

Note on concessional loans

To qualify as ODA/OA, loans must have a grant element of at least 25%, calculated against a fixed 10% discount rate. To serve as a rough guide, here are some sample loans which just qualify as aid, having a grant element of just over 25%:

- 6 year loan, annual repayments, interest rate 0.75%.
- 10 year loan, annual repayments, interest rate 3.5%.
- 20 year loan, annual repayments, interest rate 5.5%.
- 10 year loan, annual repayments, first payment after 5 years, interest rate 5%.
- 15 year loan, annual repayments, first payment after 5 years, interest rate 5.75%.

Exclusions

The following are considered to have insufficient development potential to qualify for inclusion in DAC statistics:

- Loans repayable in one year.
- Grants and loans for military purposes.
- Transfer payments (*e.g.* pensions, workers' remittances) to private individuals.

Flows originating in partner countries, for example, investments by their nationals in donor countries, are also ignored. However, partner countries' loan repayments, and repatriations of capital to the donor country, are deducted to arrive at net flows from the donor.

Stages of measurement

Flows can be measured either at the time they are firmly agreed (**commitments**) or at the time of the actual international transfer of funds (**disbursement**). Disbursements may be measured either **gross**, *i.e.* in the full amount of capital transfers to the partner country over a given period, or **net**, *i.e.* deducting repayments of loan principal over the same period. The usual measure of donor aid effort is net disbursements of official development assistance.

Data collection methods

DAC Questionnaire – A set of ten statistical tables completed annually in July by DAC members, who report the amount and destination of their flows in the previous year. Detailed information is collected regarding the destination, form, terms, sector and tying status of officials flows. A simplified form of the questionnaire is completed by multilateral agencies. There is also a one-page "Advance Questionnaire on Main DAC Aggregates" completed by DAC members each April to give early data on their flows.

Creditor Reporting System (CRS) – A system for reporting individual official transactions (both ODA/OA and other official flows) relevant to development. Reports are received directly from participating official agencies, including bilateral and multilateral agencies, development lending institutions and export credit agencies. All DAC member countries report to the CRS with 17 countries reporting fully and five countries reporting partially. Follow-up to reports on the disbursement and repayment status of loans allows the OECD Secretariat to calculate the debt burden of developing and transition countries.

Publications

There are three main paper publications of DAC statistics:

- *Development Co-operation Report* – This annual report, and especially its statistical annex, give detailed data on flows to developing and transition countries, concentrating on DAC members' aid efforts.
- *Geographic Distribution of Financial Flows to Aid Recipients* – This annual report shows the resource inflow of developing and transition countries, by source and type of flow.
- *Creditor Reporting System Regional Reports* – This annual publication – in five volumes by region – records project/activity notifications by recipient country and sector.

These publications are also available in electronic format on a CD-ROM entitled *International Development Statistics*. More information on DAC statistics is available from the internet at: *www.oecd.org/dac/stats* and comprehensive access to the databases is available by subscription through the DAC Internet site at: *www.oecd.org/dataoecd/50/17/5037721.htm*.

Table A3.1. DAC List of Aid Recipients – As at 1 January 2004

Part I: Developing Countries and Territories (Official Development Assistance)					Part II: Countries and Territories in Transition (Official Aid)	
Least Developed Countries (LDCs)	Other Low-Income Countries (Other LICs) (per capita GNI < $745 in 2001)	Lower Middle-Income Countries (LMICs) (per capita GNI $746-$2 975 in 2001)	Upper Middle-Income Countries (UMICs) (per capita GNI $2 976-$9 205 in 2001)	High-Income Countries (HICs) (per capita GNI > $9 206 in 2001)	Central and Eastern European Countries and New Independent States of the former Soviet Union (CEECs/NIS)	More Advanced Developing Countries and Territories
Afghanistan Angola Bangladesh Benin Bhutan Burkina Faso Burundi Cambodia Cape Verde Central African Republic Chad Comoros Congo, Dem. Rep. Djibouti Equatorial Guinea Eritrea Ethiopia Gambia Guinea Guinea-Bissau Haiti Kiribati Laos Lesotho Liberia Madagascar Malawi Maldives Mali Mauritania Mozambique Myanmar Nepal Niger Rwanda Samoa Sao Tome and Principe Senegal Sierra Leone Solomon Islands Somalia Sudan Tanzania Timor-Leste Togo Tuvalu Uganda Vanuatu Yemen Zambia	* Armenia * Azerbaijan Cameroon Congo, Rep. Côte d'Ivoire * Georgia Ghana India Indonesia Kenya Korea, Democratic Republic * Kyrgyz Rep. * Moldova Mongolia Nicaragua Nigeria Pakistan Papua New Guinea * Tajikistan * Uzbekistan Vietnam Zimbabwe	* Albania Algeria Belize Bolivia Bosnia and Herzegovina China Colombia Cuba Dominican Republic Ecuador Egypt El Salvador Fiji Guatemala Guyana Honduras Iran Iraq Jamaica Jordan * Kazakhstan Macedonia (former Yugoslav Republic) Marshall Islands Micronesia, Federated States Morocco Namibia Niue Palestinian Administered Areas Paraguay Peru Philippines Serbia and Montenegro South Africa Sri Lanka St Vincent and Grenadines Suriname Swaziland Syria Thailand ● Tokelau Tonga Tunisia Turkey * Turkmenistan ● Wallis and Futuna	Botswana Brazil Chile Cook Islands Costa Rica Croatia Dominica Gabon Grenada Lebanon Malaysia Mauritius ● Mayotte Nauru Panama St Helena ● St Lucia Venezuela **Threshold for World Bank Loan Eligibility ($5 185 in 2001)** Anguilla Antigua and Barbuda Argentina Barbados Mexico Montserrat Oman Palau Islands Saudi Arabia Seychelles St Kitts and Nevis Trinidad and Tobago Turks and Caicos Islands Uruguay	Bahrain	* Belarus * Bulgaria * Czech Republic * Estonia * Hungary * Latvia * Lithuania * Poland * Romania * Russia * Slovak Republic * Ukraine	● Aruba Bahamas ● Bermuda Brunei ● Cayman Islands Chinese Taipei Cyprus ● Falkland Islands ● French Polynesia ● Gibraltar ● Hong Kong, China Israel Korea Kuwait Libya ● Macao Malta ● Netherlands Antilles ● New Caledonia Qatar Singapore Slovenia United Arab Emirates ● Virgin Islands (UK)

* Central and Eastern European countries and New Independent States of the former Soviet Union (CEECs/NIS).
● Territory.

Source: www.oecd.org/dataoecd/50/17/5037721.htm.

ISBN 92-64-00761-X
Managing Aid: Practices of DAC Member Countries

ANNEX A.4

Mainstreaming Poverty Reduction and Other Cross-cutting Issues: HIV/AIDS, Gender and Environment

As outlined in Chapter 6, certain cross-cutting issues are fundamental to the achievement of overall development objectives. Issues such as poverty reduction and gender equality are cross-cutting in that they are critical to the outcome, and impact of all aspects, of the foreign assistance programme and cannot be pursued as stand-alone activities or managed as sectors. Rather, such cross-cutting issues should be integrated or mainstreamed into the overall programme of a particular development agency. This annex draws on the experience of a number of DAC member countries and OECD/DAC documents and outlines good practices for mainstreaming cross-cutting issues in general and considers a number of specific cross-cutting issues such as poverty reduction, gender equality, HIV/AIDS and environment.

Mainstreaming a cross-cutting issue means that all decisions, analytical processes, policies and planning are informed by and take full account of the issue. It is clear from this definition of mainstreaming, that mainstreaming goes beyond the integration of a cross-cutting issue and requires significant investment of time and resources. It is not feasible to mainstream multiple issues throughout a development programme without risking dilution of the significance of the issue to development outcomes. A realistic approach would be the identification of one or two issues that reflect overall policy objectives that would be fully mainstreamed into all aspects of the programme. An additional two or three cross-cutting issues could then possibly be integrated across the programme. Although not to the same degree, the integration of issues into polices and procedures would require resources, expertise and commitment as well.

To date, much experience has been gained by development agencies through their mainstreaming of gender issues. While the strategies for mainstreaming may vary according to the issue and the context (in partner countries) the gender experience provides valuable lessons. Mainstreaming cross-cutting issues involves strategies to mainstream within the policies and operations of the development agency or department, strategies to mainstream beyond the organisation *i.e.* through partner organisations including multilateral agencies and NGOs, and strategies to support mainstreaming in partner countries as part of the partnership model of working.

The most important mainstreaming strategies include the development of a clear agency-wide policy, high level commitment, the development of strategies for mainstreaming at the country level, the establishment of specialist units or the identification of specialist expertise, and the development of appropriate analytic skills. At times, in order to achieve desired outcomes, it will also be necessary to adopt issue-specific strategies.

This annex considers in some detail strategies for the effective mainstreaming of poverty reduction, many of which apply to the mainstreaming of other cross-cutting issues. The following sections consider mainstreaming strategies specific to mainstreaming of HIV/AIDS, gender, and environment which are supplementary to the core strategies outlined for the mainstreaming of poverty reduction.

Mainstreaming poverty reduction

The commitment of DAC members to poverty reduction as set out in the MDGs has led most members to formally adopt poverty reduction as the overall objective of their development co-operation. *The DAC Guidelines: Poverty Reduction* argue that tackling poverty effectively requires the mainstreaming of poverty reduction throughout agency policies, and operations. This requires changes in organisational structures, incentives, practices, system and cultures.

Strategies for mainstreaming poverty reduction[1]

The Role of Agency Leadership, Vision and Commitment

- Determined leadership at both political and policy-making levels should capture and channel the interest and commitment of all staff, other government bodies and civil society to focus more resolutely and forcefully on supporting poverty reduction in partner countries.
- Develop a clear agency vision, policy framework and strategy for attacking poverty.
- Tensions exist where agencies have multiple objectives (for example sustainable development, poverty reduction, gender equality, conflict, or national foreign policy goals). Top management needs to clarify objectives and consult widely with staff in doing so, as a way of identifying complementarities, addressing tradeoffs and resolving differences in the ensuing debates.
- It is essential to link human resources staff with policy staff: leadership must understand the practical implications of strategy and policy in terms of the way staff are managed and human resources renewed.
- There is a need for leaders at all levels of the agency – and particularly at middle management level – to clearly flag their commitment to poverty reduction.

Policy and programme development

- Align policies as closely as possible with the partner poverty reduction strategy, include poverty reduction objectives in the agency's country strategies, and include strategies for the inclusion of country level indicators.
- The goal of reducing poverty should inform all planning processes (including country strategies, sector approaches and project interventions) within the agency. Programmes and projects should be systematically assessed for their potential to reduce poverty in all agency screening and approval procedures.

- Consider revisions and additions to staff regulations that reinforce the role of reducing poverty as central to agency objectives, operations and performance.
- Promote an institutional culture that supports poverty reduction. A "disbursement" culture or a culture that treats poverty reduction with only lip-service can dilute or undermine the agency's focus on it. Develop approaches, instruments or strategies that accommodate or reduce disbursement pressures at the end of the agency fiscal year.
- Strengthen links between mainstreaming activities at the centre and the field.
- Terms of reference for research, studies or programme preparation should make links to poverty reduction goals. Build targets and standards for poverty reduction into contractual arrangements and partnership agreements with external agencies, NGOs and consultants. These agreements should incorporate incentives and sanctions, and have clear systems for monitoring results.
- Engage with multilateral partners to ensure they promote poverty reduction in agency policy and through their activities.
- Ensure institutional evaluations of multilateral partners consider the importance of poverty reduction objectives.

Developing organisational capacity

- Work with the existing agency skills set, assisting sector staff to acquire and integrate poverty reduction skills in their work.
- Focus on "new skills" building:
  - For partnership: skills in facilitation and co-ordination and in relationship building (such as active listening, consensus-building, negotiation, diplomacy).
  - For diplomatic staff: skills for understanding development issues, for taking risks, and for interacting with partners in the field.
  - For all operational staff: skills to enhance flexibility, adaptability, self-criticism, and lateral thinking.
- Addressing the many dimensions of poverty calls for building and deploying multidisciplinary teams at country level with competence and skills in many domains. Bring skills together at macro, meso and micro levels.

Staff policy

- Staff recruitment (for permanent, temporary and diplomatic staff) should focus on poverty reduction skills and performance, team-working capacities, and experience in co-ordination (facilitation, listening and negotiating skills).
- Provide additional support for focal staff based in overseas offices that may lack authority and support.

Training

- Strengthen the links between the agency's strategic objectives, its unit business plans, and individual staff performance "results agreements" to increase internal coherence and consolidate efforts.

- Country directors and programme managers should have clear poverty reduction and partnership goals in their briefs, in their performance assessments and in their criteria for assessing the performance of their staff.
- Credible performance management systems are based on objective criteria. Where poverty reduction performance is a criterion, agency evaluation systems may need to focus on developing methodologies for assessing poverty reduction impact.
- Incentive systems should be flexible and of a facilitative/regulatory nature.
- It is important to identify and understand institutional incentives and counterincentives (both explicit and implicit) when evaluating measures to increase coherence between agency poverty reduction objectives and staff performance.

Organisational structures

- Encourage team work across professional boundaries to address more effectively the multidimensional nature of poverty and to overcome narrow single-sector-driven or supply-led approaches.
- Develop structures and mechanisms for mainstreaming poverty reduction. Poverty reduction "champions" can be used to raise the profile of poverty reduction within the agency, to provide advice, to strengthen communication between and across organisational levels, and to promote good practice. Resources and authority must be vested in agency poverty reduction advocates.
- Flatter, simpler organisational structures are more compatible with trends towards team work, developing and valuing multidisciplinary competence in staff and greater reliance on information flows and networking. At the same time, some hierarchy is needed to ensure accountability, quality control and leadership.
- It is essential to understand that while organisational structures are very important, informal working methods – which determine how people work together in groups and across organisational structures – matter most.

Monitoring

- Develop monitoring systems that provide accountability against poverty reduction objectives. Marker systems have some benefits.
- Develop methodologies for assessing poverty reduction impact.

Mainstreaming HIV/AIDS

A number of DAC member countries including Canada, Denmark, Ireland and the United Kingdom regard HIV/AIDS as a key cross-cutting issue to be addressed within their development co-operation programmes. Members such as Ireland have made the policy decision to mainstream HIV/AIDS throughout their programme.

The essential strategies for mainstreaming poverty reduction also apply to the mainstreaming of HIV/AIDS. These include strategies to develop agency leadership, vision and commitment, to reflect HIV/AIDS in programme development, to build organisational capacity for mainstreaming and developing monitoring systems. In addition, there are some strategies specific to mainstreaming or that require additional attention due to the very specific nature of the issue.

Strategies for mainstreaming HIV/AIDS[2]

Policy and programme development

- Ensure that policy statements reflect HIV/AIDS as a development issue rather than as a health issue.
- Work with partner countries and key development partners to gather information on the status of the epidemic.
- Consider support for the strengthening of research capacity to increase understanding of the scale and path of the epidemic.
- Evaluate the preparedness of partners to move forward on HIV/AIDS programmes and consider how other programmes may be oriented to address HIV/AIDS indirectly.
- Consider the development of country level HIV/AIDS strategies.
- Create opportunities for dialogue at national level – the involvement of heads of country programmes and senior diplomatic staff is critical.
- In programme development consider support to non-government organisations able to work with high risk and vulnerable groups.
- Ensure the links to poverty reduction and gender programmes are made clear
- Identify how HIV/AIDS can be mainstreamed through sectoral programmes – going beyond the health sector critical.
- Consider HIV/AIDS impact assessments of all new programmes or projects.
- Include people living with HIV/AIDS in programme development and implementation where possible.
- Develop appropriate and measurable indicators and monitor impact.

Developing organisational capacity

- Develop training and awareness programmes. These are critical to the mainstreaming of HIV/AIDS as many people hold misconceptions, misunderstandings and prejudices about the causes, nature and spread of the epidemic.
- Provide specific training in advocacy and dialogue skills for staff in key positions.
- Train senior staff in overseas missions particularly at ambassadorial level as such staff are well placed to raise and discuss the issue at senior levels of partner governments despite its sensitive nature.
- Train and support capacity building in HIV/AIDS mainstreaming for consultants and NGO partners.
- Support the development of the analytic skills required to carry out HIV/AIDS impact assessments of programmes and projects.
- Prioritise the building of capacity for HIV/AIDS mainstreaming outside the health sector.
- Develop a workplace HIV programme including awareness training for staff at all levels. Good practice on workplace programmes include access to information, confidential HIV counselling and testing, and condoms, plus the development of an agency policy on access to treatment for infected staff.

Mainstreaming gender equality

The term gender mainstreaming gained widespread use after the United Nations International Conference on Women in 1995 and the adoption of the Beijing Platform for Action. The United Nations defines gender mainstreaming as:

> "The process of assessing the implication for women and men of any planned action, including legislation, policies or programmes, in any areas and at all levels. It is a strategy for making the concerns and experiences of women as well as of men an integral part of the design, implementation, monitoring and evaluation of policies and programmes in all political, economic and societal spheres, so that women and men benefit equally, and inequality is not perpetuated. The ultimate goal of gender mainstreaming is gender equality." [United Nations Economic and Social Council (ECOSOC) 1997.]

Many development agencies have been working towards the promotion of gender equality and women's empowerment for some time and considerable progress has been made in both developed and developing countries with women enjoying greater freedom and power than before. However, a recent review found that many donors' lack of accountability to gender equality processes is an ongoing obstacle to the achievement of gender equality, a failure to prioritise gender equality objectives in country strategies and a lack of guidance on how to-operationalise gender policy.[3] Gender equality needs to be constantly promoted and actively sustained as indicated by the adoption of gender equality and women's empowerment as the third millennium development goal.

Gender equality strategies must be formulated in the context of changes in development policies and approaches, change in partner countries and shifts in the international context. For example, the increasing use of aid instruments such as SWAps and direct budget support and the development of national poverty reduction strategies carry implications for mainstreaming strategies.

As indicated in the sections on mainstreaming poverty reduction and HIV/AIDS, the mainstreaming of gender equality includes strategies to develop agency leadership, vision and commitment, to reflect gender equality objectives in programme development, to build organisational capacity for the mainstreaming of gender equality and to develop monitoring systems disaggregated by sex and focusing specifically on impact on women and gender relationships. At the operational level, gender-specific activities and affirmative action may be necessary when women or men are in particularly disadvantageous position.

Strategies for mainstreaming gender equality[4]

Policy and programme development

- Formulate policies and strategies that set out the goals and means by which overall progress of support to gender equality and women's empowerment can be assessed.
- Involve gender experts in all aspects of policy development.
- Develop a shared vision of gender equality objectives with partner countries involving government, non-government and civil society stakeholders in dialogue on gender-related objectives and activities.
- Based on the participation of partner countries and high levels of ownership, ensure that country strategies reflect goals for gender equality and women's empowerment.

- Making long-term commitments to development partners and activities are an important aspect of the partnership model of development and are also critical role for sustainable progress towards gender equality at macro and micro levels.
- Ensure project documents include actions to promote greater equality of influence, opportunity and benefit.
- Identify strategic entry points for the promotion of gender equality.
- Ensure gender objectives are reflected in staff job descriptions and performance appraisals.
- Promote the involvement of women as well as men in project/programme design and implementation.
- Conduct gender impact assessment of all projects and programmes.
- Conduct gender sensitive stakeholder analysis of projects or programmes.
- Work with partner governments to generate analytical research and sex disaggregated data.

Developing organisational capacity

- Review staff capacity for mainstreaming gender equality on regular basis.
- Develop operationally relevant training programmes.
- Provide updated training courses for longer serving and senior staff.
- Develop new training programmes relevant to changes in the development context *e.g.* how to mainstream through SWAps and budget support, developing gender objectives for procedures for results based management.
- Establish a specialist gender unit and focal staff initially to provide support and expertise in aspects of gender mainstreaming.
- Ensure that in-country social and gender analysis expertise is available to undertake analysis and support the implementation and review of all strategies.
- Ensure gender equality is addressed in other training programmes *e.g.* those on poverty reduction, HIV/AIDS, agriculture.

Developing capacity in partner countries

As part of the partnership model, DAC members are concerned with enhancing national capacities in partner countries including for the mainstreaming or integration of key cross-cutting issues into policy and practice. An important element of this is the ability to identify and address gender related needs and disparities.

- Support strategies to increase partner country capacities to analyse policies, programmes and institutional cultures and to develop change strategies that contribute to gender equality.
- Assist partners in the identification of strategies to increase the representation of women at policy and decision-making levels.
- Support national statistical systems to increase the collection and availability of sex disaggregated data.
- Support the development of research capacity and operational research on issues related to gender equality of opportunity and outcome.

Monitoring

- Develop sex disaggregated monitoring indicators and impact assessment.

Mainstreaming environment and sustainable development

The protection and better management of the environment is an essential strategy for poverty reduction. Some DAC member countries provide significant external assistance to environmental issues while others address issues such as agriculture and energy which carry significant environmental implications. A number of DAC member countries aim to mainstream environmental issues as a cross-cutting issue regardless of whether they address environmental concerns directly through the programme.

The mainstreaming of environmental issues differs from the mainstreaming of the other issues discussed in two main respects. Firstly, irrespective of the extent of the environmental focus in the overall programme, the submission of all projects and programmes for Environmental Impact Assessment (EIA) screening is mandatory (OECD Council Recommendation on Environmental Assessment of Development Assistance Projects and Programmes of 1985). All members must therefore have some capacity for EIA. Secondly, most DAC members have also signed multilateral agreements on major global environmental issues. This commits members to support partner countries, through external assistance programmes, in the management of environmental concerns.

Given these differences, the main principles of mainstreaming remain unchanged but very specific approaches are needed regarding the environment. The key strategies outlined for the mainstreaming of poverty reduction, HIV/AIDS and gender remain appropriate. These include strategies to develop agency leadership, vision and commitment, to reflect environmental sustainability objectives in programme development, to build organisational capacity for the mainstreaming of environmental sustainability and to develop adequate monitoring systems. However, fulfilling the requirements for EIA and supporting partner countries on global environmental issues should be an additional concern for all DAC members.

Strategies for mainstreaming environment and sustainability issues[5]

Environmental Impact Assessment (EIA) (indicates mandatory requirements)*

- *Establish an independent unit for EIA.
- *Develop EIA guidelines in line with existing principles and DAC Guidelines (see OECD/DAC (1992) *DAC Guidelines on Aid and Environment: No. 1, Good Practices for Environmental Impact Assessment of Development Projects*).
- Promote and increase understanding of the EIA requirements among all development staff.
- *EIA screening is a requirement for all projects. It should be carried out either by the EIA unit (not by environmental specialists who are part of the project design) or by a specialist organisation sub-contracted by the EIA unit.
- Ensure adequate capacity is available for EIA.
- The size and capacity of the EIA unit should relate to the nature and volume of activities carrying significant environmental implications.
- EIA staff should be part of the policy development process.

- The EIA unit should act as a source of information and support for agency staff.
- Support capacity building initiatives in partner countries for EIA.
- Environmental Strategy at the Programmatic Level.

Policy and programme development

- Ensure policies include environmental sustainability objectives.
- Include environmental specialists in policy development.
- Ensure environmental concerns are reflected in country strategy papers and country poverty assessments.
- Inform policy development by Strategic Environment Analysis (SEA) and identify areas of potential support to reverse negative trends and reduce impact on the poor.
- Dialogue with partner country and development partners to ensure that key policies such as PRS and SWAps in all sectors take account of environmental constraints and capitalise on environmental opportunities.
- Identify opportunities for working with the private sector to raise environmental standards (*e.g.* the promotion of cleaner production by industry).
- Enhance disaster preparedness and include environmental disaster prevention and mitigation measures in national strategies for sustainable development and major long-term development projects (see OECD/DAC [1994], *DAC Guidelines on Aid and the Environment, No. 7, Guidelines for Aid Agencies on Disaster Mitigation*).
- Develop and disseminate case studies of opportunities for poverty reduction and environmental protection within the agency, to other agencies and main partners.
- Develop cross sectoral strategies to promote sustainable development (see OECD/DAC [2001], *The DAC Guidelines: Strategies for Sustainable Development*).
- Ensure linkages are made in policies and programmes between environmental sustainability, poverty reduction, HIV/AIDS and gender equality.
- Work with major multilateral partners to ensure the inclusions of sustainability targets and indicators.

Building organisational capacity

- Establish a specialist unit with expertise in strategic environmental analysis (SEA) or allocate specialist staff to key teams within the agency.
- Ensure specialist expertise available to centre and field based staff.
- Develop guidelines for strategic environmental analysis.
- Build staff capacity to analyse the environmental dimensions of policies and programmes.
- Develop analytical skills on links between environmental degradation and poverty.
- Ensure staff are adequately trained on the implications of environmentally sustainable development.

Monitoring

- Develop systems to allow monitoring of environmental impact during project or programme implementation.

Developing capacity in partner countries

- Support the inclusion of environment and sustainability issues in national poverty reduction strategies.
- Support capacity building initiatives for strategic environmental analysis.

Global environmental issues

- Support capacity building initiatives in partner countries to enable countries to fulfil their obligations and benefit from multilateral environment agreements (see OECD/DAC [1992], *DAC Guidelines on Aid and Environment, No. 4, Guidelines for Aid Agencies on Global Environmental Problems*).

Notes

1. This section draws on a number of sources notably OECD (2001), *The DAC Guidelines: Poverty Reduction*, OECD, Paris.
2. This section draws on a range of sources including the OECD/World Health Organization (2003), *DAC Guidelines and Reference Series: Poverty and Health*, OECD, Paris and the OECD (2003), *DAC Peer Review of Ireland*, OECD, Paris.
3. Hunt, J. (2004), *Effective Strategies for Promoting Gender Equality*, document produced for the OECD/DAC GENDERNET.
4. This section draws on a number of sources including Derbyshire, H. (2002), *Gender Manual: A Practical Guide for Development Policy Makers and Practitioners*, DFID, London; Hunt, J. (2004), *Effective Strategies for Promoting Gender Equality*, document produced for the OECD/DAC GENDERNET; OECD (1999), *DAC Guidelines for Gender Equality and Women's Empowerment*, OECD, Paris; and OECD (n.d.), *Gender Equality Tipsheets*, OECD, Paris.
5. This section draws on a number of sources including OECD (1995), *DAC Guidelines on Aid and Environment*, OECD, Paris; OECD (2001), *The DAC Guidelines: Strategies for Sustainable Development*, OECD, Paris; CIDA (n.d.), *Policy for Environmental Sustainability*, Available at: *www.acdi-cida.gc.ca/cida_ind.nsf/0/8d822748c6f30b31852565450065e876/$FILE/ENV-nophotos-E.pdf* and DFID (2000), *Achieving Sustainability: Poverty Elimination and the Environment*, DFID, London.

ISBN 92-64-00761-X
Managing Aid: Practices of DAC Member Countries

ANNEX A.5

Managing Development Projects and Programmes[1]

Project Cycle Management (PCM) is the process that begins with the initial conception of a project or programme and concludes with post-completion evaluation. The approach is based on a strong focus on potential beneficiaries, detailed assessment and application of the logical framework approach. Many development agencies have developed or adapted project cycle management and logical framework approaches for use within their programmes.

PCM and the logical framework approach are believed to provide a structured, logical approach to the setting of priorities and in determining the intended results and activities of an intervention. They help those in charge of project planning, implementation and evaluation to focus on the elements of an intervention considered most relevant to a successful outcome. PCM can be applied to both projects and programmes such as SWAps, as well as to local and national level interventions. PCM should apply both to directly managed development interventions as well as to those that are subcontracted to implementing agencies, consultancy firms or NGOs.

The project cycle is a detailed model of the entire lifespan of a development intervention, starting with problem recognition, intervention identification and ending with evaluation and lessons learnt. It is a continuous process in which each stage provides the foundation for the next. The division of an intervention into distinct stages helps make sure choices are based on relevant and adequate information and highlights the need for decisions to be made about whether to continue or revise plans.

There are a number of identifiable stages in the project cycle, the descriptions of which vary between DAC members, but the most important of which are identification, design, appraisal, preparation and approval, implementation and monitoring, and evaluation.

1. Identification: Development of the initial idea and preliminary design

The initial identification of a development problem or issue, and the idea for a development intervention or for financial assistance from a DAC member increasingly comes from partner country governments. However, regional or local governments, civil society groups, community, international organisations, or development agencies may still identify a problem and a need for external assistance.

Whatever the origin of the initial idea, it is important that the preliminary design is done in a participatory manner and includes an initial stakeholder analysis to establish primary and secondary stakeholders, beneficiaries and key groups who will drive the intervention. In some member countries, an initial concept note with preliminary budget must be approved before further design work can be undertaken.

2. Preparation/design: Detailed design addressing technical and operational aspects

In stage 2, the design proceeds in more detail, identifying key objectives, beneficiaries and activities, major risks, and operational considerations. Most DAC members use a logical framework or logframe as the basis for project preparation and design, and then for monitoring and evaluation.

The logical framework

The logical framework or logframe is a planning tool which sets out the basic structure of an intervention. It is a systematic method for setting and analysing the objectives of a development intervention and the assumptions behind it. Although a logframe is a key tool of project cycle management, it represents only one aspect of the project or programme cycle.

The logframe identifies the overall development objective or goal to which the intervention will contribute; the purpose of the intervention which is the specific objective of the intervention to be achieved within the life cycle of the intervention; the expected outputs or results of the intervention, the types of activities required to produce the outputs, the indicators to be used to monitor the achievement of the goal, purpose, outputs and activities; and the means of verification. The inclusion of an assumptions column is critical and identifies positive conditions in the external environment that need to be met if the goal, purpose and outputs are to be achieved.

The "logic" of the logframe flows from bottom to top, and from left to right. That is, activities should lead to outputs which should lead to achievement of the purpose and contribution to the overall goal. However, the links between the project structure and the external environment must be included and the assumptions must hold true. Hence as indicated by the arrows in the following logframe:

- If the activities are carried out and the assumptions hold true, the outputs will be achieved.
- If the outputs are achieved and the assumptions hold true, the purpose will be achieved.
- If the purpose is achieved and the assumptions hold true, then the goal will be achieved.

The "logic" and connection between the project structure and external environment or assumptions is clearer in the sample logframe shown below. In this example:

- If activity 1.1 is carried out – the group is formed – and the assumption that family members are supportive of women developing new skills holds true, then output 1 – the group will be operational – will be achieved.
- If output 1 is achieved – the group is operational – and the assumption that good quality garments are produced holds true, then the purpose – income generating activities for women – will be achieved.

Table A5.1. **The logical framework structure**

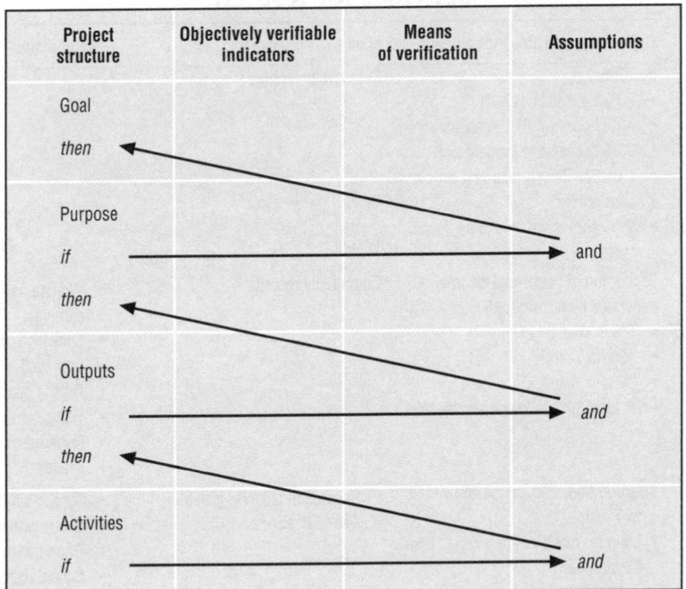

Only the major assumptions that are essential to the success of the intervention but do not require redesign or rejection of the intervention are included in the logical framework. Activities may be included in the design to anticipate and overcome a critical assumption. In the above example, activities to sensitise families to the purpose of the project and the longer term benefits to them may increase the chance of the assumption that – family members will support the women to establish their own income generating activities – holding true.

Identifying key indicators and their means of verification is also critical to the logframe and intervention design. Indicators may be identified in participation with key stakeholder groups, they may be revised during the project cycle or additional indicators developed. There is likely to be a need for both quantitative and qualitative indicators and there may be several indicators for each objective. There should also be consideration of how indicators should be disaggregated – according to gender, income level, target group etc – in order to accurately monitor project impact on a range of different groups.

Establishing the means of verification is a cross check on the choice and feasibility of measuring indicators. Where possible, indicators and means of verification should draw on national data sources. In situations of limited capacity, it may be necessary to facilitate baseline and ongoing surveys and capacity strengthening as a part of the intervention.

The logical framework approach is also relevant for complex programmes such as nation-wide or sector-wide programmes. In these cases, a master logframe may be divided into sub-logframes where the project purpose of the master framework is the same as the goal of one or several sub-components.

Table A5.2. **An example of a logical framework – establishing income generating activities for women**

Project structure	Objectively verifiable indicators	Means of verification	Assumptions
Goal: • Quality of life in fishing village improved	By 2005: • 70% houses brick built • 40% houses with iron sheet roofs • 90% decrease in incidence of common illnesses among fishing community • 90% population able to pay local taxes	Community records	
Purpose: • Income generating activities for women established	Proportion of household income generated by tailoring activities: • 5% in Year 1 • 15% in Year 2 • 30% in Year 3 • at least 30% in Year 4 and beyond	Community records	• Women have control over their earnings • Sanitation and hygiene practices improved • Fishing practices improved • Fish catch sustainable • Fishermen cease migrating to other islands
Outputs: 1. Tailoring group operational 2. Sewing machines owned by group	1. Group trading commercially within two years 2. Loan for machines fully repaid after 18 months	• Records of tailoring group • Financial records	• Trained women remain on island • Group works well together • Good quality garments produced • School uniform contract renewed • Import duty on clothes continued
Activities: 1.1 Form tailoring marketing group 1.2 Train women in tailoring skills 2.1 Train group members in loan repayment 2.2 Purchase sewing machines	1. Tailoring group: • Formed within 2 months • office holders appointed within 4 months • 35 women from fishing families attain proficiency in tailoring • Meet 3 times a week for 12 weeks 2.1 All group members attend 10 sessions (over a period of 3 weeks) 2.2 A total of 12 machines purchased within 3 months	Records of tailoring group Training Records Training Records Financial records	• Women attend training regularly • Family members supportive • Machines remain operational • School uniform contract secured • Materials for sewing available • Payments made to group on time

Source: FAO (2001), *Project Cycle Management Technical Guide*, Socio-Economic and Gender Analysis Programme, FAO available at: *www.fao.org/sd/seaga/downloads/en/projecten.pdf*.

3. Appraisal: Analysis of the project from a range of perspectives including economic, poverty impact, social, gender, institutional, environmental and HIV/AIDS

The stage of appraisal is essential for the design and implementation of any development intervention be it at project or programme level. Appraisals should determine:

- Compatibility with government policies
- Compatibility with other donor interventions.
- The viability of the intervention.
- The appropriateness of the technical design.
- The primary and secondary impact on major stakeholder groups, particularly poor and vulnerable groups.
- The likely gender disaggregated impact.
- The degree of participation of stakeholder groups.
- The likelihood of the activities and outputs being achieved in the time frame.
- The financial viability of the intervention.

- The current status of relevant institutions.
- The need for institutional capacity building activities to be included.
- Any possible environmental impact.
- Risks to achievement of the purpose.
- The sustainability of benefits beyond the life of the intervention.

4. Preparation, approval and financing: Finalising the project proposal and securing approval and funding

The final proposal will reflect the formatting and content requirements of each development agency. It will also reflect budget cycles and ceilings for a particular country programme.

5. Implementation and monitoring: Implementation of activities and on-going monitoring

Monitoring is an integral part of the project cycle and is defined by the OECD/DAC as a "continuing function that uses systematic collection of data on specified indicators to provide management and the main stakeholders of ongoing development intervention with indications of the extent of progress and achievement of objectives and progress in the use of allocated funds".[2]

Monitoring enables the review of progress and the proposal of actions necessary to ensure the achievement of the objectives. It is the responsibility of both implementing and funding organisations but should include the perspectives of stakeholders and beneficiaries. The logframe provides the basis for monitoring against the indicators and means of verification specified. Indicators measure not only the carrying out of specified activities but also the achievement of the project outputs and the extent of achievement of the project purpose at each stage of implementation. In some cases it may be necessary to collect baseline information during the initial project phase in order to provide an adequate basis for monitoring. Any changes in the external environment and the major assumptions should also be monitored.

6. Evaluation: This may be near the end of a project, upon completion or after its completion

According to the OECD/DAC an evaluation is "an assessment, as systematic and objective as possible, of an ongoing or completed project, programme or policy, its design, implementation and results. The aim is to determine the relevance and fulfilment of objectives, developmental efficiency, effectiveness, impact and sustainability. An evaluation should provide information that is credible and useful, enabling the incorporation of lessons learnt into the decision-making process of both recipients and donors."[3]

The main purposes of evaluation therefore are to provide an objective basis for assessing the performance of the intervention, to improve future interventions through the feedback of lessons learnt, and to provide accountability. For evaluations to fulfil these objectives, they must be used as learning tools within the organisation and, where necessary, used to change organisational behaviour.

Some of the main issues to be addressed during evaluation are:

- The relevance of the intervention within the context of its environment.
- The intended and unintended impact of the intervention and any contribution to achievement of the overall goal.
- The effectiveness of the intervention in achieving its purpose and the extent to which achievement of the purpose can be attributed to the intervention.
- The efficiency of the intervention in terms of the inputs used for the outputs achieved.
- The sustainability of the benefits after external assistance is ended.

Notes

1. This annex draws on a number of sources including: AusAID (1998), *Review of the Evaluation Capacities of Multilateral Organisations*, AusAID, Canberra; Dearden, P. (2001), *Programme and Project Cycle Management: Lessons from DFID and Other Organisations*, Presentation to the Foundation for Advanced Studies for International Development; European Commission (2004), *Aid Delivery Methods Volume 1: Project Cycle Management Guidelines* available at: *http://europa.eu.int/comm/europeaid/qsm/documents/pcm_manual_2004_en.pdf*; FAO/SEAGA (2001), *Project Cycle Management Technical Guide, available at:www.fao.org/sd/seaga/downloads/en/projecten.pdf;* Finland Ministry of Foreign Affairs (1998), *Guidelines for Programme Design, Monitoring and Evaluation*, Helsinki; UNDP (n.d.), *Introductory Notes about Project Cycle Management*, available at: *www.undp.sk/uploads/IntroductoryNotesaboutProjectCycleManagement.pdf.*
2. OECD (2002), *Glossary of Key Terms in Evaluation and Results Based Management*, OECD, Paris.
3. *Ibid.*

ISBN 92-64-00761-X
Managing Aid: Practices of DAC Member Countries

Bibliography

Acharya, de Lima and M. Moore (2004), *Aid proliferation: How responsible are the donors?*, Institute of Development Studies Working Paper 214, Brighton.

Addison, T., M. McGillivray and M. Odedokum (2003), *Donor Funding of Multilateral Agencies* Discussion Paper No. 2003/17, UNU/WIDER.

Cox, A., J. Healey and A. Koning (1997), *How European Aid Works: A comparison of Management Systems and Effectiveness*, Overseas Development Institute, The Chameleon Press Ltd., London.

Development Strategies (2003), Final Report: The Consequences of Enlargement for Development Policy, Volume 1, IDC, Belgium.

DFID (2002), *Working in Partnership with the World Health Organization*, DFID, London.

Nohria, N. (1991), *Note on Organisation Structure*, Harvard Business School, Cambridge, Massachusetts.

Heimans, J. (2002), *Multisectoral Global Funds as Instruments for Financing Spending on Global Priorities*, DESA Discussion Paper No. 24, United Nations Department of Economic and Social Affairs.

Jerve, A.M. and H. Selbervik (2003), MOPAN: *Report from the 2003 Pilot Exercise*, Chr, Michelsen Institute, Bergen.

Lancaster, C. (1999), *Aid to Africa: So much to do, so little done*, University of Chicago Press.

McGillivray, M. (2003), *Aid Effectiveness and Selectivity: Integrating Multiple Objectives into Aid Allocations*, World Institute for Development Economics Research Discussion Paper No. 2003/71, Helsinki.

OECD (1992), *Development Assistance Manual: DAC Principles for Effective Aid*, OECD, Paris.

OECD DAC Guidelines on Aid and Environment series:

(1992), No. 1. *Good Practices for Environmental Impact Assessment of Development Projects*, OECD, Paris.

(1992), No. 2. *Good Practices for Country Environmental Surveys and Strategies*, OECD, Paris.

(1992), No. 3. *Guidelines for Aid Agencies on Involuntary Displacement and Resettlement in Developing Countries*, OECD, Paris.

(1992), No. 4. *Guidelines for Aid Agencies on Global Environmental Problems*, OECD, Paris.

(1992), No. 5. *Guidelines for Aid Agencies on Chemicals Management*, OECD, Paris.

(1994), No. 6. *Guidelines for Aid Agencies on Pest and Pesticide Management*, OECD, Paris.

(1994), No. 7. *Guidelines for Aid Agencies on Disaster Mitigation*, OECD, Paris.

(1995), No. 8. *Guidelines for Aid Agencies on Global and Regional Aspects of the Development and Protection of the Marine and Coastal Environment*, OECD, Paris.

(1995), No. 9. *Guidelines for Aid Agencies for Improved Conservation and Sustainable Use of Tropical and Sub-Tropical Wetlands*, OECD, Paris.

OECD (1995), *Donor Assistance to Capacity Development in Environment*, OECD, Paris.

OECD (1995), *Participatory Development and Good Governance*, OECD, Paris.

OECD (1995), *DAC Orientations for Development Co-operation in Support of Private Sector Development*, OECD, Paris.

OECD (1996), *Building Policy Coherence: Tools and Tensions*, Public Management Occasional Papers, No. 12, OECD, Paris.

OECD (1996), *Shaping the 21st Century: The Contribution of Development Co-operation*, OECD, Paris.

OECD (1998), *Conflict, Peace and Development Co-operation on the Threshold of the 21st Century*, OECD, Paris.

OECD (1998), *DAC Sourcebook on Concepts and Approaches Linked to Gender Equality*, OECD, Paris.

OECD (1999), *A Comparison of Management Systems for Development Co-operation in OECD/DAC Members*, OECD, Paris.

OECD (1999), *DAC Guidelines for Gender Equality and Women's Empowerment in Development Co-operation*, OECD, Paris.

OECD (2000), *Effective Practices in Conducting a Joint Multi-Donor Evaluation*, OECD, Paris.

OECD (2001), *Evaluation Feedback for Effective Learning and Accountability*, OECD, Paris.

OECD (2001), *The DAC Guidelines: Helping Prevent Violent Conflict*, OECD, Paris.

OECD (2001), *The DAC Guidelines: Poverty Reduction*, OECD, Paris.

OECD (2001), *The DAC Guidelines: Strategies for Sustainable Development*, OECD, Paris.

OECD (2001), *The DAC Guidelines: Strengthening Trade Capacity for Development*, OECD, Paris.

OECD (2001), Conflict Prevention and Development Co-operation Papers in *The DAC Journal*, Volume 2, No. 3, OECD, Paris.

OECD (2002), *Gender Equality in Sector Wide Approaches*, OECD, Paris.

OECD (2003), *DAC Guidelines and Reference Series: Harmonising Donor Practices for Effective Aid Delivery*, OECD, Paris.

OECD (2003), *Aid Effectiveness and Selectivity: Integrating Multiple Objectives into Aid Allocations*. OECD, Paris.

OECD (2003), *Public Opinion and the Fight against Poverty*, OECD, Paris.

OECD/World Health Organization (2003), *DAC Guidelines and Reference Series: Poverty and Health*, OECD/WHO, Paris.

OECD (2004), *Development Co-operation Report 2003*, OECD, Paris.

OECD (n.d.), *Gender Equality Tipsheets*, OECD, Paris.

Princeton Survey Research Associates (2003), *Global Poll: Multinational Survey of Opinion Leaders 2002*. Washington DC.

Royal Danish Ministry of Foreign Affairs (2003), *A World of Difference*, Copenhagen.

The Simon's Committee Report (1997), *One Clear Objective: Poverty Reduction through Sustainable Development: Report of the Committee of Review*, Canberra.

United Nations (2003), Implementation of the United Nations Millennium Declaration: Report of the Secretary-General. New York. Ref. A/58/323.

United Nations Population Division (2003), *World Population Prospects: The 2002 Revision*, New York.

World Bank (2002), *World Bank Group Work in Low-Income Countries Under Stress: A Task Force Report*, World Bank, Washington DC.

World Bank/International Monetary Fund (2002), *A Review of the Poverty Reduction Strategy Paper Approach*, World Bank, Washington DC.

World Bank (2003), *World Development Report 2004: Making Services Work for the Poor*, World Bank, Washington DC.

OECD PUBLICATIONS, 2, rue André-Pascal, 75775 PARIS CEDEX 16
PRINTED IN FRANCE
(43 2005 12 1 P) ISBN 92-64-00761-X – No. 53889 2005